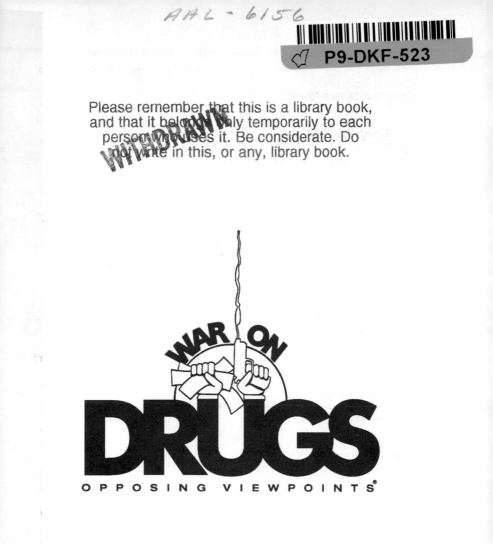

WAR ON DRUGS

OPPOSING VIEWPOINTS®

Other Books of Related Interest in the Opposing Viewpoints Series:

Central America
Chemical Dependency
Civil Liberties
Criminal Justice
The Death Penalty
Drug Abuse
Latin America and U.S. Foreign Policy
Terrorism
Violence in America

Additional Books in the Opposing Viewpoints Series:

Abortion
AIDS
American Foreign Policy
American Government
American Values
America's Elections
America's Future
America's Prisons
Animal Rights
Biomedical Ethics
Censorship
China
Constructing a Life Philosophy
Crime and Criminals
Death and Dying
Eastern Europe
Economics in America
The Elderly
The Environmental Crisis
Euthanasia
Genetic Engineering
The Health Crisis
The Homeless
Immigration
Israel
Japan
Male/Female Roles
The Mass Media
The Middle East
Nuclear War
The Political Spectrum
Poverty
Problems of Africa
Religion in America
Science & Religion
Sexual Values
Social Justice
The Soviet Union
The Superpowers: A New Detente
Teenage Sexuality
The Third World
The Vietnam War
War and Human Nature

WAR ON DRUGS

OPPOSING VIEWPOINTS ®

David Bender & Bruno Leone, *Series Editors*

Neal Bernards, *Book Editor*

OPPOSING VIEWPOINTS SERIES ®

Greenhaven Press, Inc.   PO Box 289009   San Diego, CA 92198-0009

Library of Congress Cataloging-in-Publication Data

War on drugs : opposing viewpoints / Neal Bernards, editor.
    p.   cm. — (Opposing viewpoints series)
Includes bibliographical references and index.
Summary: Presents sets of differing opinions on a range of social, political, and legal issues associated with the war on drugs.
ISBN 0-89908-458-3 (pbk.). — ISBN 0-89908-483-4 (lib. bdg.)
1. Narcotics, Control of—United States. 2. Drug abuse—United States.   [1. Narcotics, Control of. 2. Drug abuse.]
I. Bernards, Neal, 1963- . II. Series: Opposing viewpoints series (Unnumbered)
HV5825.W38128   1990
362.29'17'0973—dc20   90-39795
                                     CIP
                                     AC

"Congress shall make no law . . .
abridging the freedom of speech,
or of the press."

First Amendment to the U.S. Constitution

The basic foundation of our democracy is the first amendment
guarantee of freedom of expression. The Opposing Viewpoints
Series is dedicated to the concept of this basic freedom and the
idea that it is more important to practice it than to enshrine it.

Contents

Chapter 5: How Can the War on Drugs Be Won?

Why Consider Opposing Viewpoints?

"It is better to debate a question without settling it than to settle a question without debating it."

Joseph Joubert (1754-1824)

The Importance of Examining Opposing Viewpoints

The purpose of the Opposing Viewpoints Series, and this book in particular, is to present balanced, and often difficult to find, opposing points of view on complex and sensitive issues.

Probably the best way to become informed is to analyze the positions of those who are regarded as experts and well studied on issues. It is important to consider every variety of opinion in an attempt to determine the truth. Opinions from the mainstream of society should be examined. But also important are opinions that are considered radical, reactionary, or minority as well as those stigmatized by some other uncomplimentary label. An important lesson of history is the eventual acceptance of many unpopular and even despised opinions. The ideas of Socrates, Jesus, and Galileo are good examples of this.

Readers will approach this book with their own opinions on the issues debated within it. However, to have a good grasp of one's own viewpoint, it is necessary to understand the arguments of those with whom one disagrees. It can be said that those who do not completely understand their adversary's point of view do not fully understand their own.

A persuasive case for considering opposing viewpoints has been presented by John Stuart Mill in his work *On Liberty*. When examining controversial issues it may be helpful to reflect on this suggestion:

The only way in which a human being can make some approach to knowing the whole of a subject, is by hearing what can be said about it by persons of every variety of opinion, and studying all modes in which it can be looked at by every character of mind. No wise man ever acquired his wisdom in any mode but this.

Analyzing Sources of Information

The Opposing Viewpoints Series includes diverse materials taken from magazines, journals, books, and newspapers, as well as statements and position papers from a wide range of individuals, organizations, and governments. This broad spectrum of sources helps to develop patterns of thinking which are open to the consideration of a variety of opinions.

Pitfalls to Avoid

A pitfall to avoid in considering opposing points of view is that of regarding one's own opinion as being common sense and the most rational stance, and the point of view of others as being only opinion and naturally wrong. It may be that another's opinion is correct and one's own is in error.

Another pitfall to avoid is that of closing one's mind to the opinions of those with whom one disagrees. The best way to approach a dialogue is to make one's primary purpose that of understanding the mind and arguments of the other person and not that of enlightening him or her with one's own solutions. More can be learned by listening than speaking.

It is my hope that after reading this book the reader will have a deeper understanding of the issues debated and will appreciate the complexity of even seemingly simple issues on which good and honest people disagree. This awareness is particularly important in a democratic society such as ours where people enter into public debate to determine the common good. Those with whom one disagrees should not necessarily be regarded as enemies, but perhaps simply as people who suggest different paths to a common goal.

Developing Basic Reading and Thinking Skills

In this book, carefully edited opposing viewpoints are purposely placed back to back to create a running debate; each viewpoint is preceded by a short quotation that best expresses the author's main argument. This format instantly plunges the reader into the midst of a controversial issue and greatly aids that reader in mastering the basic skill of recognizing an author's point of view.

A number of basic skills for critical thinking are practiced in the activities that appear throughout the books in the series. Some of the skills are:

Evaluating Sources of Information. The ability to choose from among alternative sources the most reliable and accurate source in relation to a given subject.

Separating Fact from Opinion. The ability to make the basic distinction between factual statements (those that can be demonstrated or verified empirically) and statements of opinion (those that are beliefs or attitudes that cannot be proved).

Identifying Stereotypes. The ability to identify oversimplified, exaggerated descriptions (favorable or unfavorable) about people and insulting statements about racial, religious, or national groups, based upon misinformation or lack of information.

Recognizing Ethnocentrism. The ability to recognize attitudes or opinions that express the view that one's own race, culture, or group is inherently superior, or those attitudes that judge another culture or group in terms of one's own.

It is important to consider opposing viewpoints and equally important to be able to critically analyze those viewpoints. The activities in this book are designed to help the reader master these thinking skills. Statements are taken from the book's viewpoints and the reader is asked to analyze them. This technique aids the reader in developing skills that not only can be applied to the viewpoints in this book, but also to situations where opinionated spokespersons comment on controversial issues. Although the activities are helpful to the solitary reader, they are most useful when the reader can benefit from the interaction of group discussion.

Using this book and others in the series should help readers develop basic reading and thinking skills. These skills should improve the reader's ability to understand what is read. Readers should be better able to separate fact from opinion, substance from rhetoric, and become better consumers of information in our media-centered culture.

This volume of the Opposing Viewpoints Series does not advocate a particular point of view. Quite the contrary! The very nature of the book leaves it to the reader to formulate the opinions he or she finds most suitable. My purpose as publisher is to see that this is made possible by offering a wide range of viewpoints that are fairly presented.

David L. Bender
Publisher

Introduction

"The real victim [in the war on drugs] is going to be the constitutional rights of the majority of citizens."

Havery Gittler, executive director of Ohio's American Civil Liberties Union

"Constitutional liberties are in jeopardy from drugs themselves, which every day scorch the earth of our common freedom."

William J. Bennett, director of the Office of National Drug Control

The war on drugs permeates almost every level of American society. From high schools to boardrooms to bathrooms, the war on drugs is being waged by educators, business leaders, politicians, parents, and law enforcement officials. Most are concerned that the war is being lost. Drugs continue to flow into the U.S. at an alarming rate. Customs agents cannot halt the influx of drugs. Educators cannot eliminate drug dealing in high schools. And business people cannot control drug abuse by their employees.

Few leaders see easy solutions to these problems. In addition, the solutions that have been proposed are the subjects of heated controversy. The divisive debate over the war on drugs hinges on whether the government's need to preserve and protect society from the consequences of illegal drug use takes precedence over its constitutional duty to guarantee individual rights.

Hardliners in the war on drugs argue that society is being devastated by drugs. According to a national study done by the Research Triangle Institute, drug use costs American businesses $76 billion a year in decreased productivity. Countless traffic fatalities, murders, robberies, and violent crimes are also attributed directly to the influence of drugs. Some, like William Bennett and New York Representative Charles Rangel, say these facts justify the use of tough measures that may infringe on individual liberties. In the view of these hardliners, police officers must be given broad search and seizure powers, government agencies must be allowed to administer drug tests, and

13

employers must be permitted to bar drug users from positions that concern public safety.

A good portion of the American public seems to support this view. Sixty-two percent of the respondents in a 1989 *Washington Post*-ABC News poll said they would be willing to give up "a few of the freedoms we have in this country to reduce illegal drug use significantly."

Civil libertarians find this position appalling. They believe that government officials have exaggerated the danger of illegal drugs in order to rationalize an attack on people's constitutional rights. Ethan Nadelmann, a professor at Princeton University and a prominent critic of the U.S. government's drug policy, cites 1985 statistics showing that 3,562 Americans died from illegal drugs while nearly 400,000 died from legal drugs like alcohol and nicotine. Yet, according to Nadelmann, the American public has been led to believe that illegal drugs are a national crisis. He believes that tougher law enforcement is unwarranted because the cost in individual rights outweighs the seriousness of the drug problem. Nadelmann, along with noted conservatives William F. Buckley and former secretary of state George Shultz, supports the legalization of most drugs as a solution to the problem.

The War on Drugs: Opposing Viewpoints presents viewpoints from diverse sources: government position papers, newspaper columns, research studies, magazine articles, and books. The various authors address the controversial issue of how the war on drugs can best be managed. Topics debated are Is the War on Drugs Necessary? Does the War on Drugs Violate Civil Liberties? What Policies Can Reduce Teen Drug Abuse? Can the U.S. Stop International Drug Cartels? How Can the War on Drugs Be Won? As the viewpoints in this book reveal, little consensus exists concerning the war on drugs.

Is the War on Drugs Necessary?

Chapter Preface

Since 1980, the U.S. government has spent $10 billion to wage the war on drugs. There are many conflicting views, however, on whether the money has been well spent. Not everyone agrees that the war on drugs is effective.

Numerous social commentators, including columnist William F. Buckley Jr. and economist Milton Friedman, write that the war on drugs has failed. They recommend legalizing drugs as a remedy to the problem. The experiences of Jim Fyfe, a New York police officer for sixteen years, support this view. Fyfe argues that strict drug laws create an underworld of violence, organized crime, police corruption, and ineffective courts. He maintains that if drugs were legalized, most of these social ills would disappear.

Others strongly disagree with this condemnation of the war on drugs. Many lawmakers say the war on drugs is failing only because government leaders have not gone far enough. New York Representative Charles Rangel, who serves on the House Select Committee on Narcotics Abuse and Control, states, "We have never fought the war on drugs like we have fought other legitimate wars—with all the forces at our command." Rangel argues that more money and effort must be committed to win the war on drugs and assure America's survival.

As the nation's drug problem persists, these issues continue to haunt policymakers. The viewpoints in this chapter examine the controversial war on drugs.

"We must decide, as a nation, whether we really want to win our fight against drugs. . . .We believe we must win; we believe we can."

The War on Drugs Is Necessary

The Senate Task Force for a Drug-Free America

The Senate Task Force for a Drug-Free America works to shape the government's official drug policy. The group includes U.S. Senators Phil Gramm, Pete Wilson, Charles Grassley, Frank Murkowski, Pete Domenici, Rudy Boschwitz, Steve Symms, and Malcolm Wallop. Members of the task force believe that the U.S. is currently losing the war on drugs. In the following viewpoint, they argue that the war can be won by cutting American demand for drugs.

As you read, consider the following questions:

1. Why do the authors say the fight to cut the supply of drugs has failed?
2. What reasons does the task force give for continuing the war against drugs?
3. According to the authors, what penalties should drug users be given?

The Senate Task Force for a Drug-Free America, "Strategy for a Drug-Free America: A Symposium," The Heritage Foundation *Backgrounder,* September 12, 1988. Reprinted with permission.

America is losing its battle against drugs. Drug arrests, drug seizures and prison sentences for drug dealers are all up. But the price of drugs is falling, and availability is increasing. The police know we are losing the drug war. Pushers know it. Parents know it. Even school children—perhaps especially school children—know it.

In the process of losing the drug war, we are creating huge profits for organized crime, complicating relations with our allies, creating incentives to corrupt our police and enlist our young people in crime and—perhaps most importantly—we are demonstrating America's ability to fail.

Our current efforts fall far short of what is needed to win. Despite the impressive rise in law enforcement efforts, the supply of illegal drugs has increased in recent years. The demand for drugs creates and sustains the illegal drug trade. To win the war against drugs, we must deprive the drug seller of the drug buyer, the user, and thereby take the profits out of the drug trade. That goal can only be accomplished by dramatically reducing the demand for illegal drugs. Thus, winning the drug war not only requires that we do more to limit supply, but that we refocus our efforts to reduce demand.

We must decide, as a nation, whether we really want to win our fight against drugs, or just put up a good show. We believe we must win; we believe we can; and we believe we know how.

Our goal is to make America drug free by 1995. Any lesser goal is neither acceptable nor worthy of the American people.

The costs of drug use in the United States are large and growing. More than 23 million Americans use drugs at least monthly, including more than six million who use cocaine. The best available evidence is that half of all high school seniors have used illegal drugs at least once, and over twenty-five percent use drugs at least monthly.

Drugs and Society

Drug use extends throughout our society. Rural areas are nearly as heavily impacted as big cities; college-bound students nearly as likely to use drugs as non-college-bound. Forty percent of doctors in our nation's hospitals are thought to use illicit drugs. Substantial proportions of young people who apply to join local police forces show signs of cocaine use.

Those who argue for legalizing drugs ignore the tremendous costs of drugs on society as well as on those who use them. For example:

• Over 30,000 people were admitted to emergency rooms in 1986 with drug-related health problems, in
cluding nearly 10,000 for cocaine alone.

• Ten to 15 percent of all highway fatalities involve drug use.

18

- It is estimated that one of every ten Americans who went to work this morning had their productivity impaired by substance abuse.
- Drug users are three times as likely to be involved in on-the-job accidents, are absent from work twice as often, and incur three times the average level of sickness costs as non-users.
- Virtually all experts agree there is a strong link between teenage suicide and use of illegal drugs.
- The connection between drugs and crime is also well-proven. Eight of ten men arrested for serious crimes in New York City test positive for cocaine use.
- Drug use in the workplace costs our nation as much as $100 billion annually in lost productivity.

Eliminating these direct effects of drug use requires that we eliminate drugs from society.

Substantial increases in funding and resources have been made available in recent years to combat the drug problem, with spending for interdiction, law enforcement and prevention up by 100 to 400 percent. And these programs are producing results: Seizures of cocaine are up from 1.7 tons in 1981 to 27.2 tons in 1986; Drug Enforcement Administration drug convictions doubled between 1982 and 1986; and, the average sentence for Federal cocaine convictions rose by 35 percent during this same period. Federal funding has permitted programs, such as the "DARE" Program in Los Angeles, to bring drug education into thousands of classrooms. Thus, recent funding increases have not been wasted.

Continue the Battle

In 1989, the federal government released new statistics that showed a 37 percent decline in the regular use of illicit drugs in America, a fall that included every region in the nation, all races, both sexes and all social classes. With that sort of progress in the war on drugs, this is a particularly odd time to give up a battle.

The problem with drugs is drug use. Every proposed reform that makes drugs more available or acceptable is going to increase drug use. It would also increase the suffering and unhappiness that flows from drug use for both users and non-users of drugs.

Robert L. DuPont and Ronald L. Goldfarb, *The Washington Post National Weekly Edition*, February 5-11, 1990.

However, these efforts have not reduced the overall availability of drugs in America, nor produced significant reductions in drug use. The Department of Health and Human Services reports that drugs are cheaper and more available than ever, and evidence on drug use shows—at best—only modest declines. Use of the most dangerous drugs, such as inhalants and LSD, is up compared with levels in the early 1980s.

The overwhelming evidence, based both on scientific models like those used in the Rand Corporation study and on America's experience over the last decade, is that drug interdiction programs by themselves cannot raise the market price of most illegal drugs enough to reduce drug use substantially. As the Rand study pointed out, the value of cocaine is multiplied 208 times as it moves from the farm to Main Street, USA, and there are enough different growing areas and smuggling routes to guarantee that interdiction alone cannot produce victory in the war against drugs.

Attack the Demand

Similarly, while education is clearly an avenue that must be pursued, the existing evidence provides little basis for believing that education programs that simply provide information about drugs significantly reduce drug use by young people. In fact, levels of drug use appear to be very high among the best educated and most sophisticated social groups, and one comprehensive review of the available studies concluded that "by far the largest number of studies have found no effects of drug education on use."

All of the evidence we have available today suggest that efforts to attack the supply of drugs will not succeed unless they are accompanied by efforts to attack the demand. As long as strong demand is present, high potential profits will attract a supply to meet that demand.

A serious attack on the demand side will require a substantial commitment from the American public. Most of the 23 million Americans who now use drugs are not part of the "underclass" or "counterculture." Many drug users work, pay taxes and vote. Their use of drugs could not occur if it were not condoned by the rest of society. A serious attack on the demand side means telling these 23 million people to change their behavior. If we are not willing to do that, we cannot and will not win the war on drugs.

One key to success is to catch and prosecute more drug users. Given the current level of resources, drug users correctly perceive that their chances of detection are virtually nil. Moreover, they recognize that police, prosecutors and judges are reluctant to prosecute them in a system which offers few appropriate sentencing alternatives.

Penalties for drug users must be based on the principle of "measured response," with the the primary goal being deterrence. Revocation of drivers licenses, suspension of eligibility for government programs, supervised probation/rehabilitation and asset forfeiture are appropriate alternatives to prison sentences for first-time users. The key is to ensure that these penalties are actually imposed on all convicted drug users, without exception.

Clyde Peterson. Reprinted with permission.

Our approach to the drug problem must be tempered with compassion for drug addicts. But our compassion must extend as well to the victims of drug-related crime and to the millions of *potential* drug users who will suffer if we are not successful in winning this fight. Thus, while rehabilitation and treatment programs are an important component of an effective program, they should be conducted in conjunction with, not in place of, tough law enforcement.

Drug testing is clearly an effective tool for reducing use. Over 50 percent of America's Fortune 500 corporations have instituted drug testing programs, and available data indicate that these programs have resulted in dramatic reductions in usage. For example, the Southern Pacific Railroad, which has had a drug testing program since 1984, reports that drug use has been cut by 75 percent. And the Department of the Navy reports that its comprehensive testing program reduced drug use from 33 percent in 1980 to 10 percent in 1985.

Finally, winning requires a continuation and expansion of the "zero tolerance" approach. Zero tolerance is a way of stating society's commitment to succeed in the fight against drugs. Zero tolerance means that we are determined to absolutely eliminate drugs from our schools, our highways, our workplaces and ultimately from our culture.

"There seems to be no stopping drug frenzy once it takes hold of a nation."

The War on Drugs Is Unnecessary

Barbara Ehrenreich

Many opponents of the war on drugs, like Barbara Ehrenreich, believe there is a misguided pre-occupation with drug abuse. In the following viewpoint, Ehrenreich points out that alcohol and cigarettes kill more people per year than do illegal drugs. Ehrenreich, a regular columnist for the now-defunct *Ms.* magazine, argues that politicians have created a drug "frenzy" which overshadows serious discussion of the issue.

As you read, consider the following questions:

1. Why is Ehrenreich frightened by what she calls the "drug frenzy" brought on by the war on drugs?
2. According to the author, which is more dangerous, alcohol or marijuana? Why?
3. What evidence does Ehrenreich give that drug prohibition is more dangerous than drug abuse?

Barbara Ehrenreich, "Drug Frenzy, " *Ms.*, November 1988. Reprinted with permission.

If there is anything more mind-altering—more destructive to reason and common sense than drugs—it must be drug frenzy. Early signs include memory loss, an inability to process simple facts, an unnatural braying of the voice, and a belligerent narrowing of the eyes. Almost everyone is susceptible: liberals and conservatives, Presidential candidates and PTA moms, the up-and-coming and the down-and-out. In fact, even *drug users*—a category that, scientifically speaking, embraces wine-sippers and chocolate addicts—are not immune.

Drug frenzy is not, as many people like to think, just a quick and harmless high. It is an obsession, overshadowing all other concerns, and capable of leaving a society drained, impotent, and brain-damaged. . . .

It easily overwhelms poverty, homelessness, and the federal debt. The worst thing you can say about a (political) candidate is not that he's a fool or a faker, but that he isn't "tough enough on drugs." In foreign policy, drugs have replaced Communism as the scourge of the earth, and when we can't depose a Third World strongman, we indict him for dealing.

A Loss of Liberty

Our civil liberties may be the most serious casualty of the frenzy: boats and cars are being confiscated for containing as little as a tenth of a gram of marijuana. The Supreme Court has ruled that the police have a right to search your garbage—and they're not after the five-cent deposits on your soda-pop cans.

There seems to be no stopping drug frenzy once it takes hold of a nation. What starts with an innocuous "Hugs, Not Drugs" bumper sticker soon leads to wild talk of shooting dealers and making urine tests a condition for employment—anywhere. Some (government officials) would like to change a 110-year-old law prohibiting military involvement in domestic matters in order to unleash the armed forces in the "war" on drugs. There's talk of issuing "drug-war bonds," and worse talk about incarcerating drug offenders in "prison tents" to be set up in the Nevada desert. In drug frenzy, as in drug addiction, the threshold for satisfaction just keeps rising.

Now I have as much reason to worry about drugs as anyone. I am the mother of teenagers. I am also, it pains me to admit in print, the daughter of drug-abusers. Drugs disrupted my childhood home, eventually rendering it, as the social workers like to say, ''dysfunctional.'' But the drugs that worry me most, the drugs that menaced my own childhood, are not the drugs that our current drug warriors are going after. Because the most dangerous drugs in America are *legal* drugs.

Consider the facts: tobacco, which the Surgeon General categorized as an addictive drug, kills over 300,000 people a year.

24

Alcohol, which is advertised on television and sold in supermarkets, is responsible for nearly 100,000 deaths annually, including those caused by drunk drivers. But the use of all illegal drugs combined—cocaine, heroin, marijuana, angel dust, LSD, et cetera—accounted for only 3,403 deaths in 1987. That's 3,403 deaths too many, but it's less than 1 percent of the death toll from the perfectly legal, socially respectable drugs that Americans—including drug warriors—indulge in every day.

Alcohol is the drug that undid my parents. When my own children reached the age of exploration, I said all the usual things—like "no." I further told them that reality, if carefully attended to, is more exotic than its chemically induced variations. But I also said that, if they still felt they had to get involved with a drug, I'd rather it was pot than Bud.

A Hysterical Crusade

The first casualty of war, an American politician once said, is the truth. If you don't believe it, take a good look at President Bush's drug war.

There isn't a shred of honesty in his hysterical crusade. It's false in its diagnosis, false in its rhetoric, false in its remedy. Not only is it foreordained to fail, this war on drugs—like the two or three dozen before it—will worsen the problem it piously claims to address. In the process, it will diminish our freedom.

Stephen Chapman, *Conservative Chronicle*, September 20, 1989.

If that sounds like strange advice, consider the facts: unlike alcohol, cocaine, and heroin, marijuana is not addictive. Twenty million Americans—from hard hats to hippies—use it regularly. In considering whether to legalize it for medicinal purposes, a federal appeals court judge found that "marijuana, in its natural form, is one of the safest therapeutically active substances known to man." And unlike alcohol use, a frequent factor in crimes like child abuse, marijuana does not predispose its users to violence.

Not that marijuana is harmless. Although marijuana is not chemically addictive, some people do become sufficiently dependent on it to seek help. According to the National Institute of Drug Abuse, however, there are no deaths that can be unequivocally attributed to marijuana use. Five thousand "marijuana-related" hospital emergencies were reported in 1987, but 80 percent of these were known to involve another drug—most commonly alcohol. Nor is there any clear evidence that marijuana "leads to" harder drugs, unless you count alcohol and the occasional truly dire drugs, such as PCP, that have been known to

25

contaminate marijuana bought from street dealers. Taken alone, and in moderation, it is still the safest "high" on the market.

But one of the first symptoms of drug frenzy is an inability to make useful distinctions of any kind. The drug that set off the "war," the drug that is enslaving ghetto youth and enlisting them into gun-slinging gangs, is cocaine, specifically crack. But who remembers crack? We're after "drugs"! In an alarming example of drug-frenzied thinking, a *Time* magazine drug cover story lumped cocaine, heroin, and marijuana together as the evil drugs in question. Nineteen years ago, before drug-frenzy-induced brain damage set in, *Time* was still able to make distinctions, as this quote from the January 5, 1970, issue shows: ". . . the widespread use of marijuana, sometimes by their own children, is leading many Middle Americans toward a bit more sophistication, an ability to distinguish between the use of pot and harder drugs."

So what turned all these sober Middle Americans into drug-frenzied hawks? Historians point out that Americans have long been prone to episodes of "moral panic." One year it's Communism; the next it's missing children—or terrorism, or AIDS, or cyanide-laced cold pills.

Usually, the targeted issue conceals a deeper anxiety. For example, as historian Barbara Epstein has argued, the late 19th and early 20th century temperance crusade—which was every bit as maniacal as today's war-on-drugs—was only incidentally about alcohol. The real issue was women's extreme vulnerability within the "traditional marriage." Husbands leave, husbands get violent, husbands drink. But you couldn't very well run a mass crusade to abolish *husbands* or—in the 19th century—to renegotiate the entire institution of marriage. The demon rum became what the psychohistorians call a "condensed symbol" of male irresponsibility and female vulnerability—focusing the sense of outrage that might otherwise have gone into the search for radical, feminist alternatives.

Similar Messages

Drugs also play a powerful symbolic role in our culture. Generically speaking, we imagine drugs as a kind of pact with the devil: what you get is ecstasy or something pretty similar. But the price you pay is eternal thralldom, dependency, loss of self. Only a few drugs—"hard" ones—actually fit our imaginings. But in mundane, drugless, ordinary life, we're offered a deal like this every other minute: buy this—sports car, condo, cologne, or whatever—and you'll be happy, suave, sexy . . . forever!

We are talking about the biggest pusher of all—the thoroughly legal and entirely capitalist consumer culture. No street-corner

26

crack dealer ever had a better line than the one Madison
Avenue delivers at every commercial break: Buy now! Quick
thrills! You deserve it! And, of course, we love it—all those
things, all those *promises!* If we could only have a little *more!*
But, deep down, we also mortally resent it, this incessant, hard-
sell seduction. The sports car does not bring fulfillment; the
cologne does not bring love. And still the payments are due. . . .

A Phony War

The 'war' metaphor, which is a legacy from Lyndon Johnson's
'war on poverty', has never been very satisfactory. In none of
these wars is anything that could be called a final victory even
imaginable: there will always be poor people; there will always
be drugs and drug-users; there will always be civil violence. The
"war", therefore, consists of a series of gestures—a drug bust, the
capture of a cocaine shipment, an invasion of Panama—all highly
publicized, all with clear-cut good and bad guys, and all triumphs
for the good. These are just like the wars in *1984,* only adapted
to democratic conditions.

James Bowman, *The Spectator*, January 27, 1990.

Drug frenzy, we might as well acknowledge, is displaced rage
at the consumer culture to which we are all so eagerly, mor-
bidly addicted. Consider this statement in *Time* magazine by
Harvard psychiatrist Robert Coles, who is otherwise a pretty
thoughtful guy. We can't legalize drugs, he said (including, pre-
sumably, marijuana), because to do so would constitute a "moral
surrender," sending what *Time* called "a message of unrestricted
hedonism." What a quaint concern! We are already getting "a
message of unrestricted hedonism" everytime we turn on the
TV, glance at a billboard, or cruise a mall. But we can't very
well challenge *that* message, or *its* sender, even as mounting
debt—personal and social—gives that message a mean and
mocking undertone.

So we feed our legal addictions and vent our helplessness in a
fury at drugs. We buy our next chance at "ecstasy" on credit and
despise those poor depraved fools who steal for heroin or kill for
crack. The word for this is "projection," and it's the oldest, most
comforting form of self-delusion going.

The only hopeful sign I can see is the emerging debate on
drug legalization. The advocates of legalization, who include
such straitlaced types as the New York County Lawyers'
Association's Committee on Law Reform, argue that drug *prohibition* has become far more dangerous than drug abuse.
Prohibition causes about 7,000 deaths a year (through drug-re
related crime, AIDS, and poisoned drugs) and an $80 billion-a

year economic loss. And prohibition drives up the price of drugs, making dealing an attractive career for the unemployed as well as the criminally inclined.

There are problems with wholesale legalization: crack, for example, is so highly addictive and debilitating that it probably shouldn't be available. But I agree with the *New York Times* that we consider legalizing marijuana. We could then tax the estimated $50 billion spent annually on it and use the revenue to treat people who want to get off the hard drugs, including alcohol and tobacco.

But we're not even going to be able to have a sane debate about legalization until we come down off the drug frenzy. The only cure is a sturdy dose of truth, honesty, and self-knowledge—and those things do not, ancient countercultural lore to the contrary, come from drugs. Since there's no drug for drug frenzy we're all just going to have to sit down, cold sober, to face the hard questions: who's hurting, what's hurting them, and what, in all kindness and decency, we can do about it.

"The drug menace . . . threatens the whole fabric of society in a way that no other form of lawlessness does."

America Cannot Afford to Lose the War on Drugs

Reuben Greenberg

In 1982, Reuben Greenberg became the first black chief of police in Charleston, South Carolina. Greenberg's main objective as chief has been to reduce drug dealing in his city. In the following viewpoint, taken from his book *Let's Take Back Our Streets*, Greenberg describes tactics used by the Charleston police force to push drug dealers out of crime-ridden areas. Greenberg maintains that the war on drugs is a war America cannot afford to lose.

As you read, consider the following questions:

1. Into what two categories does the author divide efforts to control drug trafficking?
2. According to Greenberg, how can the police make drug dealing more difficult without arresting people?
3. In the author's opinion, why would cutting the demand for drugs dry up the supply?

Contemptible though they are, burglars are only an ugly rash on the face of society. The real cancer is drugs.

Selling drugs illegally is a crime that makes most people very angry, and that includes me. The drug menace strikes at our homes, our schools, our children, even our law enforcement agencies. It threatens the whole fabric of society in a way that no other form of lawlessness does.

The anger people feel is reflected in the remedies proposed. Some call for a mandatory death penalty for drug dealers. Others say, Call in the Navy and sink their boats; call in the Air Force and shoot their planes out of the sky! One irate Congressman even advocated machine-gunning survivors from such sunken boats or downed aircraft. These furious reactions are neither practical nor even tolerable in a civilized society, but they're understandable.

Supply & Demand

It's customary to divide drug control into two main categories: measures to curtail supply and measures to reduce demand. I'll talk a bit about these in a moment, but first I want to focus on a third area where we've had considerable success here in Charleston. This approach consists of interfering with or destroying the channels through which the drug traffic flows from the criminals who supply it to the customers who use it. Interdiction, we call it. Disruption of the lines of communication at the local level.

The best way to understand this approach is to think of the whole drug mess as a business—a sordid business destructive to many but highly profitable to others. In all businesses there must be a seller and a buyer. We have found it very hard to cut off the supply of drugs from the seller and, so far, equally hard to persuade the buyer not to buy. That leaves a third approach: separate the customers from the vendors. Create a barrier between them. Make it extremely difficult for them to deal with each other. If they can deal at all.

Visualize this: A drug dealer with a fistful of crack. A user with an outstretched hand full of money. And a blue-uniformed figure standing between them, making it very risky or very uncomfortable for the drugs to be exchanged for the money or vice versa. With this approach, no arrests are involved and no futile court proceedings are required because, as I'll explain, none are necessary. The link between pusher and user is actually a fragile one. At the local level, it doesn't take much to break it.

A little history on this whole drug situation will help make my point. The picture has changed tremendously in the past fifty years or so. Half a century ago, we had perhaps two hundred

30

thousand drug addicts in this country. Dope fiends, we used to call them. They were a scruffy lot, easily recognizable. Then, as now, they killed and robbed each other frequently. They also committed various crimes to acquire money to feed their habits: shoplifting, burglary, robbery, passing bad checks, and so on. They were a problem, sure, but it was a problem that was mostly under control. Drug dealing was profitable, but no enormous sums were involved.

Recreational Users

Today everything is different. In addition to the million to a million and a half addicts, we have a vast number of people—some say twenty-nine or thirty million—who are mainly recreational users of illegal drugs. They don't rob and steal to get the money; they have it already. Money earned from jobs of every kind: truck drivers and bankers, dentists and salesmen, stenographers and hairdressers. You can't spot them as users because they look just like the rest of us. They are not crime-committing users in the sense that they don't rob old men on park benches or break into homes, but I regard them with contempt and anger nonetheless, because these are the ones who make possible the enormous profits in the drug business. They are the ones who create the narco-millionaires and billionaires in Colombia or Mexico or Panama or Miami. Without them the drug problem would shrink back swiftly to containable proportions.

We Are the Solution

We cannot make believe that nothing is happening around us, because something is definitely happening. We cannot just sit and watch TV and read news reports about victims dropping like flies. We must not let drug gangs and thugs roam our streets and neighborhoods, turning them into battlefields, while we do nothing but lament. . . .

We can find the solution, not so much by an open declaration of war against the outside forces, but by looking within ourselves. If we honestly plumb the depths of our being and examine ourselves seriously, then we can put an end to this problem.

Tom J. Ilao, *America Under Siege*, 1988.

These are the people who speak disparagingly of crime in the ghettos and yet venture into sleazy places in the dead of night to make contact with their suppliers. And this is the pressure point that can be exploited: the point of exchange between vendor and customer. Here's how we do it in Charleston.

Most drug vendors are not anonymous; they are known to the police. The cops have arrested them before and have seen them post bond and return to their old neighborhoods almost instantly, to wait for trials that may not take place for months. The police have watched this dreary performance so often that they realize that arrest is not really the answer. The answer is to throw sand in the gears of the drug industry by making it difficult if not impossible for the customer to have access to the vendor.

One of our techniques is to put a tail on a known vendor. Not a plainclothes detective, but a uniformed cop. Wherever Johnny the Pusher goes during his "business" hours, the cop goes, too. He doesn't arrest Johnny, even though he knows the pusher is carrying narcotics. No probable cause. So when Johnny goes to Eddie's Bar and Grill, his favorite turf, the cop goes also. He does nothing, just stands there twenty feet from Johnny. Customers may come in, but they don't linger when they see a cop. They don't even say hi to Johnny. They go away and they probably won't come back. Not to deal with Johnny, anyway, because they know the cops are watching him.

Crack Houses

Is there a known crack house in some low-income neighborhood? Same technique. No need for a full-scale raid. One uniformed cop strolling back and forth outside the house will put a noticeable chill on operations. Does this represent a strain on police resources? Not really. Using a single officer is far less expensive than using a squad of detectives armed with listening devices. Pretty soon that crack house is out of business.

That kind of surveillance puts extreme pressure on the vendors. What about the well-dressed banker who drives into the ghetto area at three in the morning to pick up a supply of cocaine for a weekend party he's planning? We have an answer for him, too. We call it a checkpoint, or a road block.

I'll tell you more about this extremely effective device later on, but for the moment let's say we have decided to conduct a traffic check between ten P.M. and three A.M. of all vehicles entering a certain district where we know an established drug pusher resides. We stop cars. We ask drivers politely for licenses and registrations. We check equipment and usually find something wrong somewhere: a tail light out, a windshield wiper that doesn't work, a horn that doesn't blow, a registration that isn't signed on the back. So we give them a citation, and that establishes the time and place. Now we can prove that they were in this unsavory place in the dead of night, and they know that, and they fear the embarrassment that a newspaper account may cause.

Even if there's no cause for a citation, we ask the driver where he's going and why. If he gives an address, we can check the phone book and call the number on a cellular phone. If no one answers, then no one is at home, so why go there? If someone does answer, we usually say, "This is the Charleston Police Department. We have a person here, a Mr. So-and-So, who says he wants to visit you." When he hears the words "Police Department," the guy who answers will probably say he never heard of Mr. So-and-So. In that case, why should Mr. So-and-So go there? He may as well turn around and go home.

If Mr. So-and-So insists on exercising his constitutional rights to travel where he pleases, we say, "Okay, but just to make sure you're safe in this dangerous area, we'll go along with you and knock on the door."

Displacing Drug Dealers

In a minute, a uniformed cop is knocking on the door of the drug dealer's house. When that happens, you get all sorts of interesting reactions, such as the sound of toilets being furiously flushed. There goes the dealer's supply of drugs for the night. Sometimes he won't open the door at all. Is this a raid or what? Alarm and uncertainty have descended on that dealer.

Get Serious

This country that dreams of putting men on Mars; which has already been to the moon; which has pioneered unbelievable scientific and medical achievements, and which has shown greater compassion for people's humanity than any other in the history of the world, will now allow itself to be destroyed by drugs.

We have solved more difficult problems. It's time to get serious about this one.

Jon Kyl, *Manchester Union Leader*, February 27, 1990.

Anyway, not many customers are going to be coming around from now on. The dealer may have to find another turf altogether. But most of the good turfs are already occupied by other drug dealers. This means our displaced dealer will have to fight the established dealer. Maybe, with luck, they'll shoot each other. More likely, one or both will begin to think that Charleston is a bad location and move somewhere else.

Meanwhile, back at the checkpoint, all sorts of fascinating evidence is coming to light. We can check with headquarters by radio to see if any warrants are outstanding against a driver. We can ascertain if he has had any previous arrests. We've arrested people for carrying and using drugs while on their way to get more narcotics. All sorts of suddenly discarded drugs have been swept up from the ground and confiscated. We've arrested people for drunk driving and for possession of stolen property. Right in the front seat of the car, we've found clothing and other items shoplifted from local malls with no receipts. And illegal guns, unregistered guns, concealed weapons. Some people have even left their cars and run away when they realized they were facing a search. Of course, we ran them down and caught them. All of which is just incidental to the main purpose, which is to interdict the flow of drugs.

You don't have to set up these checkpoints every night. Hit them one night, then leave them alone for two or three nights, then hit them again. You're creating uncertainty. You're dislocating a business operation. You're putting a very big question mark into the whole sales transaction. You're introducing the element of uniformed police, which is very important, because selling drugs is one of the few ventures outside of gambling and prostitution where neither the vendor nor the customer wants the police involved. . . .

Stop the Demand

If we could persuade enough people that using crack or cocaine or heroin is basically stupid, that it's self-defeating, that only dummies get involved, that there's nothing glamorous about slowly killing yourself, then maybe the demand that fuels the whole sorry business would begin to drop. And eventually, the problem might become manageable. Demand is the key. Stop, or at least significantly diminish, the demand and you dry up the supply.

What about the well-meaning but misguided people who say we should throw in the towel and have the government distribute low cost narcotics to addicts, or even give drugs free to those who want them? I disagree completely with such proposals. The argument runs that free drugs would reduce crime, would put pushers out of business, would leave police free to deal with non-drug-related crimes. There may be some truth in such claims, but do we really want our government to supply ever-increasing quantities of drugs (most habits are progressive) to ever-increasing numbers of addicts? Do we want to be responsible for the innocent children born to such people—children who are themselves hooked on drugs? Can we be comfortable with the thought that the officials who supply those drugs will actually come to control those people's lives? Do we want to subsidize the demoralization of millions of our citizens rather than combat the drug epidemic with all the forces at our disposal?

I don't think so. I'm not ready to run up the white flag. We have proven in Charleston that we can make life very uncomfortable for user and vendor alike. We don't just rely on arrest and the snail-like performance of our courts. We use shame. We use embarrassment. We use fear. We use tactics that dislocate the drug business. We bring uncertainty and dread to the scum who profit by it and alarm and apprehension to those whose illegal purchases keep the whole miserable mechanism running.

It's a war. We may not be winning it at the moment, but we sure as hell can't afford to lose it. And some day, if we Americans put all our might and muscle, all our brains and determination into it, victory will be ours.

"When is the U.S. government going to realize that a 'war on drugs,' complete with interdiction and eradication programs, won't work?"

American Has Already Lost the War on Drugs

Kevin B. Zeese

In the following viewpoint, Kevin B. Zeese argues that America's efforts to fight illegal drugs and prosecute dealers and users have failed. He maintains that the war on drugs has in fact increased crime and done nothing to prevent drug addiction. Rather than continuing the war on drugs, Zeese supports legalizing drugs and expanding education and treatment programs. Zeese is the vice president of the Drug Policy Foundation, a group that advocates decriminalizing drug use.

As you read, consider the following questions:

1. The author writes that drug use is not the real problem. What is the real problem, in his opinion?
2. Why does Zeese oppose drug interdiction as a remedy?
3. In the author's opinion, why is social pressure against using drugs more effective than punitive laws?

Kevin B. Zeese, "Why We Can't Win," *Los Angeles Herald Examiner,* September 3, 1989. Reprinted with permission.

In Colombia, the drug lords have declared war against the government for trying to enforce its narcotics laws. During a weekend in Los Angeles, 15 people were murdered by gangs who sell drugs. In his TV speech, President George Bush, as did his three predecessors, will call on the nation to go on a "warlike footing" to stop the drug menace.

When is the U.S. government going to realize that a "war on drugs," complete with interdiction and eradication programs, won't work? Worse, that it, in effect, creates "war zones" here and abroad.

Indeed, America's drug problem is less the result of the drugs themselves than the war on them. For example, the L.A.-based drug-trafficking gangs who are expanding to the Midwest, even to Washington, D.C., are in part indebted to the South Florida Task Force that then-Vice President Bush headed during the Reagan administration. When federal law enforcement moved into Miami in the early '80s to deal with a drug-related murder rampage there, importers simply moved to Los Angeles. Now L.A.—indeed the entire country—is reporting an upsurge in drug-related violence.

Even at the street level, the war on drugs has accomplished little more than enlarging the war zones. When the police crack down in one neighborhood, dealers move to another, where they must murder other drug dealers to secure the turf. Back come the police to chase away the dealers, and the cycle is repeated. The result: More and more neighborhoods are caught up in turf wars.

All told, the two-decade history of the war on drugs overwhelmingly demonstrates that law enforcement can't limit the availability of drugs. Actually, the first great battle presaged the failures that are now commonplace.

The Nixon Approach

In 1969, the administration launched Operation Intercept, which militarized the Mexican border. One of every three cars entering the country from Mexico was searched for illegal drugs, chiefly marijuana. As a result, the pot market in Southern California temporarily dried up. But users began experimenting with other narcotics, among them amphet-amines, which quickly became the drug of demand.

In response to the border searches, smugglers switched from cars and trucks to boats and planes, thus expanding the drug war to sea and air. The marijuana market grew as well.

During the Carter administration, millions of dollars were spent spraying the herbicide paraquat on the marijuana fields in Mexico. Today, marijuana is perhaps the most valuable cash crop—estimated at $15 billion—in the United States. According to drug czar William Bennett, the American market accounts for 25 percent of the world market. Indeed, in some California counties—Santa Cruz and Humboldt—the plant is considered the largest cash crop.

The paraquat campaign added momentum to the already-burgeoning drug business in Colombia and other Latin American countries: The drug traffickers would go on to specialize in cocaine. As for Mexico, the Drug Enforcement Agency reported last year that the country was the second largest exporter of marijuana to the United States.

Reagan's Miami Vice

The administration focused its interdiction efforts in South Florida. High-tech military surveillance aircraft were recruited in the war on drugs. Colombia's traffickers quickly realized that marijuana was too bulky to ship undetected. But they also discovered that cocaine could be transported in briefcases, suitcases, even within human bodies. These methods of moving coke easily penetrated the administration's hi-tech net. The upshot was that cocaine became cheaper.

"AND YOU'RE TELLING ME DRUGS ARE OUT OF STEP WITH AMERICAN VALUES?"

Tony Auth. © 1989, Universal Press Syndicate. Reprinted with permission. All rights reserved.

Future eradication programs are likely to suffer the same failures of earlier ones. Only a tiny percentage of the land available for coca-leaf cultivation is currently being used. Even if today's entire coca crop in Colombia, Peru and Bolivia were eradicated, there is no shortage of poor farmers in other Latin American countries willing to fill the vacuum. Man-made substitutes can also be created in laboratories. Finally, a Harvard University researcher recently reported that marijuana cultivation is now so widespread that the United States could not eradicate it.

Interdiction is equally unpromising as a means to stop the drug flow. The General Accounting Office, for example, reported that the Navy and Coast Guard spent a combined $40 million in 1988 looking for drug contraband on the high seas. They seized 17 ships. The Air Force, meanwhile, used AWACS (airborne warning and control systems) survelliance, at a cost of $8 million in 1987-88, to arrest 25 suspected smugglers.

Reports out of Kennebunkport, Me., where Bush is mapping his anti-drug strategy, indicate that the president possibly recognizes the futility of interdiction efforts. By concentrating on breaking up the drug distribution networks and going after their mid-level operators, these reports say, the administration will downplay efforts to stop the flow of drugs at the border and eradicate coca plants abroad.

Use Social Pressure

Generals in the war on drugs invariably argue that drug consumers are the root of the problem. But wine dealers, beer manufacturers, tobacco growers and pharmaceutical companies aren't shooting each other in the streets. It is not drug use, then, that is responsible for the violence. Rather, it is how American society responds to drug use.

To be sure, there are various campaigns aimed at reducing Americans' reliance on alcohol, tobacco and pharmaceutical drugs. So far, they have been quite successful. At the beginning of the illegal-drug war 20 years ago, 40 percent of Americans were tobacco addicts. Today 29 percent smoke cigarettes. Half of the country's smokers have quit. Alcohol consumption, particularly hard liquor, has similarly declined.

But the statistics on illegal drug use are not so heartening. Though casual use is said to be down, the number of coke addicts has increased by more than 50 percent between 1986 and 1989, to an estimated 3 million.

The reason for the discrepancy isn't hard to fathom: The war on drugs relies on *criminal* law to achieve its aims; the campaigns against tobacco and alcohol use *social* pressure and control.

Still, what can be done?

For starters, we must admit that there simply isn't enough money to pay for all that's required—treatment, law enforcement, education, prevention, etc. Thus, what additional money is available—roughly $2 billion, according to news reports—should be spent on attainable goals.

Second, marijuana possession and personal cultivation should be decriminalized. The National Academy of Sciences recommended no less during President Ronald Reagan's drug war, as did a national commission appointed by President Richard Nixon.

Various forms of decriminalization have been sucessfully tried in 11 states, constituting a third of the population, over the last decade. A decline in marijuana use has paralleled these developments. Complete marijuana decriminalization would allow us to focus our limited resources on more serious drugs.

An Unceasing Flow

Finally, treatment programs should be fully funded. Those who want to quit drugs, but need help to do so, should not go wanting.

What's clear after 20 years of drug wars orchestrated out of Washington is that interdiction programs and eradication efforts have not stopped the flow of drugs into the United States. Quite the contrary. Drug-related violence has reached America's heartland and coke traffickers threaten to destabilize the oldest democracy in South America.

Should the Bush administration fail to learn the drug-war lessons of the past, the day may not be far off when America's drug gangs, as have their Latin American counterparts, declare war against our government.

"Drugs have always been a part of human culture. Their use, within the context of a healthy and sane community, has never hurt the culture."

The War on Drugs Damages American Society

Raul Tovares

Raul Tovares has worked as a therapist with drug and alcohol abusers. He's now the program director for Catholic Television in San Antonio, Texas. In the following viewpoint, he argues that the war on drugs, not drugs themselves, damage American society. He writes that jailing drug users only creates hardened criminals and ruins many young people's futures. Legalizing drugs is the best way to regulate the drug trade and help addicts, Tovares maintains.

As you read, consider the following questions:

1. According to Tovares, what effect did the crackdown on marijuana have?
2. Why does the author call legalization the "civilized" way to solve the drug crisis?
3. Tovares argues that jail terms for drug criminals are counter productive. Why?

Raul Tovares, "How Best to Solve the Drug Problem: Legalize," *National Catholic Reporter*, December 22, 1989. Reprinted by permission of the National Catholic Reporter, PO Box 419281, Kansas City, MO 64141.

The present hysteria over controlled substances, such as cocaine and marijuana, has clouded our thinking and caused us to support policies based more on emotion than reason. This trend, if not curtailed by calm reflection and subsequent action to implement a more sane strategy, could result in the waste of billions of dollars and the persecution of some of our community's most ambitious and intelligent young people.

The legalization of the use of cocaine and marijuana is the first step toward developing a more humane drug policy. All other attempts to curtail drug use will fail.

It should be made clear at the outset: In no way do I condone drug abuse. I support all efforts that educate persons about the dangers of drug abuse and that encourage them to refrain from using drugs. What I am against is the arrest, prosecution and incarceration of drug users.

Attempts to stop the flow of drugs into this country will not solve the problem of drug abuse. Research by Mark A.R. Kleiman of the John F. Kennedy School of Government highlights the futility of trying to suppress drug use. Kleiman found that imports of marijuana, thanks to an intensive policy of border interdictions, were reduced from approximately 4,200 tons in 1982 to 3,900 tons in 1986.

A Rise in Drug Prices

The impact of the "crackdown" was twofold: The price of marijuana went up as the risk factor for suppliers increased, and domestic production increased 10 percent within the same period. The result is that, today, one quarter of the marijuana sold in the United States is homegrown. As supply decreased, profits increased. Time and again, the increased profits have proved to be powerful incentives for dealers. For this reason, production of drugs is never eliminated; it merely moves to another state or country.

Media hype about drug busts creates a dangerous illusion. Every time we read about a major drug bust we can be sure of one thing, the profits for the dealers will go up. Major drug busts cut supply, which in turn increases demand. While the media, state and citizenry engage in victory dances in front of the television set, drug dealers are calculating their increased earnings.

Legalization of cocaine and marijuana, although the idea mortifies some, would immediately give the government more control over these substances, thus allowing it to regulate both the potency and purity of these drugs.

Those now involved in the distribution of these drugs must work outside the law. Grievances between buyers and sellers can only be settled by violence because there is no mediating body to whom either can go for assistance. If a dealer is selling less than the quantity he actually promised to deliver, he cannot be dragged into court or reported to the Better Business Bureau. Violence is the only way to settle the matter.

Legalization would open the door to a more civilized way to resolve conflicts. The issuing of licenses to sell these products would attract merchants without prior arrest records. Their primary interest would be the management of a legitimate business.

Milt Prigee. Reprinted with permission.

Clearly, the most unjust proposal for dealing with the drug problem is the incarceration of the "user." Currently, U.S. prisons house about one million people, many of them held or convicted on drug-related charges. Each cell built costs the taxpayers about $50,000. Alleviating current overcrowding would cost the state $80 billion.

The fact is, we could never afford to arrest, prosecute and incarcerate the 23 million Americans who use drugs. New York City, for example, has six judges assigned to hear 20,000 narcotics cases a year. That translates into 19,400 plea bargains and an average jail term of seven days.

In Connecticut, prisoners are being released in order to make room for incoming inmates. Those released are chosen from among the least violent. The least violent often turn out to be those imprisoned on drug charges. This pattern is repeated across the nation.

Even if state legislatures did decide to raise revenues for more prisons, such a plan could never be justified when so many of our communities are being faced with the problems of unemployment, underemployment, infant mortality, malnutrition, illiteracy and homelessness—problems that many social scientists tell us lead to drug abuse. Capital is in too short supply to be squandered on a formula we know does not work: Drug user + arrest + prosecution + prison terms = productive citizen.

Drugs are not the cause, but a symptom, of a more profound and complex set of problems we don't want to face, simply because we haven't learned to solve them: unjust economic conditions and our own addiction to consumption masquerading as "the good life."

Development of a healthy and reasonable attitude toward the drug problem begins with the acceptance of the drug user as a human being—not as a "fiend," "junkie" or "enemy." In reality, drug users are our sons and daughters, our friends and neighbors.

Politicians such as Mayor Ed Koch, who want pushers shot on the spot, and bureaucrats such as William Bennett, who have no moral problem with beheading drug dealers, appeal to our society's sense of frustration rather than offering solutions that create a sense of hope. This kind of grandstanding is the scenario for war, and wars are the result of injustice. The drug war is no exception.

Although 75 percent of the users of drugs are white, a majority of those incarcerated for drug use are either black or Hispanic.

The Real Criminals

The stereotypical drug pusher is black or Hispanic. Little is mentioned about the white bankers and investors who supply the capital for major drug deals. Between 1970 and 1976, the currency surplus (the amount of money received minus the amount lent) reported by the Federal Reserve in the state of Florida almost tripled from $576 million to $1.5 billion, according to Jefferson Morely in an article published in the Oct. 2, 1989, issue of *The Nation*. But when was the last time you heard President George Bush call for the immediate execution of bankers who take drug money or William Bennett call for the beheading of venture capitalists who fund major drug deals?

In fact, the typical drug pusher is not a strung-out gang member who lights his cigars with one-hundred dollar bills. A successful drug dealer, like any entrepreneur, is often a hard worker who likely abstains from drug use.

The explanation for this phenomenon is simple. As industry abandoned the inner city and urban areas in general, many blue-collar entry level jobs that had been available to minorities

44

and poor whites were lost. They were replaced by white-collar jobs that require higher levels of education. Inner-city school systems simply could not deliver students prepared to compete for these jobs.

With the advent of crack, a new product that could be sold for as little as five dollars, intelligent, ambitious and aggressive young people who had bought into the culture of consumerism went to work in the only service industry that didn't make them wear funny hats, and it paid 20 times more.

Drug Laws Have Failed

I favor decriminalization mainly because criminalization is amorally and materially expensive failure. It is quite ineffective, drives people to crime, corrupts law enforcement, and cost far more than it could possibly be worth, even if one assumes that all drugs are bad for anyone.

Ernest van den Haag, *Reason*, October 1988.

The rise in drug use among our nation's poor and economically disadvantaged is a direct result of our unwillingness as a community to deal with the problems of inadequate school systems, lack of good jobs and the gap that currently exists between our addition to having it all and our ability to actually pay for it all.

It is simply not fair to incarcerate those who want to live out the dream of consumption when it is our economic system that has both whetted their appetite for such a a life-style and simultaneously failed to deliver the opportunities needed to live out that dream. Besides jail terms and prison sentences, we are giving these young people prison records that will follow them for the rest of their lives. These criminal records will hinder them in their future endeavors to live as productive and fully participating members of our society. How many future attorneys, doctors, teachers and such are being cut off at an early age from ever realizing their full potential?

There is a drug problem. But it will not be solved by incarcerating young, poor blacks, Hispanics and whites. It will be brought under control only when the product they are selling is legalized and regulated just like other drugs people use today without a second thought: alcohol, caffeine, nicotine.

Next time we pick up a six-pack at the grocery store, raise our glass of champagne for a toast or fix ourselves a drink to help us relax after a trying day, we should remember that, only a few years ago, in our own nation, it was chic for politicians and bureaucrats to call for the immediate execution of users of alcohol. (Indeed, in the 17th century, the prince of the petty state of Waldeck was paying 10 thalers to anyone who turned in the drug abusers in his kingdom: coffee drinkers. During the same century, Czar Michael Federovitch executed anyone caught in possession of tobacco.)

A Sane Policy

Drugs have always been a part of human culture. Their use, within the context of a healthy and sane community, has never hurt the culture. It is only when the social system begins to break down because of economic and social factors that drugs become a point of focus for the projection of our social ills.

But a reasoned and calm analysis can forge a path through the hysteria and lead us to a sane policy for the control and distribution of cocaine and marijuana.

"Don't listen to people who say drug users are only hurting themselves. They hurt parents, they destroy families, they ruin friendships."

Drugs Damage American Society

William J. Bennett

William J. Bennett is the high-profile "drug czar" for President Bush's war on drugs. Bennett, formerly the Secretary of Education during the Reagan Administration, believes that advocates of drug legalization do not realize the dire consequences of making drugs accessible to the American public. More and more teenagers would turn to drugs and destroy their lives, Bennett contends. Rather than legalize drugs he supports stronger criminal laws against drug use.

As you read, consider the following questions:

1. Why does the author argue that legalization would not cut profits for drug dealers?
2. Why does Bennett think drug use would soar after legalization?
3. According to the author, what measures are needed to solve the drug problem?

William J. Bennett, "Mopping Up After the Legalizers," a speech before the Harvard University Kennedy School of Government on December 11, 1989.

What I read in the opinion columns of my newspaper or in my monthly magazine or what I hear from the resident intellectual on my favorite television talk show is something like a developing intellectual consensus on the drug question. That consensus holds one or both of these propositions to be self-evident: (1) that the drug problem in America is absurdly simple, and easily solved; and (2) that the drug problem in America is a lost cause.

As it happens, each of these apparently contradictory propositions is false. As it also happens, both are disputed by the *real* experts on drugs in the United States—and there are many such experts, though not the kind the media like to focus on. And both are disbelieved by the American people, whose experience tells them, emphatically, otherwise.

The consensus has a political dimension, which helps account for its seemingly divergent aspect. In some quarters of the far right there is a tendency to assert that the drug problem is essentially a problem of the inner city, and therefore that what it calls for, essentially, is quarantine. "If those people want to kill themselves off with drugs, let them kill themselves off with drugs," would be a crude but not too inaccurate way of summarizing this position. But this position has relatively few adherents.

On the left, it is something else, something much more prevalent. There we see whole cadres of social scientists, abetted by whole armies of social workers, who seem to take it as catechism that the problem facing us isn't drugs at all, it's poverty, or racism, or some other equally large and intractable social phenomenon. If we want to eliminate the drug problem, these people say, we must first eliminate the "root causes" of drugs, a hopelessly daunting task at which, however, they also happen to make their living.

Enforce Good Laws

Twenty-five years ago, no one would have suggested that we must first address the root causes of racism before fighting segregation. We fought it, quite correctly, by passing laws against unacceptable conduct. The causes of racism posed an interesting question, but the moral imperative was to end it as soon as possible and by all reasonable means: education, prevention, the media, and not least of all, the law. So, too, with drugs.

What unites these two views of the drug problem from opposite sides of the political spectrum is that they issue, inevitably, in a policy of neglect. Let me pause here to note one specific issue on which the left/right consensus has lately come to rest; a position around which it has been attempting to build national sentiment. That position is legalization.

It is indeed bizarre to see the likes of Anthony Lewis and William F. Buckley on the same side of an issue; but such is the perversity that the so-called legalization debate engenders. To call it a "debate," though, suggests that the arguments in favor of drug legalization are rigorous, substantial and serious. They are not. They are, at bottom, a series of superficial and even disingenuous ideas that more sober minds recognize as a recipe for a public-policy disaster. Let me explain.

© 1986 Joel Pett/*Lexington Herald-Leader*. Reprinted with permission.

Most conversations about legalization begin with the notion of "taking the profit out of the drug business."

But has anyone bothered to examine carefully how the drug business works? As a *New York Times* article vividly described, instances of drug dealers actually earning huge sums of money are relatively rare. There are some who do, of course, but most people in the crack business are the low-level "runners" who do not make much money at all.

A Step Up the Income Scale

In many cases, steady work at McDonald's over time would in fact be a step *up* the income scale for these kids. What does straighten them out, it seems, is not a higher minimum wage, or less-stringent laws, but the dawning realization that dealing drugs invariably leads to murder or prison. And that's exactly why we have drug laws—to make drug use a wholly unattractive choice.

Legalization, on the other hand, removes that incentive to stay away from a life of drugs. Let's be honest, there are some people who are going to smoke crack whether it is legal or illegal. But by keeping it illegal, we maintain the criminal sanctions that persuade most people that the good life cannot be reached by dealing drugs.

The big lie behind every call for legalization is that making drugs legally available would "solve" the drug problem.

But has anyone actually thought about what that kind of legalized regime would look like? Would crack be illegal? How about PCP? Or smokable heroin? Or ice? Would they all be stocked at the local convenience store, perhaps just a few blocks from an elementary school?

And how much would they cost? If we taxed drugs and made them expensive, we would still have the black market and the crime problems we have today. If we sold them cheap to eliminate the black market—cocaine at, say, $10 a gram—then we would succeed in making a daily dose of cocaine well within the allowance budget of most sixth-graders.

When pressed, the advocates of legalization like to sound courageous by proposing that we begin by legalizing marijuana. But they have absolutely nothing to say on the tough questions of controlling other, more powerful drugs, and how they would be regulated.

No Legalization

As far as marijuana is concerned, let me say this: I didn't have to become drug czar to be opposed to legalized marijuana. As Secretary of Education I realized that, given the state of American education, the last thing we needed was a policy that made widely available a substance that impairs memory, concentration and attention span. Why in God's name foster the use of a drug that makes you stupid?

Now what would happen if drugs were suddenly made legal? Legalization advocates deny that the amount of drug use would be affected. I would argue that if drugs are easier to obtain, drug use will soar. In fact, we have just undergone a kind of cruel national experiment in which drugs became cheap and widely available: That experiment is called the crack epidemic.

When powder cocaine was expensive and hard to get, it was found almost exclusively in the circles of the rich, the famous or the privileged. Only when cocaine was dumped into the country, and a $3 vial of crack could be bought on street corners, did we see cocaine use skyrocket—this time largely among the poor and disadvantaged.

The lesson is clear: If you're in favor of drugs being sold in stores like aspirin, you're in favor of boom times for drug users and drug addicts. With legalization, drug use will go up, way up.

When drug use rises, who benefits and who pays? Legalization advocates think the cost of enforcing drug laws is too great. But the real question—the question they never ask—is what does it cost *not* to enforce those laws.

Too High a Price

The price that American society would have to pay for legalized drugs, I submit, would be intolerably high. We would have more drug-related accidents at work, on highways and in the airways. We would have even bigger losses in worker productivity. Our hospitals would be filled with drug emergencies. We would have more school kids on dope, and that means more drop outs. More pregnant women would buy legal cocaine, and then deliver tiny, premature infants. I've seen them in hospitals across the country. It's a horrid form of child abuse, and under a legalization scheme, we will have a lot more of it. For those women and those babies, crack has the same effect whether it's legal or not.

A Dangerous Option

It is argued that legalization would take the profits out of drug sales. But when did legalization ever take the profits out of anything? Tobacco and alcohol—to mention two legalized narcotics—are the source of multibillion dollar profits. . . .

In any case, the major problem is not the profits made by suppliers but the damage done to drug abusers and others in our communities. When something is made legal, it becomes more accessible, and when more accessible it is consumed more. All we would accomplish by legalizing drugs is to change the suppliers and increase the number of potential consumers.

Michael Parenti, *Political Affairs*, November 1989.

Now if you add to that the costs of treatment, social welfare and insurance, you've got the price of legalization. So I ask you again, who benefits, who pays?

What about crime? To listen to legalization advocates, one might think that street crime would disappear with the repeal of our drug laws. They haven't done their homework.

Our best research indicates that most drug criminals were into crime well before they got into drugs. Making drugs legal would just be a way of subsidizing their habit. They would continue to rob and steal to pay for food, for clothes, for entertainment. And they would carry on with their drug trafficking by undercutting the legalized price of drugs and catering to teen-agers, who, I assume, would be nominally restricted from buying drugs at the corner store.

All this should be old news to people who understand one clear lesson of Prohibition. When we had laws against alcohol, there was less consumption of alcohol, less alcohol-related disease, fewer drunken brawls and a lot less public drunkenness. And contrary to myth, there is no evidence that Prohibition caused big increases in crime. No one is suggesting that we go back to Prohibition. But at least we should admit that legalized alcohol, which is responsible for some 100,000 deaths a year, is hardly a model for drug policy. As Charles Krauthammer has pointed out, the question is not which is worse, alcohol or drugs. The question is can we accept both legalized alcohol *and* legalized drugs? The answer is no.

So it seems to me that on the merits of their arguments, the legalizers have no case at all. But there is another, crucial point I want make on this subject, unrelated to costs or benefits.

Drug use—especially heavy drug use—destroys human character. It destroys dignity and autonomy, it burns away the sense of responsibility, it subverts productivity, it makes a mockery of virtue. As our Founders would surely recognize, a citizenry that is perpetually in a drug-induced haze doesn't bode well for the future of self-government.

Libertarians don't like to hear this, but it is a truth that everyone knows who has seen drug addiction up close. And don't listen to people who say drug users are only hurting themselves: They hurt parents, they destroy families, they ruin friendships. And drugs are a threat to the life of the mind; anyone who values that life should have nothing but contempt for drugs. Learned institutions should regard drugs as the plague.

That's why I find the surrender of many of America's intellectuals to arguments for drug legalization so odd and so scandalous.

The War on Drugs

Their hostility to the national war on drugs is, I think, partly rooted in a general hostility to law enforcement and criminal justice. That's why they take refuge in pseudosolutions like legalization, which stress only the treatment side of the problem.

Whenever discussion turns to the need for more police and stronger penalties, they cry that our constitutional liberties are in jeopardy. Well, yes, they are in jeopardy, but not from drug *policy*: On this score, the guardians of our Constitution can sleep easy. Constitutional liberties are in jeopardy, instead, from drugs themselves, which every day scorch the earth of our common freedom.

When we are not being told by critics that law enforcement threatens our liberties, we are being told that it won't work.

Let me tell you that law enforcement does work and why it must work. Several weeks ago I was in Wichita, Kan., talking to a teen-age boy who was now in his fourth treatment program. Every time he had finished a previous round of treatment, he found himself back on the streets, surrounded by the same cheap dope and tough hustlers who had gotten him started in the first place. He was tempted, he was pressured, and he gave in.

Virtually any expert on drug treatment will tell you that, for most people, no therapy in the world can fight temptation on that scale. As long as drugs are found on any street corner, no amount of treatment, no amount of education can finally stand against them. Yes, we need drug treatment and drug education. But drug treatment, and drug education need law enforcement. And that's why our strategy calls for a bigger criminal justice system: as a form of drug *prevention.*

Intellectual Failings

America's intellectuals—here I think particularly of liberal intellectuals—have spent much of the last nine years decrying the social programs of two Republican administrations in the name of the defenseless poor. But today, on the one outstanding issue that disproportionally hurts the poor—that is wiping out many of the poor—where are the liberal intellectuals to be found?

They are on the editorial and op-ed pages, and in magazines like *Harper's,* telling us with a sneer that our drug policy won't work.

The current situation won't do. The failure to get serious about the drug issue is, I think, a failure of civic courage—the kind of courage shown by many who have been among the main victims of the drug scourge. But it betokens as well a betrayal of the self-declared mission of intellectuals as the bearer of society's conscience. There may be reasons for this reluctance, this hostility, this failure. But I would remind you that not all crusades led by the U.S. government, enjoying broad popular support, are brutish, corrupt and sinister. What is brutish, corrupt and sinister is the murder and mayhem being committed in our cities' streets. One would think that a little more concern and serious thought would come from those who claim to care deeply about America's problems.

Recognizing Statements That Are Provable

From various sources of information we are constantly confronted with statements and generalizations about social and moral problems. In order to think clearly about these problems, it is useful if one can make a basic distinction between statements for which evidence can be found and other statements which cannot be verified or proved because evidence is not available, or the issue is so controversial that it cannot be definitely proved.

Readers should be aware that magazines, newspapers, and other sources often contain statements of a controversial nature. The following activity is designed to allow experimentation with statements that are provable and those that are not.

The following statements are taken from the viewpoints in this chapter. Consider each statement carefully. *Mark P for any statement you believe is provable. Mark U for any statement you feel is unprovable because of the lack of evidence. Mark C for any statements you think are too controversial to be proved to everyone's satisfaction.*

If you are doing this activity as a member of a class or group, compare your answers with those of other class or group members. Be able to defend your answers. You may discover that others will come to different conclusions than you do. Listening to the reasons others present for their answers may give you valuable insights in recognizing statements that are provable.

P = provable
U = unprovable
C = too controversial

1. One-third fewer high school seniors use cocaine now then five years ago.

2. The "Just Say No" anti-drug campaign has been very successful.

3. Since 1983, illegal drug use within the military has dropped by two-thirds.

4. The war on drugs will not work.

5. The crackdown on marijuana encourages drug users to experiment with cocaine and other drugs.

6. Eleven states have decriminalized the possession of small amounts of pot.

7. Domestic drug production has increased by ten percent since border searches became more common.

8. Building more jails to alleviate overcrowding from drug arrests would cost taxpayers $80 billion.

9. A majority of people imprisoned on drug charges are black or Hispanic.

10. Few drug dealers actually earn much money.

11. Over 100,000 deaths per year can be attributed to alcohol.

12. No drug therapy in the world can keep addicts from using if cheap drugs are available.

13. Reducing the demand for drugs is the only way to solve the drug problem.

14. Ten to fifteen percent of all highway fatalities involve drug use.

15. Drug education programs do little to reduce drug use among young people.

16. The police have a right to search your garbage for signs of drug use.

17. Drug prohibition kills more people than drug legalization ever would.

18. Tobacco, an addictive drug, kills over 300,000 people each year.

19. The two-decade history of the war on drugs overwhelmingly demonstrates that law enforcement can't limit the availability of drugs.

20. The war on drugs is succeeding. The U.S. must continue to fight against drug abuse.

21. Drug prohibition causes about seven thousand deaths per year through drug-related crime, AIDS, and poisoned drugs.

55

Periodical Bibliography

The following articles have been selected to supplement the diverse views presented in this chapter.

William J. Bennett	"A Response to Milton Friedman," *The Wall Street Journal,* September 19, 1989.
George J. Church	"Thinking the Unthinkable," *Time,* May 30, 1988.
Michael S. Gazzaniga	"The Federal Drugstore," *National Review,* February 5, 1990.
Victor Gold	"The Year They Legalized Drugs," *The American Spectator,* November 1989.
Stephen J. Gould	"The War on (Some) Drugs," *Harper's Magazine,* April 1990.
Tim D. Kane	"Costs of Drug Warfare," *USA Today,* July 1988.
Michael Kinsley	"Glass Houses and Getting Stoned," *Time,* June 6, 1988.
Jacob V. Lamar	"Where the War Is Being Lost," *Time,* March 14, 1988.
Lewis H. Lapham	"A Political Opiate," *Harper's Magazine,* December 1989.
Tom Morganthau	"Should Drugs Be Legal?" *Newsweek,* May 30, 1988.
Jefferson Morley	"Aftermath of a Crack Article," *The Nation,* November 20, 1989.
Ethan A. Nadelmann	"Shooting Up," *The New Republic,* June 13, 1988.
The New Republic	"The Quack Epidemic," November 14, 1988.
Andy Plattner and Gordon Witkin	"The Enemy Up Close," *U.S. News & World Report,* June 27, 1988.
A.M. Rosenthal	"Tale of Two Mayors," *The New York Times,* March 14, 1989.
Kurt L. Schmoke	"A War for the Surgeon General, Not the Attorney General," *New Perspectives Quarterly,* Summer 1989.
Verne E. Smith	"A Frontal Assault on Drugs," *Newsweek,* April 30, 1990.
Mike Tidwell	"Murder Capital," *The Progressive,* July 1989.
James Q. Wilson	"On the Legalization of Drugs," *Commentary,* May 1990.
Mortimer B. Zuckerman	"The Enemy Within," *U.S. News & World Report,* September 11, 1989.

CHAPTER

2

Does the War on Drugs Violate Civil Liberties?

Chapter Preface

The Fourth Amendment of the U.S. Constitution guarantees citizens the right to be protected from unreasonable searches and seizures. But what constitutes an unreasonable search or seizure has been controversial since the Fourth Amendment was adopted. One of today's hottest debates is whether testing people for drug use violates the Fourth Amendment.

Many people believe that random drug tests are unreasonable searches because people's bodily fluids are tested even though there may be no cause to suspect a person of any wrongdoing. In addition, they believe that drug testing regulates not just work-related behavior, but off-duty recreational activities as well. Since drug tests may detect traces of drugs for up to seventy-two hours, employees may test positive even if they used drugs on weekends and their work was not affected. Loren Siegal, a staff member at the American Civil Liberties Union, writes, "The increasingly routine use of tests in the work-place—urinalysis, polygraphs, AIDS antibody tests, genetic screens, psychological and personality profiles—is a development with frightening implications for individual liberties." Siegal and others view drug testing as an ominous and unwarranted invasion of personal privacy.

Others contend that the dangers of drug abuse necessitate drug testing. Robert L. DuPont, the director of the National Institute on Drug Abuse, writes, "Drug-using workers are three to four times as likely to have an accident on the job, two to three times as likely to be absent from work, and three times as likely to file medical claims." DuPont and others point to the many accidents caused by people who use drugs, and the innocent lives that are lost in such accidents. They conclude that when other people's safety is at stake, it is constitutional and appropriate for employers to test their employees for drugs.

The authors in this chapter debate the issues of drug testing and other civil-liberties questions relating to the war on drugs.

1

"The politics of the War on Drugs generates proposals that only a few years ago would have been repudiated as either absurd or excessive."

The War on Drugs Violates Civil Liberties

Steven Wisotsky

Steven Wisotsky is a professor of law at the Nova University Law Center in Florida and is a scholar of constitutional rights and criminal justice. In the following viewpoint, Wisotsky writes that U.S. political leaders are willing to sacrifice Americans' civil liberties in the name of fighting illegal drugs. Wisotsky argues that Americans should oppose this trend, lest the right to freedom from undue government interference be lost.

As you read, consider the following questions:

1. In Wisotsky's view, why was President Reagan's tough talk about the war on drugs significant?
2. What specific instances does the author cite to justify his concern that the war on drugs threatens civil liberties?
3. Why does Wisotsky worry about the growing level of frustration with the war on drugs?

Since the early 1980s, the prevailing attitude has been that cracking down on drugs is imperative. As a result, the three branches of government have deferred very little to constitutional and nonconstitutional limits on the exercise of governmental power in the domain of drug enforcement. What Laurence Tribe describes as the Constitution's "pivotal, even mythological place in our national consciousness" is rapidly being eroded by a positivist, bureaucratic attitude that we can—must—do whatever is deemed necessary or expedient in waging the War on Drugs. This situation would be bad enough if the War on Drugs worked effectively to control the supply of illegal drugs. It is tragic when the curtailment of "zones of privacy" is accompanied by the tripling of cocaine imports to the United States, the emergence of marijuana as a leading domestic agricultural product, and insistent demands for yet further escalations in the War.

Tough Talk

The story begins on October 2, 1982, with a Presidential speech denouncing illegal drugs: "The mood towards drugs is changing in this country and the momentum is with us. We're making no excuses for drugs—hard, soft, or otherwise. Drugs are bad and we're going after them." President Reagan continued this hard-line rhetoric in another speech that month, pledging an "unshakable" commitment "to do what is necessary to end the drug menace" and "to cripple the power of the mob in America."

Legal scholars rarely pay much attention to Presidential rhetoric in analyzing legal developments. But, in this situation, it would be a serious mistake to disregard the tough talk and political posturing. Attitude, above all else, drives the counterrevolution in criminal law and procedure. The idea that the end of "getting" drug traffickers justifies just about any means seems an idea whose time has come. One federal judge, in a 1977 opinion, adumbrated the evolving jurisprudence of hostility in condemning drug dealers as "merchants of misery, destruction and death" whose greed has wrought "hideous evil" and brought "unimaginable sorrow" upon the nation. He concluded his opinion by denouncing drug crimes as "unforgivable." This attitude propels the trend toward creating a drug "exception" to the law: if conduct is literally unforgivable, then draconian measures are justified. . . .

Drug Testing

The latest "imperative" in the War on Drugs is compulsory and sometimes random urine sampling for traces of illegal drugs, a practice now followed by one-fourth of Fortune 500 companies, by many local governments, and by the United States of America for its employees and the employees of federal contractors. The practice of watching an employee or applicant pee into a jar would seem to implicate rights of privacy recognized by the fourth amendment, and most federal courts have ruled that some showing of individualized suspicion is required to compel a public employee to submit to urinalysis. But exceptions have been carved out for some classes of employees, and the view that the right of privacy does not protect bodily wastes has gained some support. Whatever the final resolution of the issue, the private sector will remain largely free to require such tests. Drug testing, of course, is only part of a much larger picture. The real question is this: what happens when drug testing is absorbed into the culture without noticeable effect on the black market in drugs? What will the next round of escalation bring?

Tony Auth. © 1988, Universal Press Syndicate. Reprinted with permission. All right reserved.

That question, ultimately, shows the truly insidious quality of the War on Drugs: the drug enforcement system can never have enough power or resources to win the war. In the futile quest to control the uncontrollable, the government follows an imperative to expand. Legislative reforms, doubling of "troops," administrative directives, task forces, executive coordination—all of these have proven ineffective in controlling the drug supply. Yet the reflexive response of the system is always to do more, always to expand. "In one sense," said former Attorney General William French Smith, "to deal with this problem, we have to blanket the world."

Blanketing the world, of course, begins at home. When one initiative after another fails to produce any discernible or lasting impact on the black market in drugs, the frustrated impetus for control carries the system to its next "logical" extension. The internal logic of the War on Drugs, coupled with its insatiable appetite for resources and power in its futile pursuit, leads inevitably to repressive measures. The authoritarian logic of drug control was noted, although not endorsed, by the President's Commission on Marijuana and Drug Abuse more than a decade ago:

> Under certain conditions, perhaps, law enforcement alone might eliminate the illicit market in drugs. To achieve this, though, would require, at the least, multifold increases in man-power, a suspension of Fourth Amendment restraints on police searches, seizures and wiretaps, wide-scale pretrial detention, abolition of the exclusionary rule and border controls so extreme that they would substantially hinder foreign commerce.

In a nutshell, the Commission suggested, a successful drug enforcement program requires a police state.

In the United States, warnings about a police state sound a bit excessive, if not jejune, if one has in mind the nations of the Soviet Bloc. Our contemporary reality is quite different. The gradual accretion of enforcement powers moves so slowly as to be invisible to the untrained eye. The rights of citizens recede by gradual erosion, by relentless nibbling, rather than gobbling. Yet the danger to civil liberties is no less real, especially in the realm of criminal justice.

Erosion of Rights

Magistrate Peter Nimkoff of the Southern District of Florida dramatized that reality in his resignation from the federal court in protest of the continued erosion of the rights of those accused of crime. In an exit interview with the press, Nimkoff focused on the War on Drugs as the source of governmental abuses of power: According to Nimkoff, many people have decided "that because drugs are such a horrible thing, we will bend the Constitution in drug cases," or "that there are two constitutions—one for criminal cases generally, and another for drug cases. . . . I think that's wrong. . . . It invites police officers to behave like criminals. And they do."

Among his specific areas of concern are:

• Government sting operations in which it is considered "sound police practice to get people to do bad things in order that they can then be accused," Nimkoff said.

- Use of informants who pretend to be criminals during on-going investigations and then testify about what they did. Nimkoff said that the use of civilian informants and assignment of police as undercover agents are "very, very dangerous" practices.

Erosion Of Civil Liberties

In cities like Kalamazoo, Michigan, ordinances *banning* gatherings of three or more people—supposedly to combat drug dealing, have been passed. In 1986, one-half of all court-authorized orders for wiretaps covered drug-related cases.

The Bush administration's anti-drug strategy shows the campaign's "law-and-order" intent.

Among other provisions, the $11.6 billion bill calls for: the death penalty for drug "kingpins," whether or not they are connected to murder; stepped up policing along the Mexican border from California to Texas; creation of a National Drug Intelligence Center to coordinate the exchange of intelligence information between law enforcement agencies; and a 37.6 percent increase in military spending for drug interdiction.

Socialist Worker, February 1990.

"Justice Brandeis said about 60 years ago that government is the omnipresent teacher, especially in a democracy," he said. "And that the police practices of our government teach moral lessons to our society. And I think it is wrong and dangerous for the police to make a norm of deception. . . ."

"It's a very dangerous practice for the police to begin to behave like criminals in order to catch criminals, and to encourage the commission of the offense instead of preventing its occurrence."

Nimkoff said he's also troubled by the Comprehensive Crime Control Act of 1984, which he said undercuts the presumption of innocence and removed the traditional presumption that a defendant is entitled to bond before trial.

Human Freedom

Although most criminal defendants are eventually found guilty, Nimkoff said, "I'm very reluctant to discard the presumption of human freedom or the presumption of innocence. . . . To discard them is to engage in classically authoritarian behaviors."

Magistrate Nimkoff's resignation, however unusual, reflects a traditional concern. Even Justice Hugo Black, an advocate of aggressive enforcement against the drug trade, warned of its ready capacity for excess: "The narcotics traffic can too easily cause threats to our basic liberties by making attractive the adoption of constitutionally forbidden shortcuts that might suppress and blot out more quickly the unpopular and dangerous conduct." As the War on Drugs converts paramilitary rhetoric into social reality, the nation's threshold for extremist ideas rises. Thus, the politics of the War on Drugs generates proposals that only a few years ago would have been repudiated as either absurd or excessive.

A Climate of Repression

In this climate of repression, politicians advocate capital punishment for drug dealers, or isolating them in Arctic Gulags, or simply shooting drug planes out of the sky without charges or trial. What will tomorrow's political agenda find tolerable? A bill in the Florida Senate proposed to prohibit the sale of "any magazine or other printed matter the dominant theme and purpose of which, taken as a whole, is to advocate, advise, encourage, or glorify the unlawful consumption, purchase, or usage of any controlled substance. . . ." Despite the bill's analogy to valid antiobscenity statutes, it almost certainly violates the right of free speech under existing case law—even advocacy of the violent overthrow of the government finds protection under the first amendment, absent a "clear and present danger" of intended imminent violence. But case law and history also demonstrate that war-time emergencies can justify curtailment of constitutional rights, and the analogy to the War on Drugs beckons. "When a nation is at war many things that might be said in time of peace. . .will not be endured. . . ." Or when "our shores are threatened by hostile forces, the power to protect must be commensurate with the threatened danger."

After a few more years of frustration with the War on Drugs, extremist proposals may not seem so far-fetched. Repeated expansions of governmental powers have already gained acceptance as reasonable or "necessary" measures to fight the War on Drugs. Given the nature of the beast, we can expect the demands for more power to spiral upward towards infinity. There is no light at the end of the law enforcement tunnel.

Already, some of the authoritarian methods mentioned by the National Commission on Marijuana and Drug Abuse, such as pretrial detention, have become law. Why not go further and abolish the exclusionary rule altogether, authorizing drug agents to search for drugs, tap telephones, or seize financial records without warrant, probable cause or reasonable suspicion? Why not adopt a bounty hunter system for suspected drug dealers and teach school children to report their parents for drug possession? Why not, in fact, bypass entirely the cumbersome criminal justice system, with its tedious set of impediments to investigation, prosecution, and conviction, and substitute a control system consisting of civil sanctions: fines, asset seizures and forfeitures. Control over the offender's future conduct would come, as one law professor has already proposed, through a civil injunction forbidding the defendant from violating the drug laws in the future. Violation of the injunction would be proved in a civil contempt proceeding by a mere preponderance of the evidence, rather than by proof beyond a reasonable doubt as required in a criminal prosecution: no need for grand jury indictment, right to counsel, or even for trial by jury. After all, if the United States Code is the "enemy," it must be overcome.

Giving Up Liberties

Americans who want to give up their liberties to fight cocaine are sure to get their wish. Anytime the populace starts to resemble a gargantuan lynch mob, we run the risk that the zeal for revenge will override our better judgment—as when we locked up innocent Japanese-Americans during World War II. But the danger is especially great in the drug war.

It's possible, in both theory and practice, to crack down on robberies or murders or noisy mufflers without shredding the Bill of Rights. But it's almost inconceivable that the government can vigorously enforce the drug laws without tromping on privacy and personal freedom.

Stephen Chapman, *Conservative Chronicle*, September 27, 1989.

Personal freedom is the inevitable casualty of the War on Drugs. The zealous pursuit of drug offenders is manifested in the adoption of increasingly stringent punishments for existing drug offenses, the proliferation of new drug-related criminal legislation by Congress, more aggressive investigative and prosecutorial initiatives, generally supported by judicial validations. Taken together, these developments suggest that the legal system is evolving to take the paramilitary rhetoric of the War on Drugs at face value. Like the wartime curtailment of civil liberties during both World Wars, the War on Drugs is used to justify the application of *force majeure*. In short, the War on Drugs is producing a political-legal context in which drug enforcement constitutes an exception to the principle that laws must comport "with the deepest notions of what is fair and just." In drug enforcement, most anything goes. This dishonors our legacy of limited government and natural rights, those "principles of justice so rooted in the tradition and conscience of our people as to be ranked as fundamental." It also sets a very dangerous precedent, for it is doubtful that drugs can be treated as *sui generis* in the long run. Inevitably, the drug exception will spill over to other areas of the law. We clearly face the danger of losing the ability, in James Madison's immortal phrase, to "oblige [the government] to control itself."

2

"Law enforcement officers can return to traditional police practice . . . with renewed confidence in the constitutionality of their actions."

The War on Drugs Does Not Violate Civil Liberties

Kimberly A. Kingston

Police officers have used many techniques to apprehend drug traffickers, including road blocks, searches, and drug tests. The following viewpoint is by Kimberly A. Kingston, a special agent for the Federal Bureau of Investigation's legal counsel division. In it, she maintains that these law enforcement techniques do not violate the Constitution and that the rights of privacy and freedom from unreasonable search and seizure remain protected. She contends that American society is better served by arresting drug dealers than by strictly observing the Fourth Amendment.

As you read, consider the following questions:

1. In the author's opinion, how has the Supreme Court redefined the term "search"?
2. According to Kingston, why did the Court rule that using drug-sniffing dogs at airports was not intrusive?
3. In the author's view, is one's garbage covered under the right of privacy? Why or why not?

Kimberly A. Kingston, "Reasonable Expectation of Privacy Cases Revive Traditional Investigative Techniques," *FBI Law Enforcement Bulletin*, November 1988.

The fourth amendment of the U.S. Constitution guarantees the right of the people to be secure from unreasonable searches and seizures. Over the years, the U.S. Supreme Court has expended considerable time and energy in an effort to interpret the fourth amendment and to define its terms. Specifically, the Court's efforts have often focused on the task of defining the term "search" as it is used in the amendment. Whether an action is a search under the the fourth amendment is of particular importance to the Courts and law enforcement officers, because only those actions which amount to a search fall within the parameters of the fourth amendment, and consequently, only those actions need be reasonable.

Prior to 1967, the Supreme Court defined the term "search" as a governmental trespass into a constitutionally protected area. Although this interpretation, when applied to fourth amendment cases, did little to protect individual privacy, it did lead to very effective and confident use of traditional investigative techniques. Law enforcement officers could use electronic surveillance, physical surveillance, or any other investigative technique they chose without concern for the proscriptions of the fourth amendment as long as they steadfastly avoided any trespass into constitutionally protected areas such as homes and offices.

In 1967, however, the constitutionality of these investigative techniques was questioned when, in the case of *Katz v. United States*, the Supreme Court redefined the term "search." In *Katz*, the Court recognized that the fourth amendment was designed to protect people, not places, and concluded that the then current interpretation of the amendment did not accomplish this purpose. Therefore, the Court revised its definition of the term "search" in order to make the protections of the amendment more responsive to the needs of individual privacy. No longer would the application of the fourth amendment depend upon physical trespasses into certain protected areas. Rather, the Court in *Katz* held that the purpose of the amendment would be better satisfied if all governmental intrusions into areas where individuals legitimately expected privacy were required to be reasonable. The Court achieved this goal by redefining the term "search" to include any governmental action which intrudes into an area where there is a reasonable expectation of privacy. . . .

Open Fields

A good example of the confusion that resulted from the decision in *Katz* is demonstrated by the lower courts' conflicting interpretations of the open fields doctrine in the case of *Oliver v. United States*. In *Oliver*, two police officers, acting on a tip that marijuana was being grown on defendant's farm, went to the farm to investigate. While there, the officers drove onto defendant's property, and ignoring a "No Trespassing" sign and a locked gate, located a marijuana field approximately 1 mile from defendant's house. The marijuana was seized and defendant was arrested and indicted for manufacturing a controlled substance.

A BETTER WAY TO LOOK AT

DRUG PUSHERS AND USERS...

© Tom Gibb/Rothco. Reprinted with permission.

Prior to trial, defendant moved to suppress the marijuana seized from his property on the grounds that it was discovered as a result of an unreasonable, warrantless search. Applying its interpretation of *Katz*, the district court found that the entry into defendant's field was indeed a search. Because the search was conducted without a warrant, it was deemed unreasonable and the evidence was suppressed. The district court's conclusion that a search of defendant's property had occurred was based on its belief that defendant "had a reasonable expectation that the field would remain private because [defendant] 'had done all that could be expected of him to assert his privacy in the area of the farm that was searched.'"

On review, the Sixth Circuit Court of Appeals applied its own interpretation of *Katz*, concluded that no search of defendant's property had occurred, and reversed the district court order suppressing the evidence. In reaching this conclusion, the court of appeals reasoned that the "human relations that create the need for privacy do not ordinarily take place" in open fields. Because there normally was no need for privacy in an open field, the court found that it would be unreasonable to expect such privacy, and thus, open fields do not come within the protection of the fourth amendment.

The U.S. Supreme Court resolved the apparent conflict which existed in the lower courts when it reviewed the facts of *Oliver* and, agreeing with the court of appeals, determined that no search had occurred. . . .

In practice, the Supreme Court's determination that there is no reasonable expectation of privacy in open fields has effectively removed all physical entries into such areas from fourth amendment scrutiny. Law enforcement officers can now, when the situation dictates, confidently resume the practice of making warrantless entries into open fields without fear of contravening fourth amendment proscriptions. What must be remembered, however, is that the home and the curtilage, that is the area immediately surrounding and associated with the home, remain under the protection of the fourth amendment. Consequently, any governmental entry into the home or curtilage must comply with fourth amendment standards by being conducted under the authority of a valid warrant or by falling into one of the recognized exceptions to the warrant requirement. . . .

Dog Sniffs

The use of specially trained dogs to detect the odors of explosives and narcotics is another example of a law enforcement practice that has caused some concern in the courts over the years since *Katz*. This concern was at least partially alleviated by the Supreme Court when it gratuitously addressed the issue of using specially trained dogs in the case of *United States v. Place.*

In *Place*, law enforcement officers at New York's LaGuardia Airport lawfully detained defendant on a reasonable suspicion that he was carrying a controlled substance. When defendant refused to consent to a search of his luggage, he was given the opportunity to accompany his luggage to the office of a Federal judge where a search warrant would be sought. Defendant declined the offer but requested and received a telephone number where the officers could be reached. After defendant left the premises, his luggage was taken to Kennedy Airport where it was subjected to a "sniff test" by a trained narcotics detection dog. In response to the dog's positive reaction to one of the bags, a warrant was secured. The subsequent search of the bag revealed a substantial quantity of cocaine. The defendant was later arrested and indicted for possession of cocaine with intent to deliver.

After the district court denied defendant's motion to suppress the evidence seized from his luggage, defendant entered a plea of guilty but reserved his right to appeal the denial of his suppression motion. On review, the U.S. Court of Appeals for the Second Circuit reversed on the grounds that the lengthy detention of defendant's luggage exceeded permissible limits and consequently amounted to a seizure in violation of the fourth amendment. The U.S. Supreme Court affirmed.

Reasonable Questions

Some court cases have involved narcotics officers who board buses passing through a city. The officers go down the aisle questioning every passenger, often asking permission to open bags. . . .

"The (D.C. Circuit) Court of Appeals has made it clear that randomly asking a citizen to cooperate in an investigation of this type is reasonable," Washington, D.C. District Court Judge Royce Lamberth said in a ruling from the bench. "No articulable suspicion is necessary."

Tracy Thompson, *San Francisco Chronicle*, May 8, 1990.

Although resolution of the dispute in *Place* did not require the Court to address the use of "dog sniffs," a majority of the Court took the opportunity to clarify the issue. The analysis used by the Court in *Place* was similar to the analysis discussed in previous cases. First, the Court looked and found that defendant had a subjective expectation of privacy in his luggage. Next, the Court considered whether the use of a specially trained dog to detect the odors emanating from the luggage violated any expectation of privacy that society was willing to protect. Of particular significance to the Court was the fact that the "dog sniff" did not require the opening of defendant's luggage. Furthermore, the Court made the following observations:

> [The 'dog sniff'] does not expose noncontraband items that otherwise would remain hidden from public view, as does, for example, an officer's rummaging through the contents of the luggage. Thus, the manner in which information is obtained through this investigative technique is much less intrusive than a typical search. Moreover, the sniff discloses only the presence or absence of narcotics, a contraband item. Thus, despite the fact that the sniff tells the authorities something about the contents of the luggage, the information obtained is limited. This limited disclosure also ensures that the owner of the property is not subjected to the embarrassment and inconvenience entailed in less discriminate and more intrusive investigative methods.

Obviously, what impressed the Court the most about the "dog sniff" was its limited intrusiveness. The sniff can tell law enforcement officers only one thing—whether there is contraband in the item tested. According to the Court, this single fact is something society is not willing to protect. Consequently, under the circumstances present in *Place*, the use of a trained detection dog did not violate any reasonable expectation of privacy, and therefore, was not a search under the fourth amendment.

In *Place*, the Court did not go so far as to say that no dog sniff would ever be considered a search. There remains some room for doubt. For instance, some courts have held that the reasoning in *Place* is not controlling when a detection dog is used to sniff a person or an individual's home. It is clear, however, that when an item of personal property, such as luggage, is brought into a public place and thereafter subjected to the special talents of a detection dog, no fourth amendment concerns arise. Accordingly, the "dog sniff" continues to be a widely used, effective law enforcement investigative technique.

Field Tests

Shortly after announcing its decision in *Place*, the Supreme Court, in *United States v. Jacobsen*, used the same rationale to sanction the law enforcement practice of conducting warrantless field tests of suspected controlled substances. In *Jacobsen*, a package that was being shipped by Federal Express was damaged in transit. In accord with company policies, an employee opened the box to inspect for further damage. Inside the box, the employee found 10-inch tube of duct tape containing a number of plastic bags. One of the plastic bags held a quantity of a white power. Suspicious of the powdered substance, the employee contacted agents of the Drug Enforcement Administration (DEA) who responded quickly when advised of what had been found. However, before agents arrived at the Federal Express office, the employee replaced all the items he had taken from the box.

When agents arrived on the scene, the items were once again taken from the box. The plastic bags were opened, and a knife was used to remove a small amount of the white powder. A field test identified the powder as cocaine. Armed with the results of the field test, agents obtained a warrant to search the place corresponding to the address on the package. The warrant was executed and defendant was arrested.

After being indicted on charges of possession with intent to distribute, defendant moved to suppress the evidence on the grounds that the warrant was the product of an illegal search of the damaged package. Defendant's motion was denied, and he was subsequently tried and convicted. On appeal, the Eighth

Circuit Court of Appeals reversed defendant's conviction on the basis that the field test of the white powder was a search under the fourth amendment and a warrant was required. Because "field tests play an important role in the enforcement of the narcotics laws," the Supreme Court agreed to review the case, and ultimately, reversed the decision of the court of appeals.

Not a Search

In reaching its conclusion, the Court noted first that the opening of the package by the Federal Express employee was not a "search" governed by the fourth amendment, inasmuch as it was not performed by a government actor. Next, the Court found that the subsequent opening of the package by DEA agents was not, in and of itself, a "search" because defendant's reasonable expectation of privacy in the package had already been frustrated to some extent by the Federal Express employee. What concerned the Court was whether the DEA agents made any significant invasion of defendant's privacy when they exceeded the scope of the Federal Express employee's actions by field testing the controlled substance. More precisely, did the field test itself intrude into an area where defendant had a reasonable expectation of privacy remaining, thereby making the warrantless test an unreasonable search under the fourth amendment?

Restoring Rights

In Chicago, under Operation Clean Sweep, public housing projects have been sealed off, house-to-house inspections have been carried out under housing regulations, and residents have been required to show identification in order to enter. . . .

"We are not infringing on rights; we are restoring rights," said Vincent Lane, chairman of the Chicago Housing Authority. "We are restoring our residents' rights to a safe and decent environment."

Seth Mydans, *The New York Times*, October 16, 1989.

There was no doubt that the defendant expected privacy, not only in the package itself but also in the nature of the white powdered substance contained therein. Nevertheless, the Court was quick to point out that "the mere expectation, however well justified, that certain facts will not come to the attention of the authorities" is critically different than the "concept of an interest in privacy that society is prepared to recognize as reasonable." The question thus became whether the field test at issue violated an expectation of privacy that society is willing to protect. Answering this question in the negative, the Court relied on its knowledge that "the field test could disclose only one fact previously unknown to the Agent—whether or not a suspicious white powder was cocaine. It could tell him nothing more, not even whether the substance was sugar or talcum powder." Because the test could reveal only this one fact, the Court concluded that it did not compromise any legitimate interest in privacy.

By refusing to characterize the field test as a "search," the Supreme Court added this investigative technique to the list of law enforcement practices that have been removed from fourth amendment scrutiny.

The law enforcement investigative technique that has undergone recent judicial review is the warrantless inspection of discarded trash. In *California v. Greenwood*, the Supreme Court upheld such inspections when the trash was left for collection outside the curtilage of the home. In *Greenwood*, law enforcement officers received information indicating that defendant was involved in drug trafficking. Surveillance of defendant's home added to the officers' suspicions. In an effort to develop probable cause to search defendant's premises, officers arranged to have the local trash collector segregate defendant's trash bags during the regular scheduled pickup so that the bags could be inspected for evidence. The warrantless inspection resulted in discoveries which, when recited in an affidavit, supported the issuance of a search warrant. The subsequent search of defendant's home resulted in the seizure of cocaine and hashish. Defendant was thereafter arrested on felony narcotics charges.

Narcotics Charges

While defendant was out on bail, law enforcement officers continued to receive reports of suspicious activities at defendant's home. Consequently, a trash pickup identical to the previous one was conducted and again evidence of narcotics trafficking was found. A second search warrant was executed and additional evidence was seized from defendant's residence. Once more, defendant was arrested on narcotics charges.

Prior to trial, the evidence seized pursuant to the warrants was suppressed on the theory that the warrantless trash searches violated the fourth amendment, and all charges against the defendant were dismissed. Both the suppression of evidence and dismissal of charges were upheld by the California Court of Appeals. After the California Supreme Court denied the prosecution's petition for review, the U.S. Supreme Court agreed to hear the case.

On review, the Supreme Court simply applied the two-part analysis it had used in previous cases and came to the conclusion that although defendant may have had a subjective expectation that his trash was private, that expectation was not objectively reasonable because it was not an expectation of privacy that society was willing to recognize and protect. The Court's conclusion that society would not recognize defendant's expectation of privacy as reasonable was based in large part on the belief that defendant had "exposed [his] garbage to the public sufficiently to defeat [his] claim of Fourth Amendment protection." The Court found it to be "common knowledge that plastic garbage bags left on or at the side of the public street are readily accessible to animals, children, scavengers, snoops, and other members of the public." Because the contents of the trash bags were so "readily accessible," the Court held, as a matter of law, defendant "could have had no reasonable expectation of privacy in the inculpatory items that [he] discarded."

It is important to reiterate that the Court's holding in *Greenwood* is applicable only in situations where the trash bags in question have been left for collection outside the curtilage of the home. The Court did not condone law enforcement intrusions into curtilage areas for the purpose of collecting the desired trash bags. Nevertheless, despite the dissenting Justice's opinion that "scrutiny of another's trash is contrary to commonly accepted notions of civilized behavior," the majority in *Greenwood* has preserved the warrantless inspection of discarded trash as an effective, if not particularly attractive, investigative technique.

Constitutional Actions

The decisions of the Supreme Court were not, in any way, intended to diminish the protections of the fourth amendment. On the contrary, the Court has repeatedly stressed both the importance of complying with fourth amendment proscriptions and the desirability of obtaining warrants whenever possible. However, in those instances where reliance on a warrant is an impossibility, the Court has cleared the way for the use of certain less intrusive investigative techniques. Specifically, the Court has approved the warrantless use of those investigative techniques which merely intrude into areas that society is not willing to protect. As a result, law enforcement officers can return to traditional police practices such as those discussed herein with renewed confidence in the constitutionality of their actions.

"Drug laws . . . are focused on primarily young, exclusively poor, by and large exclusively Black and Latino and people of color."

The War on Drugs Is Racist

Stanley Cohen

The following viewpoint is taken from a statement Stanley Cohen presented at the October 1988 conference, "War on Drugs: A Dangerous Trap." Conference participants were lawyers, black activists, students, and professionals who oppose the war on drugs. In this viewpoint, Cohen argues that police officers' racist attitudes can be seen by examining who the police target when enforcing laws against drug abuse. According to Cohen, the police focus on minority neighborhoods and arrest small-time users and dealers, while allowing wealthy white traffickers to go unpunished. Cohen is a New York attorney and a former community organizer and social worker.

As you read, consider the following questions:

1. According to the author, how does a "nuisance" bail unfairly punish poor arrestees?
2. Why does Cohen consider police acts like seizures of property racist?
3. In the author's view, what is the effect of police sweeps through minority neighborhoods?

Reprinted by permission of the author from a paper presented to the 1988 conference "War on Drugs: A Dangerous Trap" and published in the October 17, 1988 issue of *Revolutionary Worker*.

Primarily, what we're beginning to see is a return to the demand for the increased and enhanced sentencing, focused not on major "dealers" or on people who don't reside in the community, or don't reside in the Black and Latino communities that are making millions of dollars in profits off of these monies, namely politicians, corrupt police officials, government agents. What we're seeing is a clamor for return in New York to what was, at one time had been called, the Rockefeller drug laws. Those focus specifically on individuals who were addicted. They're not focused on large-scale profiteers. They're focused on primarily young, exclusively poor, by and large exclusively Black and Latino and people of color. Laws in which people caught with the smallest amounts—now the new crisis drug is crack—are being prosecuted for felonies, are being subjected to the most extraordinarily severe sentences, are being housed under bail which is designed to serve as preventive detention.

But, worst of all, the local police departments, who have served as occupation forces, oppressor forces in ghettos of this country for years are being given even a greater hand at this point. They're invited in by so-called community leaders. They engage in the most racist, offensive, and violent conduct—all because they know what the end is, that the end justifies their means. They brutalize the young, they intimidate the young. Those young, and those addicted who don't fall at their feet, so to speak, and welcome them as conquerors are beaten, are brutalized, are arrested, are framed, are jailed, are harassed. . . .

Buy and Bust Operations

In New York City they're setting up this massive new force which is known under any number of acronyms. But the long and the short of it is they've brought hundreds of thousands of cops into the ghettos in what are called "buy and bust" operations. As a defense attorney who has represented in one way or another hundreds of people over the years in these "buy and bust" cases, most of these cases are nonsense. Many of them "buy" money which is marked money, which is established to make a case, is never recovered from individuals. They're prosecuted as felons. A vicious cycle in these "buy and bust" operations is that it comes down to an undercover agent who says he sold it or she sold it. And if they need to make a case they will, if they need to plant money they do, and if they need to plant extra drugs, they do.

The courts have become part and parcel of this whole process of oppression, and out of concern for their own public image and their own reelections or reappointments, they in fact have become the drum majors in the parade of this oppression. So you have hundreds of young Blacks and Latinos and poor people being brought before judges in New York City with a "nuisance bail" being set, bail which to white middle class kids could be posted in a matter of hours, but to poor people in the amounts of $500 to $1,000 results in their languishing in jail for weeks and months on end. . . .

Matt Wuerker. Reprinted with permission.

Until you address the quintessential issue of poverty and racism, there's going to be a drug problem. Until you make available to hundreds of thousands, if not millions of Black and Latino and poor people in this country opportunities that are denied them, there's going to be a drug problem. Until you begin to commit yourself, not through piecemeal programs, but through a real war on the drug problem, which is a war on poverty, until you begin to commit yourself as a society to eradicating racism and to equality of opportunity, and to the notion of social justice, drugs of one form or another are going to be here. Now, if the middle class, or the ruling class, or the legislative body in this country is truly desirous or interested in eradicating or addressing the drug problem, then they have to commit themselves to the war on poverty, and they have to commit themselves to recognizing that it ultimately comes down to racism and classism in the communities. . . . There are community groups, and there are community people that are community based, that have the heartbeat of their community, and that can deal with the drug problem in a way that poses not just band-aid solutions but provides true opportunity to deal with it in a realistic, in a non-racist, in a non-classist, and in a possibly successful manner. Let me just add one thing. Now, my perspective is not just as a defense attorney in the South Bronx for a good number of years. But for over a decade I was a community organizer, a social worker, and a director of a large drug program. So the positions that I'm taking do not by any means come from the isolated framework of the law, or as an attorney, but come from ten, twelve years of working in the community on a community-based level, dealing in a multifaceted approach to problems of drugs in this country.

Seizure of Property

There's no doubt in my mind that the evictions [from housing where drugs are sold] are part of a demagogic response of politicians on their surface. But when you look behind them, they're a pretense. These evictions are being used, in particular in New York City, to again focus on seizing an already almost zero housing market—displacing poor people and turning it over to either the city or to private interests who are involved in gentrification, who are involved in making millions of dollars by taking properties that are evicted, turning them into co-ops and condos for yuppies. So there's a hidden agenda. It appears very sexy on the surface: "We keep going into these places if they keep dealing, we're gonna shut them down and we're gonna take away a base of operations." It sounds good, but it's nonsense for many reasons. Number one, many of these so-called drug dens are quasi-abandoned buildings in which poor people live, in which poor addicts live, in which people who may possess small amounts of narcotics, who may use small amounts of narcotics, or who may even deal small amounts of narcotics are forced to reside in. They're cold-water flats, they are abandoned buildings, they are hazardous to their health. And what they in effect do is they take thousands of poor people, they put them out into the streets in a city such as New York where there are already hundreds if not thousands upon thousands of homeless people. They are then taken over by the city which sits on them and redevelops them with a view towards the upper classes. They're turned over to private interests who reap tremendous profits on these properties. All in the name of addressing the drug problem. I would note that you don't see those types of evictions when people are convicted of white collar crimes, people who are predators who live off the poor in this city and other cities. They make deals with the federal government, they pay fines, and they go back to their homes. . . .

An Attack on Civil Rights

Drug Tsar William Bennett demonstrated his racial and class priorities by serving eviction notices to 60 low-income, mostly Black, residents of public housing projects in southeast Washington for reported use of drugs in their apartments. Similar actions have been taken in Chicago and other cities.

Moreover, military-style weekend police sweeps into Black and Latino neighborhoods have become commonplace in Los Angeles.

This emphasis on attacking the consumer, the petty drug dealer, and the worker on the job constitutes another prong of the attack on civil rights and living standards.

Paul D'Amato, *Socialist Worker*, October 1989.

This is a system that reacts only to community pressure. This is a system that reacts only to the presence of united numbers of folks. If there's gonna be demonstrations, then not only should we be demonstrating on a local level, but on the national level. Because the fact of the matter is, the enemy and the real profiteer and the whole so-called drug crisis in this country are the powerful that run this country. The people that profit from racism and classism and sexism and oppression are the largest importers and distributors of narcotics in this country. There's not a doubt in my mind they're involved with the government and police on a national and local level. . . .

I just hope I've made it clear enough that historically in this country, the so-called leadership, the police forces, and military have used pretexts to further oppress and to expand and use their stranglehold on people of color. Whether it's expropriation of Native American land, whether it's slavery, which is the most obvious, whether it's economic slavery, each and every time the so-called leadership of this country has had a chance to make further inroads in controlling the aspiration and the independence of communities, populated by people of color, they do it. . . .

The other thing that's become very widely used—the other police tactic used in the ghettos of New York City now—is what are called sweeps. These are situations which are particularly active during the summer time, when hundreds of thousands of poor kids are on the streets. And what the police do is they will literally pull police buses, and sometimes they've even used private buses. They will close off entrances and exits to square-block areas, and they will send hundreds of cops into this area, rounding up poor people, lining them up against walls, charging them all with one sort of crime or another because it has to be cost effective. You can't go in there with 100 or 150 cops during a six-hour operation and come out with two so-called drug busts. So what they do is that they sweep away 100, 150, 200 kids, young people, charge them with anything and everything. Interestingly enough, the vast majority of young kids primarily busted in these raids get nailed for disorderly conduct and resisting arrest. They are beaten. Drugs which may be found are tagged to ten and fifteen and twenty people at the same time. Now, not only is this another means of removing poor people from the streets during the summertime but it is also part and parcel of the government sending a message that "We control your communities, we control your destiny, you are not free to do as you wish."

Divide and Conquer

And lastly, the other point I'd like to raise . . . is probably one out of every four people in this country are poor and oppressed directly. Now you better believe that the powerful in this country are sensitive to this tremendous number—sixty, seventy million so-called North American citizens, and I say that because they're certainly not accorded with any of the rights and benefits which purportedly go with that type of citizenship. They represent a tremendous untapped potential, which the government of this country is very frightened of. If sixty million people ever got their act together politically, that's more than enough to shift the balance of power in this country. It's more than enough to make the privileged few begin to worry about their status. So, this police attack on the poor people in this country in ghettos and barrios and reservations should also be kept in the broader context of another in the government's design to divide, to conquer, and to prevent the types of coalition development which poses a threat to the powerful in this country. And that, along with the agenda that we talked about earlier, is clearly what this so-called War on Drugs is about.

"An alternative explanation to the racism charge is that the police are simply responding to (black) community pressure to 'do something' about the problem."

The War on Drugs Is Not Racist

William Wilbanks

William Wilbanks is a professor in the criminal justice department at Florida International University in Miami. He is also the author of the book, *The Myth of a Racist Criminal Justice System*. In the following viewpoint, Wilbanks counters the common charge that the war on drugs is racist. He maintains that many black communities have demanded that the police step up their efforts to stop drug trafficking in minority neighborhoods. Thus he writes that when the police sweep through minority neighborhoods and arrest people, they are responding to local pressure.

As you read, consider the following questions:

1. In Wilbanks's view, why are public surveys taken on drug use often flawed?
2. According to the author, what is the link between drug use and criminality?
3. Wilbanks admits that more black drug dealers are arrested than white dealers. What explanation does he give for this?

William Wilbanks wrote "The War on Drugs Is Not Racist" specifically for inclusion in this book.

For years many black leaders, defense attorneys, civil libertarians, etc. have claimed that blacks are targeted for arrest far out of proportion to their representation in the "offender pool". This more general criticism of the police arrest process has intensified in recent years—during the War on Drugs—as the race gap has widened while the U.S. prison population has more than doubled in the decade of the 70's. The Sentencing Project reported that 23% of black (vs. 10% of Hispanic & 6% of white) men in their 20's were under the control (i.e., in prison or on probation or parole) of the criminal justice system at any point in time. This chorus of criticism from the left is beginning to find support from the political "mainstream" as two "establishment" newspapers have raised questions as to whether the War on Drugs is racist.

USA Today reported on December 20, 1989, on its own analysis of FBI [Federal Bureau of Investigation] nationwide arrest data and claimed that the criminal justice arrest process is racially biased since 38% of drug arrests in the U.S. in 1988 were of blacks while blacks comprised only 12% of the U.S. population and only 12% of drug users. Reporter Sam Meddis also claimed that racial inequalities in arrests widened between 1984 and 1988 as cocaine/heroin arrests doubled for whites but jumped four-fold for blacks. Further, when only cocaine arrests were considered, blacks made up 57% of arrests for sale and 44% for possession.

The Statistics

The *USA Today* article claimed that the racial gap in arrests was a clear indication of racism since blacks and whites are equally (i.e., proportionate to population figures) involved in regular drug use and sales. The newspaper pointed to the annual household survey conducted by the National Institute on Drug Abuse which found that about 12% of whites and blacks admitted to regular drug use. Thus the newspaper attributed the greater arrest propensity of blacks (in the face of an equal drug using propensity) to racist arrest policies. The newspaper also suggested that blacks and whites were equally likely to be involved in drug sales and thus that over 80% of cocaine salesmen are white though only 43% of cocaine sale arrests are of whites.

USA Today focused on drug arrest, use and sales figures and made little attempt to explain why current policy has produced this racial disparity. By contrast, *Los Angeles Times'* reporter Ron Harris devoted most of his lengthy April 22, 1990, article to explanations for this racial disparity in arrests provided to him during interviews with 100 persons in and outside of the criminal justice system.

Reporter Harris accepted as a given that "whites sell most

of the nation's cocaine and account for 80% of its consumers while "it is blacks and other minorities who continue to fill up America's courtrooms and jails." He concluded that the nation's War on Drugs "has in effect become a war on black people.". . .

Serious Flaws

The statistical claims and conclusions (the War on Drugs is racist) of the two newspaper articles make a good story (how "newsworthy" would a story about even-handed justice in the War on Drugs be?) but are seriously flawed. Let me make six points that argue against the claims put forward by *USA Today* and the *Los Angeles Times*.

A Community Fights Back

Whenever discussion turns to the need for more police and stronger penalties, [American intellectuals] cry that our constitutional liberties are in jeopardy.

Well, yes, they are in jeopardy, but Americans—many of them poor, black or Hispanic—have figured out what the armchair critics haven't. Drugs may threaten to destroy their neighborhoods, but *they* refuse to stand by and let it happen. *They* have discovered that it is possible not only to fight back, but to win.

William J. Bennett, speech before the Kennedy School of Government at Harvard University, December 11, 1989.

First, the claim that blacks and whites are equally likely to regularly use drugs is based on figures from the annual household surveys conducted by the National Institute on Drug Abuse (NIDA). The *interpretation* (not the studies themselves) of the NIDA surveys have recently come under strong attack from Dr. Eric Wish of the U.S. Dept. of Justice and Dr. Mark Kleiman of Harvard University who point out that the most serious (i.e., those who combine criminality with drug use) abusers of drugs are part of populations (i.e., criminals, homeless, inmates) not counted in NIDA surveys and when criminal abusers are interviewed they are not likely to tell "the nice man from the government that they smoked crack recently." The Wish and Kleiman criticisms of the interpretation of data from NIDA surveys are included in a report ("Hard-core Cocaine Addicts: Measuring—and Fighting—the Epidemic") by the U.S. Senate Judiciary Committee and in the March 5, 1990, issue of *U.S. News & World Report*.

Thus the best research available indicates that the "regular users" of drugs according to the NIDA survey are a different type of population from the types of addicts typically arrested. Thus there is no basis for suggesting that since blacks are only 12% of drug users they should be only 12%—not 38%—of drug arrests. We do not know what percentage of *criminal drug abusers* in the U.S. are black vs. white and thus we do not have a figure to compare to the 38% black drug arrest figure. No competent drug researcher (including NIDA staffers) would draw the kind of comparisons made by the two newspapers.

Black Crimes

Second, the link between regular drug use and criminality is not as simple as newspapers would have us believe. There is no evidence that regular drug use inevitably—or even usually—leads to criminality. It is much easier to predict drug use from criminality (i.e., most criminals regularly use drugs) than criminality from drug use (i.e., most regular drug users do not commit crimes—other than drug use). But arrest policy focuses on those involved in crime (robbery, drug sales, etc.) rather than those simply involved in illegal drug use.

Victim survey data from the Dept. of Justice indicates that blacks are disproportionately involved in crime (on the order of 6:1 for violent crime and 4:1 for property crime) and thus it follows that blacks are more likely to be caught up in "drug arrests". The FBI figures may simply indicate that blacks—being more likely to be involved in crime and drug use—are also more likely to be caught up in the "police net" designed to catch criminal addicts and sellers.

Third, the NIDA survey sex difference in regular cocaine use is approximately 2:1 (male vs. female) while the sex ratio for drug arrests (according to *USA Today*) is 5:1. This difference does not represent the "sex discrimination" factor but the fact that female drug users are less often involved in crimes that subject them to arrest. Again, the baseline for what "should be" (in a criminal justice system devoid of race and sex bias) the proportion of arrests by race or sex is not the proportion of admitted usage according to NIDA surveys.

Community Pressure

Fourth, it is interesting to note (even in the *Los Angeles Times* article) that cities with black police chiefs and mayors are just as likely—perhaps more likely—to "produce" disproportionate numbers of drug arrests of blacks. If police surveillance and arrest policies are racist those policies are even more pronounced when blacks are designing and implementing the policy. An alternative explanation to the racism charge is that the police are simply responding to (black) community pressure to "do something" about the drug problem.

Surely one cannot characterize the black community's demands for more police action as a demand for greater implementation of a racist policy? And one can only imagine the reaction police would receive if they went to a "crime watch" meeting in a black community plagued by drugs and told the audience that police presence would have to be reduced as the department had decided that resources would have to be shifted to white areas to avoid charges of racism.

Poverty, Not Race

To the extent . . . that "high-crime areas" are populated by racial minorities and the economically disadvantaged, it will be blacks, Hispanics, the poor, and other inhabitants of such areas whose conduct will take on sinister meaning. Poor people and minorities who pass glassine envelopes to one another at West 128th Street and Eighth Avenue in Manhattan will be suspect; the residents of communities where the crime rate is lower, and the socioeconomic status generally higher, will be able to pass such envelopes without risking lawful seizure by a police officer. . . .

Research suggests that while the police do tend to arrest blacks at a higher rate than they do whites with whom they come into contact, it is probable that race, in itself, is not the explanatory factor. It is more likely that poverty and a low socioeconomic status, with which race tends to be associated, figure importantly into the police arrest decision.

James R. Acker, *Criminal Law Bulletin*, January/February 1987.

If the black community is being destroyed now by the cocaine epidemic one can only speculate as to what would happen if the police decided to cast their "surveillance net" elsewhere (primarily in the white suburbs). The black community does not want less police attention or even more "equal" police attention. Many black residents (and black police) might agree that "the police should go after the rich whites who control the drug trade" but at the same time they do not want a reduction of police presence in their area. The demand is for greater police protection and those who criticize the War on Drugs for unwanted or unjustified police presence are simply out of touch with the black community. In short, "leaders" who charge that the War on Drugs is racist simply do not speak for the vast majority of residents in the black community.

Begging the Question

Fifth, it is misleading to label as racist any process that produces a disparate impact on blacks as racist *in operation if not in intent*. The term institutional racism is often applied to policies that produce disproportionate negative outcomes for blacks. But such a term "begs the question" (i.e., assumes what should be proven) in that it assumes that race had some (perhaps subtle or unconscious if not conscious) part in the decision-making process without proof of bias.

But the concept of institutional racism, if "equally" applied, would also lead to the conclusion that major universities are guilty of institutional racism since Asians and Jews are over-represented and Blacks and Hispanics under-represented and that the National Basketball Association and the NAACP [National Association for the Advancement of Colored People] are institutionally racist since whites are under-represented. In short, the label of institutional racism would seem to be required where black and white "representation" does not conform to a rigid quota system based on numbers in the general population.

Drug Markets

Sixth, the local police do focus (but not exclusively) on low-level street dealers but only with the knowledge that other agencies (i.e., the U.S. Drug Enforcement Agency) are going after the big dealers. Local departments do not have the resources or jurisdiction to target upper-level dealers. And even if the police gave equal attention to upper-level dealers (who might be mostly white) the numbers of low-level dealers (who might be mostly black) are so much greater that such a policy would still result in more drug arrests of black dealers.

Police drug sting operations concentrate in poor (usually black and Hispanic) areas because open drug markets are generally confined to those areas. Many whites are arrested trying to buy drugs in black areas. Those whites choose to take the risk of being mugged, robbed, shot, etc. in a high crime area because they want the drugs which are not as readily available in middle-class and white areas. Middle-class areas will not tolerate open drug dealing and thus most whites (without "connections") are forced to travel to a black area to buy their drugs.

"Blood and urine testing ensures that the first, and worst, casualty of the war on drugs will be the precious liberties of our citizens."

Drug Testing Violates Civil Liberties

Leonard H. Glantz

Leonard H. Glantz is a professor of health law at Boston University's School of Public Health. In the following viewpoint, Glantz condemns the arbitrary nature of drug testing and argues that it constitutes an unnecessary search of many innocent people. He writes that the Constitution guarantees individual liberty over the state's need to enforce the law, even in the war on drugs.

As you read, consider the following questions:

1. What evidence does Glantz offer that drug testing constitutes a search?
2. Does the author believe that drug testing is an effective deterrent? Why or why not?
3. What objection does Glantz have to testing workers in certain "sensitive" occupations?

Leonard H. Glantz, "A Nation of Suspects: Drug Testing and the Fourth Amendment," *American Journal of Public Health,* October 1989. Excerpts reprinted with the author's permission.

One of the weapons in the drug war arsenal is drug testing in the workplace. The pretext is often detection of worker impairment, but this is seldom the true motivation. Much of the impetus for the current drug testing rage comes from the 1986 President's Commission on Organized Crime report, *America's Habit: Drug Abuse, Drug Trafficking and Organized Crime,* which recommended that "Government and private sector employers who do not already require drug testing of job applicants and current employees should consider the appropriateness of such a testing program." In the context of a report on organized crime, workplace drug testing becomes a tool for attacking the drug problem from the demand side. If users can be stopped, then the drug traffickers and dealers will have no one to whom to sell their drugs. President Ronald Reagan underscored this approach in ordering a drug-free federal workplace, declaring that ilegal drug use on or off duty by federal employees is not acceptable for a variety of reasons, and directing the head of each executive agency to establish programs to test for the use of legal drugs by employees in "sensitive positions." One of the goals is to recruit employers, both public and private, into the war on drugs. Former Attorney General Edwin Meese even suggested that employers "undertake surveillance of problem areas, such as locker rooms, parking lots, shipping and mailroom areas, and nearby taverns if necessary."

A Demeaning Procedure

As a result of this fervor, the pace of workplace drug testing has notably increased. Workers from groups as diverse as firefighters, police officers, nuclear power plant employees, school bus aides, probationary school teachers, and computer programmers have been subjected to mandatory drug testing. There has understandably been a complementary increase in the number of lawsuits brought by workers to halt what they feel is a demeaning and intrusive procedure. The courts have been divided in their determination of the legality of mandatory drug tests. The vast majority of the cases have been brought by governmental employees, since their employers are subject to the restrictions against unreasonable searches and seizures found in the Fourth Amendment of the US Constitution:

> The right of the people to be secure in their persons, houses, papers, and effects, against unreasonable searches and seizures, shall not be violated, and no Warrants shall issue, but upon probable cause, supported by Oath or affirmation, and particularly describing the place to be searched, and the persons or things to be seized.

Not *all* searches are forbidden by the Fourth Amendment— only unreasonable ones. Where a search warrant is secured upon probable cause from a judicial officer, a search becomes reasonable. Over the years, however, the courts have carved out exceptions to both the warrant and probable cause requirements and have, at times, looked at other circumstances to determine if a search is reasonable and, therefore, lawful.

Dan Wasserman. © 1989 Reprinted by permission of Los Angeles Times Syndicate.

The initial question was, is a urine test a search or seizure at all? In one case, which upheld drug testing of police officers in limited circumstances, a concurring judge argued that requiring a person to urinate on demand could not be a search or seizure since a person could not "retain a privacy interest in a waste product that, once released, is flushed down a drain" and that one could not have a "subjective expectation of privacy in a body waste that must pass from his system." However, no majority of any court has reached this conclusion, and all that have decided the issue have concluded that a mandatory urine, blood or breath test constitutes a search under the Fourth Amendment. The focus of the courts, therefore, has been on the "unreasonableness" of the "search" that is involved in drug testing.

Drug testing can be conducted in a variety of ways. It can be done by examining the urine, blood, or breath of an individual.

The urine can be collected by allowing the person to urinate privately, while someone listens for the normal sounds of urination, or under direct observation. People can be tested randomly, as a result of behavior that indictates impairment due to drug use, as part of pre-employment or annual physicals, as a result of known procedures, or through sheer whim and surprise. A positive test can lead to a re-test, a warning to stop drug use, voluntary or mandatory drug treatment programs, termination of employment, or criminal prosecution. Given the possible various combinations of these factors, it is not surprising that courts have split on the "unreasonableness" of drug testing in various situations.

The depth of a court's feeling that mandatory drug screening is demeaning, intrusive, or a violation of a person's general right to be free from governmental intrusions, also affects its decision. For example, in one case the Plainfield, New Jersey, Fire Department entered a city firehouse at 7:00 am, secured and locked all the station doors, awoke all the firefighters on duty and ordered them to submit a urine sample while under surveillance. There was no notice of any intent to require urinalysis, there was no written directive, policy or procedure, and nothing in the collective bargaining agreement regarding drug tests. All firefighters who tested positive for "controlled substances" were immediately terminated without pay. They were not told of the particular substance found in their urine or its concentration, nor were they provided with copies of the actual laboratory results. The city had no reason to suspect that any of the tested firefighters had used drugs or were impaired in any way. There were no complaints from the public about inadequate fire protection and no increase in the incidence of accidents. In short, there was no reason for this surprise raid. . . .

The Supreme Court

Given the diversity of opinions and approaches used by various courts across the country, it was only a matter of time before the United States Supreme Court would enter the fray. On March 21, 1989, the Court handed down the first two of what is likely to be a series of opinions on drug testing.

The first case, *Skinner v. Railway Labor Executive Association*, involved the constitutionality of a drug testing scheme directed at railway workers. While the tests were to be performed by private railways on their employees, the tests implicated Fourth Amendment concerns because they were either mandated or authorized by the Federal Railroad Administration (FRA). In 1985, the FRA promulgated regulations addressing alcohol and drug use by certain railway employees. The regulations forbid these employees from using or possessing alcohol or any controlled substance while on the job, and prohibit employees from reporting to work while under the influence of, or impaired by, controlled substances or alcohol, or having a blood alcohol level of .04 or higher. These regulations were issued in response to evidence that a significant proportion of railroad workers report to work impaired by alcohol or got drunk while working, that 23 percent of operating personnel were "problem drinkers," and that from 1972 to 1983 at least 21 significant accidents resulting in fatalities, serious injury and multimillion dollar property damage involved alcohol and drug use as a "probable cause or contributing factor.". . .

No Balance of Rights

Drug testing is what happens when the government, faced with a national crisis it doesn't know how to handle, decides that individual liberties are an obstacle to the nation's salvation. And the Supreme Court has gone along. Making this mugging of the Constitution appear praiseworthy are such eminently respectable institutions as *The New York Times*, which has declared the Court's dragnet drug search decisions a proper balance of "privacy rights against public safety."

But once you can force blood and urine tests on someone without a wisp of an indication that person has done anything wrong, there is no balance of rights. There are no privacy rights left.

Nat Hentoff, *The Village Voice*, May 2, 1989.

In its analysis, the Court recognizes that blood, urine and breath testing are an invasion of employee privacy interests and are a "search" for the purposes of the Fourth Amendment. The Court also recognizes that to perform a search, a warrant or at least probable cause is usually required. But at times, as the Court has held in the past, the government may have "special needs" beyond normal law enforcement that may justify departures from the usual warrant and probable cause requirements. The opinion then discusses the "special needs" in this case. First, the employees to be tested are engaged in "safety-sensitive tasks." Second, the purpose of the tests is not to aid in prosecution of employees, but rather to prevent accidents. Third, those charged with administering the test have minimal discretion and, therefore, there is only a minimal chance of arbitrary or unfair use of the testing procedure. Fourth, railroad investigators are not familiar with the Fourth Amendment or warrant requirements. Fifth, if a warrant was required, the delay in obtaining the warrant might allow the needed evidence to be dissipated. Sixth, although urine tests invade an "excretory function traditionally shielded by great privacy," the regulations do not require the direct observation of a monitor, and it is not unlike similar procedures performed in the context of a "regular physical examination." Seventh, the expectations of privacy of employees is "diminished by reason of their participation in an industry that is pervasively regulated to ensure safety." Eighth, the interests of the government to test are "compelling" because the employees can cause "great human loss before any other signs of impairment become noticeable to supervisors." Ninth, the regulations will be an effective means of deterring employees from using alcohol or drugs. Finally, the testing procedures will help railroads obtain "invaluable information about the causes of major accidents."

Individual Rights

This is a remarkably utilitarian approach to the Fourth Amendment, as the dissent notes. Essentially, it holds that the Fourth Amendment safeguards are not applicable to situations where the government has good reasons to want information and the intrusion on the person is not great. It makes no effort to distinguish between the searches of places or things, and searches of persons. As the two dissenters argue, "The majority's acceptance of dragnet blood and urine testing ensures that the first, and worst, casualty of the war on drugs will be the precious liberties of our citizens." The dissent points out that the Fourth Amendment was designed to make governmental searches of citizens difficult, and that it is all too easy to balance away individual rights for the good of the state. However, that balancing. was done by the Founders in favor of the individual. The dissenters agree that if the police were freed from the constraints of the Fourth Amendment, the resulting convictions would probably prevent thousands of fatalities. But "our refusal to tolerate this spectre reflects our shared beliefs that even beneficient governmental power—whether exercised to save money, save lives, or make the trains run on time—must always yield to a resolute loyalty to constitutional safeguards."

The dissenters were unconvinced that there is any evidence that drug testing is a deterrent or provides useful evidence of the causes of accidents, and were even more concerned with the majority's standardless and shifting balancing of individual rights and state powers to invade those rights, and its "cavalier disregard" for the text of the Constitution: "There is no drug exception to the Constitution, any more than there is a Communism exception or an exception for other real or imagined sources of domestic unrest.". . .

The fear that these opinions have no principled boundaries was expressed by Justice Antonin Scalia when he pointed out that automobile drivers, construction equipment operators, and school crossing guards all have safety-sensitive jobs. Could they be drug tested based on the speculative injuries that they might cause if under the influence of drugs? Could states require physicians or nurses to be drug tested as a condition of licensure? There is more evidence of drug use by physicians and medical students than there was evidence of drug use by customs workers. If the court is serious about upholding drug testing to ensure the integrity of a program and prevent the possibility of bribery, then certainly it is judges who should be tested, since they are the ultimate arbiters of imprisonment or freedom for accused drug dealers. One could go on indefinitely making lists of potential job categories that might be eligible for drug screening using the Court's rationale.

Expanding the Reach of Government

This is not idle speculation or liberal hysteria. The drug testing cases have already been used to expand the reach of government into the lives of individuals. For example, a licensed practical nurse was fired when he refused to submit to an HIV (human immunodeficiency virus) test, or to disclose the results of a test he had taken earlier. His employer, a public hospital, had learned that his lover had recently died of AIDS (acquired immunodeficiency syndrome), and wanted to know his HIV status in order to decide what duties he could perform. While the procedures he regularly performed could hardly be deemed invasive, this did not deter the hospital. One of the nurse's claims was that the hospital's demand violated his Fourth Amendment rights. Citing the hospital's desire to provide a "safe and efficient workplace," and pointing out that the nurse was in a "safety-sensitive" position, the court readily upheld the hospital's demand based on the appellate courts' decisions in the railroad workers and Customs Service cases. The result would seem to be supported by the Supreme Court's decisions.

In our well-intended desire to stop the flow of drugs into the country and reduce drug abuse, we are rapidly becoming a nation of suspects. Perfectly law abiding citizens who are under no suspicion of drug use are increasingly being called upon to prove their innocence. This activity extends the scope of those who are victims of the drug war.

"The sobriety checkpoints, and drug and alcohol testing are all designed to deter . . . drug or alcohol abuse . . . which could result in the killing or maiming of innocent people."

Drug Testing Does Not Violate Civil Liberties

Paul Glastris

Every year thousands of Americans die in car, boat, train, and plane accidents because of operators under the influence of drugs or alcohol. Proponents of drug testing claim that random tests of all train engineers, bus drivers, and airline pilots would make travel safer. In the following viewpoint, Paul Glastris, a former editor for *The Washington Monthly*, writes that drug tests are not an unreasonable search. Glastris chides the American Civil Liberties Union for fighting the issue in court. He maintains that drug tests save lives and prevent innocent Americans from being killed by drunk or stoned mass-transit drivers.

As you read, consider the following questions:

1. According to the author, what is the difference between a strip search and passing through a metal detector? How does he connect this issue to drug testing?
2. What specific reasons does Glastris give for arguing the ACLU is wrong to fight drug testing?

Paul Glastris, "The ACLU and the Right to Die in a Train Wreck," *The Washington Monthly*, March 1988. Reprinted with permission from *The Washington Monthly*. Copyright © by The Washington Monthly Company, 1611 Connecticut Avenue NW, Washington, DC 20009, (202) 462-0128.

Does the Average Guy worry when he steps through an airport metal detector? Sure he does. He worries about business. He worries about the rising cost of season tickets. He worries about making his flight. He worries about his Walkman as it passes through the x-ray machine. And when the overhead buzz goes off because he forgot to divest himself of his keys, and the young female attendant asks if he would please empty his pockets and pass through again, he worries if she thinks he's good looking.

What he probably does *not* worry about is whether the metal detector search violates his civil liberties. And that is what petrifies the American Civil Liberties Union. The group states its fear in ACLU policy #270: "Perhaps the most troublesome aspect of the airport search question is the readiness with which most people, civil libertarians included, have accepted and indeed welcomed such procedures. It reflects a disturbing tendency to accept any measures, such as routine searches in public places, which are supposedly devised to protect our safety. Such an atmosphere of acquiescence poses the greatest threat to all our civil liberties."

Misdirected Zeal

Supposedly devised? The gravest threat to all our civil liberties? The passion that the ACLU has historically marshalled to combat censorship and racial bigotry is now leading it to fight even the most benign safety measures. As we grope for what to do about hazards such as drunk driving and kids routinely toting pistols down school corridors, and as we seek to stem drug and alcohol abuse by the people who operate our trains and aircraft, the ACLU puts up its dukes as if it were mixing it up with Bull Connor.

When talking about public safety, ACLU officials can sound like nothing so much as Chicago School economists drearily insisting that padded dashboards and pollution controls might save lives but can't be tolerated because they threaten free enterprise. Similarly, the ACLU can't see metal detectors as the modest act of a democratic government to thwart hijackings and murders. It insists on seeing each measure "supposedly" meant to protect health and safety as another dangerous step towards fascism.

What is dangerous is the ACLU's reading of the Constitution, specifically its interpretation of the Fourth Amendment's prohibition of "unreasonable" searches and seizures. The ACLU has dismissed random searches, like those at the airport, as unconstitutional. But not all random searches are created equal. Surely, we have the common sense to recognize the difference between random searches with the rational aim of protecting public safety and searches with the irrational aim of persecuting minorities or minority opinion. There is also an important distinction between searches that employ outrageous techniques, like strip searches, and those that are "minimally intrusive," such as passing through a metal detector. And, finally, there's an important common sense distinction between searches so humiliating or terrifying that the innocent fear them and those that only the guilty fear. . . .

Awhile back, the Reagan administration, in its zeal to root out drugs, started testing the urine of federal employees, even those who push paper all day. Uncle Sam, it seemed, was becoming Big Brother and the ACLU rightly stepped in to fight. But even when it came to drug testing, the ACLU had an uncanny ability to stake out the most indefensible terrain.

Justified Testing

I believe that courts and legislatures that outlaw the random testing of safety-sensitive employees, public or private, are doing America a great disservice. Doesn't it make simple common sense that the public's right to safety and life itself should outweigh an individual's questionable right to abuse drugs?

I'm not arguing that we should toss the constitution out the window in our fight against drug abuse. I can understand, for example, why the random testing of *all* employees or *all* citizens is a dangerously intrusive invasion of privacy. But I do believe that testing is a vital tool with safety-sensitive employees who could kill or maim others if they're messed up on drugs.

John W. Johnstone Jr., speech delivered at the White House conference on Public/Private Partnerships, December 1, 1988.

The government has no pressing need to know about the drug habits of most of its work force. But is it fascism for the government to ensure that air traffic controllers, railroad engineers, and others who make the difference between life and death are unimpaired by drugs and alcohol? Too often they are stoned and drunk. Amtrak passengers, who take 20 million train trips a year, would be shocked to learn of the extent of the drinking problem in the railroad industry. A 1979 study found 23 percent of railroad operating employees were problem drinkers and many of those got drunk on the job. Drug abuse is also a serious problem. According to the Federal Railroad Administration (FRA), between 1975 and 1984 there were 48 train accidents, causing 37 fatalities and 80 injuries, in which drugs or alcohol were "directly affecting" causes.

So in 1986 the Transportation Department ruled that railroads had to begin testing employees for drugs as a condition of employment, after an accident and when trained supervisors had "reasonable cause" to believe an employee was impaired by drugs or alcohol. One final precaution was rejected: random testing. Officials from the railroad unions and the FRA felt random testing wasn't necessary.

Deadly Accident

All those precautions, however, failed on January 4, 1987 when the brakeman and engineer of a three-engine Conrail train shared a joint of marijuana on duty. Both were veteran railmen in their thirties. Both had just come under the gaze of a supervisor trained to spot signs of drug and alcohol use. ("Reasonable cause testing is keyed to the ability of a supervisor to detect symptoms," says a FRA study of the accident that was to follow.) Despite several warning signals, the impaired engineer failed to slow his train, instead driving through an intersection and onto a track in Chase, Maryland, just ahead of an Amtrak passenger train traveling at 105 miles per hour. The collision of the Amtrak train into the back of the Conrail locomotive left 16 people dead and 174 injured.

This crash and other data led Congress and the Transportation Department to reconsider the drug testing program. Government labor union leaders still oppose random testing. But significantly, Senators Paul Sarbanes and Barbara Mikulski, liberal Democrats from Maryland, a state with both a huge constituency of government employees and a lot of grieving family members of the train wreck victims, wound up supporting the random testing bill. So did the National Association of Rail Passengers, a public interest group.

The head of the FRA, John H. Riley, reversing himself, now favors random drug use testing. The reason: after a 24-month program of testing based on "reasonable cause," FRA studies show that 4 percent of all rail employees involved in accidents had recently used illicit drugs, and 1 percent had alcohol in their blood. "Although these numbers are relatively low," he said, "they represent a hard core of alcohol and drug users who have not been persuaded by prevention campaigns, have not been willing to take advantage of employee assistance programs, have avoided detection in scheduled testing conducted by the railroads, and have not been deterred by the reasonable cause testing program."

Dangerous Travel

Drugs and alcohol threaten our skies and roads too. In 1986, the Insurance Institute for Highway Safety asked 300 truck drivers in Tennessee to be tested. Thirty percent (of the 88 percent who volunteered) tested positive for "drugs with potential for abuse"; 14 percent tested positive for marijuana, 11 percent for speed, 2 percent for cocaine. In 1983, Greyhound, during a strike, took applications from experienced bus drivers: 30 percent tested positive for marijuana. The airline industry is also plagued. While there have been no big commercial air carrier accidents attributable to drugs or alcohol, there are risks to the Americans who take 418 million plane trips each year. Tests of general aviation pilots killed in fatal accidents found alcohol a contributing factor 10.5 percent of the time. And an inspector general's report revealed that more than 10,000 FAA [Federal Aviation Administration] certified pilots had their automobile licenses suspended or revoked for driving while intoxicated during the previous seven years.

" . . .in conclusion, it is this court's opinion that drug testing would put the constitutional rights of railroad employees in danger."

Henry Payne. Reprinted by permission of UFS, Inc.

The whole notion of testing people for drugs—"lifestyle choices" as one ACLU lawyer puts it—drives the Union crazy. ACLU attorneys have been burning out word processors writing court briefs and motions to defend workers. Sometimes, the Union has been on the side of the angels, as in their suit on behalf of postal service job applicants rejected on the basis of drug urine tests. The postal service has many problems, but the occasional stoned mailman misdelivering a letter is not one of them. More to the point, mail delivery is not a health or safety function. For the same reason, you have to like the ACLU for taking on the Tippecanoe County, Indiana, school system for forcing its cheerleaders to submit urine samples. But in 1987 it fell short of sainthood, filing an amicus brief supporting federal workers who were suing the Transportation Department over its planned random testing of safety-sensitive government employees, mostly in the FAA. The ACLU opposes a bill passed by the Senate that would extend random tests to key railroad workers, pilots, truckers, and bus drivers.

Reliable Tests

Here again, the ACLU plays the "effectiveness" game. It points to the high error rate for initial drug screening tests and sloppy lab work as reason enough to reject drug use testing. Yet the Senate bill mandates elaborate and reliable confirmation tests, done at federally certified labs, to determine if an initial screening was accurate. The Union also points to electronic devices that test worker dexterity as an alternative to urine testing—though they don't endorse the use of these devices, either. But what if—as is likely—urine tests, or a combination of urine and dexterity tests, proved better than dexterity tests alone in deterring drug and alcohol use and saving lives? "Under no circumstances would we approve of urinalysis," said ACLU special assistant Loren Siegel, "no matter what the occupation."

When it comes to public safety, judges have, for the most part, resisted the most extreme arguments of the ACLU. (Don't expect to read headlines declaring airport metal detectors unconstitutional.) But the ACLU has been effective at conning the courts, state legislatures, regulatory agencies, and law enforcement offices into some lousy policies. (Consider the ban on surprise searches and the shooting of Chester Jackson in Detroit.) On drug testing, for instance, courts have issued a wide range of rulings—everything from approving random testing for racehorse jockeys to rejecting testing rail employees even after they have been in an accident. Is this any way to protect the nation's welfare?

Because the ACLU's arguments have at least in part been heeded, many of the safety procedures we do have are less effective than they might be. The crucial element of surprise, for instance, has been taken out of many of these measures even though it would ensure more safety with no infringement on personal liberty. Those warning signs at sobriety checkpoints hand the drunken driver a splendid opportunity to take a U-turn and threaten motorists on another road. Similarly, it seems odd that someone who sets off the alarm of an airport metal detector is allowed to waltz out of the terminal without being so much as questioned by airport security guards, let alone detained by police. Anyone unglued enough to try to sneak a pistol through a metal detector might be likely to use it on his way out the door. . . .

If the ACLU would focus on the real dangers, it would see that the safety measures it is opposing so fanatically pose absolutely no threat to our political or religious liberties. The purpose of these measures is not to discover whether we are Republicans, Democrats, or Communists, or Protestants, Jews, or Catholics, or in any way inhibit us in the exercise of our political and religious freedoms. Nor do these safety measures pose any threat to the innocent. The metal detectors, the school sweeps, the sobriety checkpoints, and drug and alcohol testing are all designed to deter or apprehend those guilty of carrying concealed weapons, or of drug or alcohol abuse, all of which could result in the killing or maiming of innocent people. These measures do not even put the innocent in fear, as would, say, police pounding on our door in the night. Only the guilty have anything to fear. What is wrong with having the guilty worry about what they are doing and perhaps change their behavior as a result? What is wrong with keeping them from harming the rest of us? What is wrong with the ACLU?

Understanding Words in Context

Readers occasionally come across words they do not recognize. And frequently, because they do not know a word or words, they will not fully understand the passage being read. Obviously, the reader can look up an unfamiliar word in a dictionary. However, by carefully examining the word in the context in which it is used, the word's meaning can often be determined. A careful reader may find clues to the meaning of the words in surrounding words, ideas, and attitudes.

Below are excerpts from the viewpoints in this chapter. In each excerpt, one or two words are printed in italics. Try to determine the meaning of each word by reading the excerpt. Under each excerpt you will find four definitions for the italicized word. Choose the one that is closest to your understanding of the word.

Finally, use a dictionary to see how well you have understood the words in context. It will be helpful to discuss with others the clues which helped you decide each word's meaning.

1. Since the early 1980s, the prevailing attitude has been that cracking down on drugs is *IMPERATIVE*. Tough measures must be taken to solve urban problems.

   IMPERATIVE means:

   a) unnecessary   b) overwhelming
   c) essential   d) mistaken

2. What will the next round of enforcement bring? That question shows the truly *INSIDIOUS* quality of the war on drugs: the drug enforcement system can never have enough power to win the war.

   INSIDIOUS means:

   a) sour   b) treacherous
   c) attractive   d) hideous

3. The hysteria of the war on drugs generates proposals that only a few years ago more rational people would have *REPUDIATED* as either absurd or excessive.

REPUDIATED means:

a) rejected   b) upheld
c) considered   d) accepted

4. Prior to trial, the defendant moved to *SUPPRESS* as evidence the marijuana seized from his property. He argued that the evidence not be used against him because it was discovered as the result of an unreasonable, warrantless search.

SUPPRESS means:

a) remove   b) grow
c) exclude   d) smoke

5. The Supreme Court ruled that the police do not violate the Fourth Amendment when they enter open fields to search for drugs. Thus, once again, the police can search farms without worrying about *CONTRAVENING* Fourth Amendment *PROSCRIPTIONS*.

CONTRAVENING means:

a) discussing   b) meeting
c) stepping on   d) violating

PROSCRIPTIONS means:

a) prescriptions   b) suggestions
c) bills   d) restraints

6. U.S. courts *VACILLATE* between supporting tough antidrug measures and rejecting them as un-Constitutional. The courts have not been consistent.

VACILLATE means:

a) choose   b) advocate
c) condemn   d) waver

7. The government's right to punish deviants like drug users is a value *INTRINSIC* in civilized societies. There should be little need for discussion.

INTRINSIC means:

a) forgotten   b) inherent
c) old-fashioned   d) isolated

Periodical Bibliography

The following articles have been selected to supplement the diverse views presented in this chapter.

George J. Annas	"Crack, Symbolism, and the Constitution," *The Hastings Center Report*, May/June 1989.
Jeffrey Chamberlain	"Legal Aspects of Employee Drug Testing," *USA Today*, May 1988.
B.D. Colen	"What Price Drug-Free?" *Health*, May 1988.
Robert L. DuPont	"Never Trust Anyone Under 40," *Policy Review*, Spring 1989.
Ebony	"War! The Drug Crisis," August 1989.
Gerry Fitzgerald	"Dispatches from the Drug War," *Common Cause Magazine*, January/February 1990.
David R. Gergen	"Drugs and White America," *U.S. News & World Report*, September 18, 1989.
Judith Havemann	"Catching Innocents in the Federal Drug Net," *The Washington Post National Weekly Edition*, February 29-March 6, 1988.
John Hoerr et al.	"Privacy," *Business Week*, March 28, 1988.
Tamar Jacoby	"Drug Testing in the Dock," *Newsweek*, November 14, 1988.
Tamar Jacoby	"When Cops Act on a Hunch," *Newsweek*, October 10, 1988.
Andrew Kupfer	"Is Drug Testing Good or Bad?" *Fortune*, December 19, 1989.
Richard Lacayo	"A Threat to Freedom?" *Time*, September 18, 1989.
Thomas Moore	"Dead Zones," *U.S. News & World Report*, April 10, 1989.
Tom Morganthau et al.	"Children of the Underclass," *Newsweek*, September 11, 1989.
Richard Morin and Jodie Allen	"Americans Are Ready to Drop 'The Bomb' in the War on Drugs," *The Washington Post National Weekly Edition*, July 4-10, 1988.
The Nation	"Body Invaders," January 8, 1990.
The Progressive	"Phony War on Drugs," October 1989.
William Saletan	"Jar Wars," *The New Republic*, October 2, 1989.
Alain L. Sanders	"A Boost for Drug Testing," *Time*, April 3, 1989.
Elaine Shannon	"A Loose Cannon's Parting Shot," *Time*, August 7, 1989.
Chris Spolar	"Drugs and the Workplace," *The Washington Post National Weekly Edition*, January 23-29, 1989.

What Policies Can Reduce Teen Drug Abuse?

Chapter Preface

Overall drug use among seniors in high schools has dropped significantly since 1980, according to the University of Michigan National High-School Seniors Survey. The regular use of marijuana, hallucinogens, tranquilizers, and stimulants has been almost halved among high school students. Unfortunately, alcohol and cocaine use remain high. Dr. Lloyd Johnston, a social research director at the University of Michigan, points out that between 1975 and 1985 alcohol use remained constant while cocaine use doubled. Educators, politicians, parents, and counselors are troubled by this trend and remain divided on how to address continuing chemical abuse among America's youth.

Hard-liners like William J. Bennett, director of the Office of National Drug Control Policy, advocate straightforward education programs, stiff penalties for students caught with drugs in school, and a strong antidrug message from adults. Bennett thinks traditional education programs have been too weak. He writes, "No videotape, no matter how useful, and no curricular package, no matter how well-conceived, can substitute for the action and example of educators, parents, and other adults in the community who teach young people the lesson that drug use is wrong."

Many social researchers disagree with this approach, however. Psychologist Carol Tavris argues against hard-line education programs because she believes they are designed to scare teens.

Tavris maintains that such programs give drugs a mystique that encourages young people to experiment with the forbidden substances. She contends that drug education should teach young people "responsible use of alcohol and 'social drugs' in controlled settings." Tavris asserts, "Lower rates of alcohol and drug abuse have been associated with approaches that emphasize moderation and education."

As the problem of teen drug abuse persists, the debate on how to reduce the problem intensifies.

"The principal way to curb the demand for drugs is education."

Education Can Reduce Teen Drug Abuse

William DeJong

Two well-known anti-drug programs that started in the 1980's include Project DARE (Drug Abuse Resistance Education) and Project SPECDA (School Program to Educate and Control Drug Abuse). Both programs use local police officers to educate fifth through seventh graders about the dangers of drug use. In the following viewpoint, William DeJong writes that graduates of Project DARE and Project SPECDA are less likely to use drugs than are students who have not attended the program. DeJong, an analyst at the Education Development Center, prepared this study for the National Institute of Justice.

As you read, consider the following questions:

1. Why does DeJong argue that enforcing anti-drug laws is not enough to stop drug abuse?
2. According to research cited by the author, is Project SPECDA effective? How?
3. Why does DeJong believe that police officers are qualified to teach courses on drug use?

Reprinted from William DeJong, *Arresting the Demand for Drugs: Police and School Partnerships to Prevent Drug Abuse*, published by the U.S. Department of Justice, National Institute of Justice, Office of Communication and Research Utilization, November 1987.

Law enforcement agencies across the nation spend millions of dollars each year to control the distribution and sale of illicit drugs. By any measure, that effort is paying off. Each year, tons of narcotics are seized. Vast sums of cash, weapons, boats, and planes are confiscated. Thousands of arrests are made.

Nevertheless, the drug trade continues to flourish.

Drug traffickers face risks. But they also know that, with the demand for drugs so high, there is lots of money to be made. To them, the risks seem worth it.

Thus, for every smuggling route closed, a new avenue is opened. For every arrest made, for every conviction won, a new trafficker eagerly fills the void. For every ton of drugs seized, several more slip through the enforcement net and reach the streets.

Certainly, our efforts to attack the processing, distribution, and sale of illegal drugs must continue. But there is also a need to focus on arresting the demand for drugs. Until there is a drop in demand, law enforcement officials, by their own admission, are fighting a war they cannot possibly win.

The principal way to curb the demand for drugs is education. Recognizing this fact, top police administrators in both Los Angeles and New York initiated collaborations with their respective school departments to develop, implement, and evaluate drug prevention education programs that bring police officers into the classrooms as regular, full-time instructors. . . .

Project DARE

A joint project of the Los Angeles Police Department (LAPD) and the Los Angeles Unified School District, Project DARE (Drug Abuse Resistance Education) is designed to equip fifth-, sixth-, and seventh-grade children with the skills and motivation needed to resist peer pressure to use drugs, alcohol, and tobacco. DARE's instructors are uniformed police officers on full-time duty with the project. All are veteran officers, volunteers, carefully selected by DARE's supervisory staff and then fully trained by experienced officers and specialists from the school district.

Beginning with the 1986-87 school year, a DARE officer is assigned to teach in every elementary school under the LAPD's jurisdiction, offering the 17-session core curriculum to either fifth- or sixth-grade students. A junior-high program for seventh-graders, which includes early intervention with students deemed at risk, is also at full implementation in 58 junior high schools.

In bringing the core curriculum to the elementary schools, DARE officers are assigned to five schools per semester, and they visit each classroom once a week. Beyond this, the officers conduct one-day visits at other schools for an assembly program and follow-up visits in individual classrooms; hold formal training sessions on drug abuse for teachers; and conduct evening parent meetings.

Evaluations conducted on behalf of Project DARE by Evaluation and Training Institute (ETI) in Los Angeles reveal great enthusiasm for the project among principals and teachers and a widespread conviction that it has been successful in making students less accepting of substance use and better prepared to deal with peer pressure. Across all of ETI's evaluations, tests of students' knowledge, attitudes, and self-esteem have shown marked improvement by students who had received DARE.

Marked Improvements

The most recent ETI evaluation suggests that students receiving the DARE elementary curriculum show greater improvement in grades for work habits and cooperation during their first semester of junior high, compared to non-DARE students. Moreover, evidence from one elementary school showed that, compared to a control group of non-DARE students, the DARE students' academic grades also significantly improved during the semester they received the DARE lessons.

A Drop in Use

Researchers at the Rand Corporation in Santa Monica, Calif., studied 3,900 students at 30 junior high schools. Pupils were followed in seventh and eight grades and were given questionnaires four times.

Two-thirds attended eight 50-minute anti-drug classes in the seventh grade, and three the following year. The rest attended no such classes.

In schools with programs, pupils who had not tried cigarettes or marijuana were 30 percent less likely to start.

The programs appeared to cut frequent marijuana use among pupils who had tried cigarettes or marijuana by seventh grade. And, the number of experimenting smokers who became regular smokers was 50 percent to 60 percent lower.

Dan Sperling, USA Today, March 16, 1990.

William DeJong conducted a short-term evaluation for the National Institute of Justice to assess the impact of Project DARE on the knowledge, attitudes, and behavior of seventh-grade children who received the DARE core curriculum during sixth grade. Compared to a control group, students who had

DARE reported significantly lower scores on an overall index of substance use since graduation from sixth grade. These findings were especially strong for boys.

In response to questions in which students were to imagine friends pressuring them to use alcohol or drugs, those who had DARE were significantly less likely to indicate acceptance of the offer made. Refusal strategies used by that group more often included the student saying he or she needed to be somewhere else, walking away, and suggesting an alternative activity—all strategies promoted by the DARE curriculum.

Project SPECDA

Project SPECDA (School Program to Educate and Control Drug Abuse) in New York City is a collaborative project of the city's Police Department and Board of Education. A 16-session curriculum, with the units split evenly between fifth and sixth grade, imparts basic information about the risks and effects of drug usage, makes students aware of the social pressures that cause drug use, and teaches acceptable methods of resisting peer pressure to experiment with drugs.

Weekly 45-minute classes are taught by SPECDA instructional teams, each comprised of a police officer and a drug counselor employed by the schools. The police instructors are veteran officers who are selected from volunteer applicants and assigned full-time to the program. Special police officer teams also conduct assembly programs for students not receiving the full classroom curriculum, with follow-up discussions in individual classes about drugs and peer pressure.

With strong support from the Mayor's Office, Project SPECDA expanded to 28 of the Board of Education's 32 school districts by the early part of 1987.

SPECDA is a two-track program. Concurrent with the education program is an increased effort by the police department's Narcotics Division to create safe passage to the city's schools by increasing arrests for drug sales and closing so-called "smoke shops" within a two-block radius of the schools. Within the first six months of the program, over 3,500 arrests were made in the vicinity of 310 schools, the majority being in the vicinity of elementary schools. Students themselves have accounted for only a tiny fraction (4%) of those arrested. Nearly four out of every five arrested were over 20 years of age.

Research Results

A SPECDA pilot program was evaluated in April 1985 by the Criminal Justice Center of the John Jay College of Criminal Justice. The researchers obtained data from classroom observations, interviews, and pre- and post-test questionnaires administered to the SPECDA students. Findings include:

111

1. SPECDA students showed significant gains in factual knowledge about drugs and the nature and scope of drug abuse. Most important, SPECDA students expressed a greater awareness of the risks of drug use, including one-time or occasional use, and the role that peer pressure plays in drug abuse. A majority of students interviewed attributed this enhanced awareness to their participation in SPECDA.

2. At the conclusion of the pilot program, SPECDA students showed strong positive attitudes toward SPECDA police officers and drug counselors, though not toward police officers in general.

3. On both the pre- and post-test questionnaires, students asserted that they were unlikely to use drugs within the next year. A majority of the students who were interviewed volunteered that SPECDA had strengthened their resolve to become or remain drug free. . . .

Good Teachers

What makes both Project DARE and Project SPECDA especially innovative is the use of veteran police officers as full-time instructors. These officers, because of their "street experience," and because of the respect they typically receive from fifth- and sixth-grade children, can bring a credibility to such instruction unmatched by regular classroom teachers.

Confronting Social Problems

Education's role in preventing drug abuse goes much deeper than lectures about just saying "No" and movies on the horrors of addiction. Schools must prepare young people for the multiple challenges of life in a changing world. Schools need to keep up with accelerating leaps in technology and knowledge. At the same time, they must cope with some of the knottiest social problems that our society has ever produced. In addition to all this, many expect our nation's schools to strengthen our children's self-image, contribute to the formation of values, and help them carve paths for themselves into a satisfying and productive adult life. Fulfilling these hopes would require major investments—of time, attention, and money—in the education of the nation's children.

Friends Committee on National Legislation, *Washington Newsletter*, February 1990.

Equally important, the officers are good teachers. They are carefully selected, trained by experienced officers and specialists from the school district, and carefully monitored by their supervisors. Because these programs involve police officers in positive, non-punitive roles, students are more likely to develop positive attitudes toward police officers and greater respect for the law.

Of course, however talented they may be, good teachers can only be as effective as the lesson plans from which they work. Both DARE and SPECDA employ core curricula for fifth- and sixth-graders that are at the forefront of recent innovations in substance abuse education. Instructional units include: (1) factual information on alcohol, tobacco, and drugs and the consequences of use; (2) promoting self-awareness and self-esteem; (3) assessment of risks and decision-making skills; (4) media and peer influences that encourage substance use; (5) techniques for resisting peer pressure; and (6) positive alternatives to substance use.

A growing consensus among experts in education and public health holds that substance abuse prevention must begin early, well before children have been led by their peers to experiment with drugs and alcohol. Both DARE and SPECDA introduce their core instruction just at the time when this peer pressure begins to mount.

"The best defense in the war against drugs on the school grounds is firm, fairly enforced policies against the use and sale of drugs."

Enforcing School Codes Against Drugs Can Reduce Teen Drug Abuse

The Heritage Foundation

Many experts on drug abuse believe that America's schools need to play a central role for the war on drugs to succeed. In the following viewpoint, a writer for the Heritage Foundation publication, *Education Update*, states that schools must adopt and strictly enforce codes prohibiting drug use. The author argues that education programs alone are insufficient. The Heritage Foundation is an influential think tank in Washington, D.C.

As you read, consider the following questions:

1. Why does the author write that schools are uniquely suited to fight the war on drugs?
2. How does the author think "zero tolerance" will work in schools?
3. What evidence does the author give that drug education programs do not work?

The Heritage Foundation, "Stopping Drugs in Schools: Tough Policies Work," *Educational Update*, Fall 1988. Reprinted with permission.

After years of disappointing results in its efforts to win the war against drugs, the U.S. is launching a major new offensive against drug use, based on a hardheaded understanding of the economics of the drug trade. As long as there is a strong demand for drugs, the current thinking goes, there will always be someone willing to supply them. Seize one cargo, or jail one supplier, and another appears. But halt the demand for drugs, and the market dries up.

A central feature of this "demand side" emphasis is action to cut drug use among the young; government officials, legislators, and policy experts are mobilizing to find solutions to the spread of drugs in the schools. It is an uphill battle. Countless studies have been written over the years, conferences held, and legislation introduced. But most parents and school administrators still are in the dark when it comes to mounting an effective campaign. They want the answer to the question: "What works?"

Tough Response

If America's school kids stop using drugs, the demand for drugs will shrivel. Legislation passed overwhelmingly by the House of Representatives on September 22, 1988 aims to decrease the supply of drugs through tough new penalties. The measure includes drug education efforts targeted at young Americans from members of street gangs to college students. But most important, the legislation strengthens penalties for users by such means as cutting off federal benefits to those convicted, fines of up to $10,000 for possession of even small amounts, and other deterrents such as random drug testing for convicted felons. The actions taken have been lauded by proponents of stringent reform, which most experts agree is essential to prevent drug abuse from further undermining America's schools, especially those in the inner cities. And according to most research on the subject, illegal drug use is essentially an activity of the young. Few adults over age 35 use illegal drugs.

Former Education Secretary William J. Bennett argues that schools are "uniquely situated to mobilize" the community against the drug problem. While schools are not equipped to do the job alone, they can make substantial progress in concert with educators, parents, students, law enforcement officials, and community groups. And, he adds, adults are the key to how the children will behave. Adults must make consistent efforts to show that drug use is bad.

The evidence shows that the best defense in the war against drugs on the school grounds is firm, fairly enforced policies against the use and sale of drugs. The White House Conference for a Drug Free America was mandated in May 1987 by Ronald Reagan as part of a national effort against illegal drug use.

Conferees appointed by both Congress and the White House spent a year interviewing thousands of Americans about the problem, seeking specific recommendations for a national assault on drugs. The Conference issued its final report in June, 1988. Among its recommendations, strict enforcement policies head the list. "Schools and local boards of education must establish and enforce policies and procedures for students, teachers, administrators, and staff that clearly forbid the sale, distribution, possession or use of all illicit drugs and alcohol on school property, or at school sponsored functions." The recommendation also urges that students be made part of the effort against drugs, and that alternative classes be held during nonschool hours, so that those with a serious problem can be counseled and not left "out on the street."

Treat Users Firmly

Schools need clear policies against the use and sale of drugs. The most effective policies call for suspension of students caught using drugs and harsher penalties for those who sell drugs. These policies must include the involvement of parents, law enforcement personnel, and drug abuse treatment professionals. The point is not simply to punish young people who become involved with drugs. The fact is that when a young person begins using drugs he tends to spread his drug use to friends and to other students. In order to prevent drug use from expanding, a user must be treated firmly, so that he cannot involve non-users, and so that his own drug use ceases.

In the simplest terms, effective drug prevention rests on teaching the lesson that drug use is wrong and that it poses dangerous risks both to those who take drugs and to society.

William J. Bennett, remarks at the Second Annual Conference on Drug Free Schools, May 24, 1988.

About 57 percent of the youth in the U.S. have used drugs by the time they graduate from high school according to the Justice Department's Bureau of Justice Assistance. Although there has been a steady decline in use, the numbers are still unacceptably high. And not surprisingly, surveys show that most students who use drugs are likely to do poorly in school and that many drop out. Students report that, while drugs are readily available at school, strong penal measures would deter them from using drugs.

Some schools prefer to handle drug-related problems internally and not involve law enforcement agencies. But it is those schools that have brought in community law enforcement officials to back up strict drug policies in the school buildings that report the best results. Take Joe Clark's Eastside High School in Paterson, New Jersey, for example. When Clark became principal of Eastside in 1982, drugs were sold openly in the classrooms. But because of tough action by Clark and his faculty, and Clark's decision to call in local law authorities to enforce his policies, drug use has been cut significantly at Eastside High and the academic performance of its students has improved dramatically.

The Reagan Administration has adopted the principle of "zero tolerance" at the federal workplace; it also can work in the schools. The most effective policies against drug use among school children are suspension for those caught using drugs and harsher penalties, such as expulsion or serving time at a corrective institution, for those caught selling drugs. But the job cannot be left solely to the schools. Parents must be willing participants in the schools' anti-drug policies, and must be prepared to contribute time to supervising after-school activities and becoming more involved in their children's efforts at school. At a number of forums, reformed students have testified that their families were not aware that they had been using drugs—even, in some cases, when they took drugs in their own homes. Schools need to enlist the support of parents, but they also need to make parents aware of effects of substance abuse, from symptoms to behavior. Administrators must explain to parents that punishment is intended to help the offenders. Thus the programs need to rehabilitate students caught with drugs, so they will be able to continue their education and reenter school.

Programs That Work

Tough drug programs work. Drug-laden Northside High School in Atlanta, Georgia, for example, decided in 1987 to take a zero tolerance approach to the problem. The new principal, Bill Rudolph, enlisted outside authorities to rid the school of drugs. When students were caught with drugs, he called in the police and notified families immediately. Parent-peer counseling groups were formed, and parents were used to monitor their children's extracurricular activities. There are few reports of drug incidents in Northside today, and achievement test scores have increased dramatically.

Combatting peer pressure is another key to the success of such zero tolerance programs. Students must be counseled to resist the pressure of bad or illegal activities, according to an Education Department study, *Schools Without Drugs*.

Programs work best if the consequences of possession and drug use are emphasized strongly. Every student should know exactly what will happen if he or she is caught with drugs. And the school must make it clear to students that it is determined to stamp out drug use. Samuel Gompers Vocational-Technical High School in New York City's South Bronx is one school that turned around after a well-designed "show of force" approach. In 1977, the school was a "war zone," with drugs visible in every area. After principal Victor Herbert took over that year, security guards were stationed outside each restroom, and "hall sweeps" for drugs were conducted while the exits were guarded. In addition to such tough and visible actions, drug awareness programs were organized involving the community. Herbert persuaded companies located near the school, like IBM, to hire drug-free students for part-time work. This gave non-offenders the incentive to avoid drugs, because of the prospects of employment and other positive community relationships. The results are impressive. School achievement at Samuel Gompers has broken records, and today there are no known incidents of drug use or related violence on school grounds.

Tighten Discipline

I think our schools could tighten up on discipline all down the line. I know of one high school that gives a student a warning for the first infraction of the drug rules, suspension for the second, then expulsion for the third offense. But why wait for the second or third offense? That just gives the student one free shot at using drugs—or ten or twenty, so long as he isn't caught.

Reuben Greenberg, *Let's Take Back Our Streets*, 1989.

In contrast with these tough, often controversial approaches, the more popular drug "education" programs, which have sprouted nationwide thanks to increases in federal funding, seem to have yielded little or no impact on actual drug use or sales. A 1987 report by the National Institute of Justice, for instance, found no evidence that drug education programs alone contribute to a decrease or increase in students' drug use. Most of these programs assume that highlighting the negative aspects of drug use will be sufficient to dissuade students from using narcotics. But without tough penalties and other actions to back up such education, it appears to be ineffective. Indeed, there is even evidence to suggest that such education programs can breed cynicism among students, making it more likely that young people actually may try drugs instead of avoiding them.

A No-Nonsense Solution

A no-nonsense campaign to eradicate drugs from America's schools can succeed. The resources are available. There are publications, videos, volunteer organizations, and national, state, and federal organizations dedicated to helping the nation's youth out of the drug crisis. In every major urban area, there are peer counseling groups, parent education groups, and community support organizations. In more rural areas, the schools themselves form the nucleus of guidance programs. There is no shortage of information; what is needed is leadership from the community and leadership from the schools. Drug education programs work if they provide the right message, if they are attended, and if they are backed up with firm anti-drug use school policies. And the evidence shows that strong leadership and role models from among parents, teachers, and the community can change attitudes—even in the worst cases.

"*Simply saying no is not enough. Children need to be empowered.*"

Enhancing Teens' Self-Esteem Can Reduce Teen Drug Abuse

Robert Schwebel

Just Say No, Project DARE and S.M.A.R.T. are three popular anti-drug programs many schools use to teach students to avoid drugs. Some critics believe that these programs are misdirected. In the following viewpoint, Robert Schwebel argues that young people need substantive reasons why they should not use drugs. He believes that "Just Say No" is a superficial answer to a serious problem. Schwebel is a clinical psychologist with over twenty years experience counseling people with substance abuse problems. He also serves as the vice chairperson of the School Chemical Abuse Prevention Interagency Committee for Arizona and writes a weekly column for the *Arizona Daily Star* on families and relationships.

As you read, consider the following questions:

1. Why does Schwebel think it is important for children to talk to their parents about drugs?
2. According to the author, what message should adults send young people about drug use?
3. In Schwebel's opinion, what kind of information and education do children need to remain off drugs?

Robert Schwebel, *Saying No Is Not Enough.* New York: Newmarket Press, 1989. Excerpted with permission.

Thirteen-year-old Daniel has a choice to make. It's Saturday night. He's sitting in his kitchen at home with his two best friends, Kevin and Michael. Kevin wants to smoke some marijuana that he got from his older brother. Michael suggests they wash it down with a cool beer from the refrigerator, Spuds McKenzie style. No adults are home. No one will notice.

This comes as a shock to Daniel, who never seriously thought about using drugs. He is scared and confused. Although he never discussed drugs with his parents, he knows from some of their comments that they would tell him to "just say no." He has seen scary television commercials suggesting that drugs "fry" your brain, but that message seems to be contradicted by Kevin's brother, who smokes pot, apparently without harm.

Personal Decisions

Beer doesn't scare Daniel. Marijuana does. But what worries him more is being called a "chicken" by his friends. So he smokes the joint and drinks the beer.

Did Daniel turn into a druggie that night? No, certainly not. In fact he gagged on the smoke and disliked the taste of the beer. But the episode was significant because Daniel, at age thirteen, had broken the barrier of using illegal drugs. He also committed an act that he kept secret from his parents.

Whether Daniel ever becomes harmfully involved with chemical substances in the future will depend to a great extent on his own personal development. The determining questions include: Will he become informed about drugs? Will he discuss drugs with mature and loving adults? Will he learn to meet his needs without drugs? Will he learn to resist peer pressure? Will he learn to make wise decisions?

Daniel's situation is similar to those faced by many of his peers. Like apples in the Garden of Eden, drugs are readily available to even the youngest and most vulnerable among us. Twelve-, thirteen-, and fourteen-year-olds, and often younger children, have important decisions to make. Even if they don't seek substances, it's likely that something—marijuana, a can of beer, or a stronger drug—will be placed in their hands. Regardless of their parents' wishes, they will have to decide for themselves.

Most children, like Daniel, were not prepared in their early years for decisions of this magnitude. Many decide about drug use without ever talking with an adult. . . .

Positive Attitudes

Empowering young children means promoting positive attitudes such as high self-esteem. It also means teaching life skills such as problem solving and assertiveness. The development of these attitudes and life skills begins during early childhood, long before chemical substances are available. These attitudes and skills prepare children for the important decisions that lie ahead, including decisions about drugs.

Empowering teenage children means giving them a certain amount of freedom and responsibility, along with solid information, guidance, and supervision to help them learn to make good decisions on their own. Dialogue between parents and children is especially important during this period.

Steve Artley. Reprinted by permission of Artley Cartoons.

Too often the drug issue tears families apart. It doesn't have to be that way. Discussions about drugs can become an opportunity to help your children learn to think clearly and to develop a sense of true identity. Good discussions promote this type of personal growth and family closeness.

Drugs are not just a family problem. The availability and acceptance of drugs in our communities is also a major social problem, one that will not soon be solved. Long-term solutions include community action and changes in community standards. . . .

I believe that adults should give a clear message: *The use of alcohol and other drugs is not for children.*

Drugs affect mood, concentration, and cognitive functioning, including memory. They can interfere with learning and impair school performance. They can disrupt healthy development. Furthermore, children have not yet attained the maturity needed to manage powerful chemical substances, and therefore are more vulnerable to drug problems than adults.

Young adolescents and teenagers have access to drugs at a time in their lives when they are struggling with their sense of personal identity, separating from their parents, and moving toward adulthood. They are beginning to find their own answers to these basic questions: Who am I? What is important to me? Where do I fit in the world? Without a fully established, firm sense of identity, adolescents are susceptible to peer pressure and likely to "do what everyone else does," instead of what might be best for them. When friends are using drugs, they will be tempted to do likewise.

Besides forming their own identity, adolescents are also involved in mastering the mental ability to think through *all* the implications of *all* possible actions. Until they have mastered this logical ability, they are not fully equipped to think through *all* the implications of their own actions, including the use of drugs.

Another concern about young people experimenting with drugs is that teens and preteens have trouble setting limits for themselves. Some adults can limit their consumption of chemical substances to weekends or other carefully selected times when alcohol or other drugs will not disrupt their lives. They may, for example, only drink an occasional cocktail or glass of wine with dinner or at a social gathering. Other adults cannot control themselves. Since children have less self-control than most adults, they are even more vulnerable to problems. Once children decide to experiment with drugs, they might find that it is difficult to stop. . . .

Emotional Cripples

Considering the level of maturity of young adolescents, the availability of drugs, and the age at which drugs are first used, it is not surprising that a substantial number of them develop serious drug problems.

Once this happens, the effects are devastating. Drugs shield children from dealing with reality and mastering developmental tasks crucial to their future. The skills they lacked that left them vulnerable to drug abuse in the first place are the very ones that are stunted by drugs. They will have difficulty establishing a clear sense of identity, mastering intellectual skills, and learning self-control.

The adolescent period is when individuals are supposed to make the transition from childhood to adulthood. Teenagers with drug problems will not be prepared for adult roles. They will lose the benefits of important years of schooling, leaving them ill-prepared for the job market. They will not deal directly—that is, with a clear head—with the emotional and social issues of dating. This means they will be ill-prepared to establish a committed, loving relationship. In short, they will chronologically mature while remaining emotional adolescents.

However, all of this can be prevented.

"Just Say No"

Much has been said about the "Just Say No" campaign made famous by Nancy Reagan. Even before this particular campaign was launched, studies had shown that learning to say no was part of an effective way that children could resist negative peer pressure. The former first lady used the slogan to rally public support against children using drugs and has no doubt made a valuable contribution to public awareness of this enormous problem.

A Meaningless Phrase

Listen to the comment of a particularly perceptive teenager. It touches on an important facet of the drug problem. "Telling kids to 'just say no' is meaningless," this young person said. "Kids use dope because they are unhappy. Just saying no won't help that. You can shut off the supply of cocaine or heroin. Kids will find something else—even if they have to make it themselves!"

Clayton Steep, *The Plain Truth*, January 1989.

It is important that young children hear the "Say No" message, as in: "Do what we tell you to do. We know what is best. Say no to drugs." But young children need more than a slogan. They need positive role models. They need to feel good about themselves. They need to know how to have fun and how to cope with stress, without drugs. In short: Saying no is not enough. Young children need a broad range of experiences to help them learn positive attitudes and basic life skills. They need support in succeeding at home, in school, and in their social life. By providing these experiences, parents go a long way toward assuring that their children are part of the vast majority of children—those who do not develop drug problems.

With adolescents, the "Just Say No" approach is entirely misdirected. Adolescents who are developing their own identity and learning to make their own decisions do not necessarily benefit from the campaign nor take it seriously.

Teenagers need clear standards of behavior and an objective presentation of the facts. They need an opportunity to think for themselves and to discuss their thoughts. They need to learn to make good decisions on their own about drugs and, for that matter, all health issues. Instead, they are being served one-sided information—all negatives about drugs—and therefore are not prepared when they start hearing the positives. And they are told what to do—"Just Say No." This is not very helpful advice considering that rebelliousness is a major correlate of drug use by teenagers.

Simply saying no is not enough. Children need to be empowered. Young children need an opportunity to learn positive attitudes and basic life skills. Teenagers need dialogue and discussion with their parents. Given an opportunity, all children can learn to make wise decisions about their health.

"Parents . . . must arm children against drugs just as they do against fire."

Parents Can Reduce Teen Drug Abuse

Vic Sussman

Many drug programs focus on schools, peers, or the media, to prevent drug abuse when they should concentrate on families, according to Vic Sussman, the author of the following viewpoint. Sussman, a reporter for *U.S. News & World Report*, argues that parents must use their influence to prevent their children from using drugs. He writes that parents serve as important role models, educators, and sources of information for their children.

As you read, consider the following questions:

1. In what ways does Sussman think parents should get involved with drug abuse prevention?
2. What evidence does the author give to support his theory that parents can influence their children?
3. Why does Sussman write that drug use of today is different than drug use twenty years ago?

Not my kid. Not my kid. *Not my kid.*

It is both incantation and denial, this parental mantra. But whether it is murmured as a prayer or sputtered in outrage, the headlines and statistics shout: Yes, your kid. If not today, maybe tomorrow.

From the primary grades on, virtually every child knows another who regularly uses drugs and booze. In a Gallup poll released in August 1989, more than 4 million youngsters between 13 and 17 years of age said they had been offered illicit drugs in the previous 30 days. The average age at which children first try alcohol or marijuana is 12. And in a 1987-88 survey of over 200,000 junior and senior high-school students by the National Parents' Resource Institute for Drug Education (PRIDE), over 45 percent said they drank liquor. A third of the drinkers said they "got bombed" when they drank.

Parents' Duties

These are not youthful high jinks. Getting stoned kills teens in auto wrecks, drags them into alcoholism and seduces many into a deadly dance with crack. And only one weapon, say researchers, can mount a true counterattack against this chemical warfare: Parents. They must arm children against drugs just as they do against fire. To determine the practical steps parents can take, *U.S. News* interviewed drug-abuse educators, counselors, clinical researchers and recovering addicts struggling to keep their kids clean and sober. Their advice will sound obvious, even simplistic, because what works as drug prevention is based on common sense and parental control.

The problem is that parental common sense often comes up short when it comes to drugs. Most parents got their basic training in child rearing from being reared themselves. But their parents never dealt with a drug epidemic, so today's parents find coping with young children who use drugs an alien experience. Thus, ignorance and denial are typical. "Parents often deny their child is on drugs because it makes them look like bad parents, but they should be getting help," says Shirley Coletti, cofounder of Operation PAR (Parental Awareness and Responsibility) at St. Petersburg, Fla.

Parents cannot teach their children safe passage in a world awash in booze and crack until they learn how to navigate it for themselves. They can read drug-abuse pamphlets; they can get involved in school programs; they can confront their own use of alcohol and other drugs; they can seek family therapy. Once parents recognize the risks, they can get serious about prevention.

The first step is to look in the mirror. "Start by assessing yourself and your family history," says Scott McMillin, director of the Addiction Treatment Center at Suburban Hospital in Bethesda, Md. "Having a family pattern of drug or alcohol abuse quadruples the risk that your children will continue the cycle."

Researchers are unsure whether the link is genetic, environmental or both.

The Lure of Drugs

The lessons of substance abuse should begin no later than in the third grade. "Attitudes are formed very young," says David Robbins, a community prevention specialist in the U.S. Office of Substance Abuse Prevention. "If information isn't shared and if limits are not set at an early age, children are going to be more susceptible to the lure of drugs."

Drug education can begin with preschoolers by teaching them about health and cautioning them not to accept medication from anyone without parental permission. Third graders on up can learn how to identify various drugs, their effects and their dangers. This is also a time when parents must assess the messages their children are getting about drugs and alcohol from baby-sitters, day-care providers, relatives and friends. Many schools have drug-prevention programs, and parents can reinforce these lessons at home by using school literature.

A Commonsense Approach

Because parents dramatically can affect their children's choices, prevention programs often include a segment that teaches them to monitor their offsprings' behavior, use appropriate discipline when there are undesirable actions, and reward good behavior in a consistent manner. Research indicates that this common-sense approach works—children become more attached to their parents and exhibit less problem behavior at school and at home.

Stuart Greenbaum, *USA Today*, November 1989.

Scare tactics and hysteria do not work at any age. Telling children that smoking marijuana will kill them, for example, may backfire when they glean more-accurate information from their peers. Parents must explain, truthfully and in detail, that while not everyone who uses drugs or alcohol becomes an addict or dies as a result, many do. "Research tells us that kids who perceive drugs as potentially harmful are less likely to use them," says Dr. Martha Morrison, who treats drug abusers in Atlanta and once used a dozen different drugs herself every day, including alcohol, Valium and marijuana. Her book, *White Rabbit: A Woman Doctor's Story of Her Addiction and Recovery*, tells her story.

One way to teach about drugs is to seize "teachable moments," using television reports of drug busts, alcohol-related auto accidents and similar news items to stimulate conversations about the dangers of alcohol and drugs. TV commercials suggesting that unpopularity can be erased by the right pill or cosmetic or that hoisting a cold one is the key to good times present ripe teachable moments.

Important Groundwork

Although family life changes dramatically when adolescence storms into the home, teens do not forget all they were taught as little children; it only seems so. The information is still in their heads, forming an important groundwork. Parents can build on this by addressing a teen's changing needs. For example, when the *Weekly Reader* National Survey on Drugs and Drinking asked teens in 1987 to name the most important antidrug action parents can take, 44 percent said parents should talk with kids about their problems. Providing information about drugs came next. Yet no matter how carefully they have been reared, teens may still try that first beer or joint.

Realistically, parents can only influence teenagers, not control them, particularly when cars enter the picture. Parents must know their children's friends and determine the attitudes of the friends' parents on drugs and alcohol. Many parents are themselves substance abusers; others ignore or supply alcohol at teen parties. Giving up in frustration, letting kids do as they will, may surrender them to drugs. Authoritarian rules, on the other hand, not only alienate kids but fail to teach them how to control their behavior. However difficult, parents must be ready to intervene at the first sign of alcohol and drug use. Here are the classic danger signals, according to the federal Office for Substance Abuse Prevention:

- Abrupt changes in mood or attitude.
- Continuing slump at work or school.
- Continuing resistance to discipline at home or school.
- Cannot get along with family or friends.
- Unusual temper flare-ups.
- Increased borrowing of money.
- Shoplifting or stealing money.
- Heightened secrecy.
- A completely new set of friends.

Telltale Signs

Some of these signals, of course, characterize normal adolescent looniness. Volcanic temper tantrums and Oscar-winning emotional eruptions can stem from a hormone-suffused brain or coping with The High School from Hell. Nonetheless, all flash an alert that something is making your child miserable, and that is reason enough to investigate.

But the cardinal rule is that all substance abusers lie, even your kid. How can you tell if the problem is drugs? "You know your kid best," says Lee Dogoloff, executive director of the American Council for Drug Education and a clinician who treats drug abusers. "Talk with other parents about their experiences with their children. Discuss the situation with teachers. But in the end, you have to trust your gut. And if something doesn't feel right, you have to do something." It might mean searching the child's room. Many parents balk at this benevolent despotism, afraid that such a blatant invasion of privacy may anger their children. Perhaps, but drug use could kill them.

Parents Are the Key

Wars on crime and drugs, if they are to be successful, must target children.

Research clearly demonstrates that children who are taught early to respect the property of others, to delay gratifications of the moment if they conflict with long-term goals and to understand the negative consequences of drug and alcohol abuse are unlikely to abuse drugs or commit criminal acts, no matter what the criminal justice system looks like. The same research shows that children not taught these things are likely to run into trouble with the law.

Parents, not police, are the key to the drug crisis.

Michael Gottfredson and Travis Hirschi, *The Washington Post National Weekly Edition*, September 18-24, 1989.

Urine tests are another option. Properly analyzed, urine can reveal traces of marijuana, amphetamines, Valium and other drugs for days after their use. It will probably not show evidence of alcohol, the major drug of choice among teens, because it leaves the body within 24 hours or less. But like a room search, urine testing sends a signal to children that you are dead serious about prevention. They may hate it, but cannot complain you don't care about them. A random "whiz quiz" also provides a surprisingly welcome way for kids to fend off peer pressure and further drug use—the ancient but effective My Parents Will Kill Me excuse. Drug-abuse clinics, drug-prevention organizations and some pediatricians all can steer you to labs that do urine testing and help you get the appropriate follow-up if the test is positive. The cost for a broad-spectrum test is under $50, with results back in less than a week.

Such a strategem may seem extreme to those who had their fling years ago and may still use an occasional joint. "Parents often say, 'Well, I snorted a little coke, drank, dropped acid, smoked marijuana, and I'm O.K.,'" says San Mateo Union High School District drug-education coordinator Benjamin Westheimer. "But things are profoundly different for kids today. Your experiences don't matter."

For one, kids start much earlier now, and smoke marijuana packed with four to 10 times more of the major psychoactive ingredient, THC, than a decade ago. "It's easier to get higher and stay stoned all the time, maintaining a higher blood level of THC with less smoking than was possible a decade ago," says Richard Hawks, who heads the National Institute on Drug Abuse's (NIDA) Research Technology Branch, which has tracked marijuana potency for several decades.

Scientists have studied marijuana for nearly 20 years, concluding, among other things, that smoking a couple of joints a day produces lung damage and cancer risks comparable with smoking tobacco. Animal studies also show, says neuroscientist David Friedman, that chronic marijuana use destroys cells in the brain's memory center. "We don't know how much marijuana or how long it will take for humans," says Friedman, deputy director of NIDA's Division of Preclinical Research, "but the evidence suggests that marijuana will damage human brains."

Role Models

Obviously, adults must recognize that they are role models. Parents who smoke, drink or use drugs are the likeliest to have children who mimic their behavior. And all parents must watch their children for the first evidence of the "gateway drugs," tobacco, alcohol and marijuana. Sophisticates may still laugh at this, but every drug counselor and drug-education expert interviewed agrees that a drug or alcohol abuser who did not begin with at least one gateway drug is virtually unknown. Some youngsters can confine their alcohol and drug use to experimentation or weekend use, but others, more susceptible, cross over to preoccupation with drugs. Experts point to two reasons: Using forbidden drugs gradually transforms the illegal into the acceptable, while getting stoned or drunk converts harsh reality into an increasingly tempting escape. No one can predict who will cross the threshold to chronic abuse.

Parents may not be able to stop their kids from experimenting with drugs and alcohol, but they can get tough before the situation goes too far. The longer kids avoid having drug problems—preferably at least through high school—the more likely, say experts, that they will grow into adults free of addiction.

There are no guarantees. The one certainty, says Dogoloff, is that "every child in this country between the ages of 12 and 14 will be called upon to make a decision about drugs and alcohol. The only option is what decision they will make." Parents who do nothing to help kids make that decision, who merely hope for the best, who blithely assume Not My Kid now and forever, are abandoning their children at the edge of a whirlpool.

"Peer pressure, a powerful force in the adolescent drive for establishing identity, may be a positive as well as a negative influence."

Positive Peer Pressure Can Reduce Teen Drug Abuse

Donald Ian Macdonald

Donald Ian Macdonald, a pediatrician, served on President Ronald Reagan's White House staff as the Director of the Drug Abuse Policy Office. In the following viewpoint, Macdonald writes that peer pressure during adolescence can be used positively to steer teenagers away from drugs. He argues that rebellion often causes teens to ignore their parents' advice, thereby making the peer group the most influential factor in a young person's life. Macdonald gives examples of various drug prevention programs that have succeeded by using positive peer pressure.

As you read, consider the following questions:

1. In the author's view, why is peer pressure so influential during adolescence?
2. What causes teens to be susceptible to drugs, according to Macdonald?
3. How does the author think peer-led programs can be effective in reducing drug use?

Donald Ian Macdonald, *Drugs, Drinking, and Adolescents.* Second Edition. Chicago: Yearbook Medical Publishers, Inc., 1989. Excerpted with permission.

"The single main determinant of whether a young person uses marijuana is whether or not his best friend uses it [asserts Mitchell Rosenthal]," Peer pressure is a strong force indeed. It is felt by all ages, but by the adolescent most of all. In testing new behaviors and seeking to establish his identity, he has a particularly strong desire to relate to and be accepted by people his own age. Peer pressure is generally seen as a negative force, but it need not be. . . . . To avoid peer pressure, as some would suggest, would require placing children in glass bubbles.

Peer pressure affects us all. Codes of dress and style may vary widely, but within each group there are norms and standards ignored only by the eccentric, the clod, or the trend setter. Neckties, for example, serve little useful purpose other than meeting certain group standards for business and social functions. The child who is looking for his own identity most often finds it in establishing his position within a peer group.

Peer Influence

Young people do not talk about peer pressure in the same way adults do. They talk about looking for acceptance and wanting to fit in and belong. Adolescent drug users are often asked why they began drug use. Their answers are most often vague and should not be considered highly reliable. Peer influence objectively and observably influences drug use, but the drug-using teenager will not necessarily perceive this as a causal factor.

If smoking and drinking are considered acceptable and are indulged in by a child's friends, he is in jeopardy. Where keg parties for 16-year-olds have become fashionable, it is much harder for a child to say "no." Young people need the friendship and acceptance of other teenagers. The desire to be popular is very strong, and if the popular crowd drinks, the child looking for acceptance will be strongly tempted. In order to counteract this pressure, efforts should be aimed at making drinking and other drug use unfashionable.

While peer pressure may be the main factor leading children to experiment with drugs, immaturity and other intrapersonal factors are the main causes of their high rate of chemical dependency. Normal adolescent behavior and developmental immaturity make teenagers more at risk than adults. Those who have inappropriate attitudes and lack coping skills are even more susceptible. Modified and/or reinforced parenting skills and efforts may go a long way toward helping these marked children. Efforts aimed at diminishing or eliminating harmful attitudes and building appropriate skills can make children stronger. . . .

Many seem to have forgotten that adolescents are different from adults. A society where 12- and 13- year-old girls are paid huge sums of money to look suggestively older and more experienced in the ways of the world needs a refresher course in child development. There is more than the normal adolescent's search for identity and independence that make him particularly susceptible to drugs and alcohol.

What makes children most susceptible to drugs is the fact that they are children. When a child falls into chemical dependency, his progress to mature independence will be interrupted, and he may remain a child forever. Acting like a teenager at age 13 is appropriate. At age 27, it is not.

What Parents Can Do

Help direct your child toward quality friendships. "If Jennifer insists you drink or smoke pot against your will just because she does, that's not being a good friend. A true friend respects others' decisions." Teach by example; discuss with your youngster your own relationships and what makes them work.

When kids bring their pals home, they are to abide by the household rules. Your sixteen-year-old daughter's best girlfriend is allowed to smoke cigarettes? Not in your home. Period. And you know to keep an eye on her, for children who use tobacco frequently advance to other dependency-producing drugs.

Ken Barun and Philip Bashe, *How to Keep the Children You Love Off Drugs*, 1988

Normal teenage attitudes such as their love of danger, the "group" and the "here and now" also increase the risk of drug use. Observe a teenager on a dirt motorbike or at a roller coaster park, and you will gain some increased appreciation of the thrill they get from challenging fear. Observe the hairstyles, dress fads, and musical tastes that identify each generation of adolescents, and see young people looking for an identity of their own, separate from their parents and from the teenagers who preceded them. Teenagers do not see long distances into the future. Scare tactics that talk about long-range consequences such as the relationship of lung cancer to cigarettes are given low priority on their rating scale. What counts most is now.

Adolescent Rebellion

Comparing, competing, testing, experimenting, looking for thrills, and tuning out parental advice and instructions have always been a part of adolescence. Warnings, which are often the result of past parental experience, may be disregarded by young people looking for their own answers. A certain amount of rebellion is normal. When maturity is reached, most adolescents come to realize that their parents were not so dumb after all or are surprised that their parents have learned so much over the course of a few adolescent years. . . .

135

Too often the pleasure-seeking behavior typical of drug use is viewed as characteristic of all teenagers. It is hard to ignore such behavior, but there is more to the well-rounded teenager than thrill seeking. If all adolescents are labeled self-seeking hedonists, the idealism and enthusiasm so typical of many may be overlooked. Teenagers have much to offer and appear willing to do so. Drug prevention efforts aimed at providing alternative highs have merit, but those aimed at putting adolescent idealism and energy to work should do more. Positive peer pressure approaches do not ask children whether they need help, but instead ask if they are willing to help.

Drug prevention efforts utilizing positive peer pressure and young people's desire to help may be divided into four general groups: (1) peer influence programs, (2) peer participation programs, (3) "kids teaching kids," and (4) peer counseling. The first two may offer great hope. Proof of their value, however, is still lacking, as there are few, if any, mature and effective programs 5 years old.

Peer Influence Programs

Peer influence programs provide options. Courage is required by those teenagers who are the early organizers of these peer activities, which are outside the mainstream of popular adolescent activity. Parental support and encouragement is important and must precede adolescent action. The goal is to reach young people who either do not want to be involved with drugs, have not yet made a decision, or who are minimally involved. Without reinforcement many of these young people will be unable to withstand social pressures pushing them to experimentation and "recreational" use.

Successful parties have been arranged for teenagers where the price of admission was observance of no-drinking-or-drugging rules. In Palo Alto, Calif., a small group of teenagers began meeting weekly and worked to plan a drug-free party. They hoped 30 would attend and had a crowd of 250. In Grand Junction, Colo., 500 came. Those who did attend had fun, and many agreed to sponsor drug-free parties at their own homes. No young person was excluded on the basis of his reputation as long as he agreed to arrive sober and stay that way. The large numbers who showed up may have pushed attendance beyond the ideal number for teenage parties, but illustrate clearly that interest exists. Whether this sort of interest is curiosity or a desire for options must await the test of time.

Some peer participation programs are working; others are not. Channel One, a coordinated effort of government and the private sector, involves adolescents and community leaders. Young people analyze community needs and decide what they want to do for their community. Adults assist. Prudential and the Metropolitan Life Insurance Companies have offered strong support to Channel One projects. Other major corporations are becoming involved in an expanding program of putting young people to work constructively in the community.

Student Groups

In Kansas City, Mo., student leaders with training in alcohol and drug abuse approach new students and tell them it is not necessary to do drugs at their high school. They reach out to these susceptible young people and inform them of alternative parties and activities.

In Minneapolis, young people between the ages of 12 and 18 are used as health educators to teach younger children the facts about drug effects. The adolescent teachers receive job training from qualified leaders. In reality, the student teachers benefit more from the program than those they teach, but this in no way makes the program less valuable.

Teens Telling Teens

The "social pressures model" is one that has become increasingly popular since the late 1970s. This model attempts to counter the impact of peer pressure as a factor leading to the use of drugs through programs that teach adolescents skills and offer support for rejecting peer pressure and saying "no." These programs are more effective when the message is delivered by other teenagers. Many use teen-sponsored drug-free clubs and social events to implement this strategy.

Eli Ginzberg, Howard S. Berliner, and Miriam Ostow, *Young People at Risk*, 1988.

A fourth approach is peer counseling, which is based on the belief that many adolescents trust their peers more than adults and would benefit from trained listeners.

In Illinois, several hundred campus leaders selected as peer counselors attend the Illinois Teenage Institutes, where they spend 6 summer days training with teachers and administrators. They are taught to support and listen. Operation Snowball, sponsored by the Illinois Alcoholism and Dependence Association, was designed to build on the enthusiasm generated by the summer institutes and carry prevention programs back to local schools. Groups similar to Operation Snowball exist in New York City, Minneapolis-St. Paul, and elsewhere.

Hastily thrown together and poorly supervised peer counseling programs can be dangerous. Counseling requires maturity and knowledge of when and how to refer emergencies such as possible suicides. An inclination on the part of peer counselors to provide therapy in contrast to listening and supporting must be discouraged. Advocating moderation or responsible use are also not in keeping with drug-prevention efforts. In the course of peer counseling, major benefits may accrue to the counselors themselves. Many are enthusiastic about peer counseling. Others view peer counseling as a way to stay in touch with drug use and drug problems, but contributing nothing directly to cure or rehabilitation. Caution in selection, training, and supervision of peer counselors should be urged.

A Powerful Force

Adolescents have traits of adventurousness and willingness to test danger that make them particularly susceptible to drug use. This susceptibility is increased when they are younger and have low self-image. If they communicate poorly, are unable to separate needs from wants, and see no relationship between their actions and their consequences, the risk is increased. Peer pressure, a powerful force in the adolescent drive for establishing identity, may be a positive as well as a negative influence. To be successful in drug abuse prevention, one must address these issues. The best approaches will work on building and employing adolescent strengths and providing adult support and encouragement.

Distinguishing Between Fact and Opinion

This activity is designed to help develop the basic critical thinking skill of distinguishing between fact and opinion. Consider the following statement as an example: "By the age of eighteen, most American teenagers will have tried alcohol or illegal drugs at least once." This statement is a fact which could be verified by checking recent studies on teen drug abuse. But consider another statement about teenage drug use. "Any high school student caught using or dealing drugs should be required to spend time in a juvenile detention center." This statement expresses an opinion on how to deal with teen drug abuse. People who support counseling and treatment for first-time drug users may disagree with this recommendation.

When investigating controversial issues it is important that one be able to distinguish between statements of fact and statements of opinion. It is also important to recognize that not all statements of fact are true. They may appear to be true, but some are based on inaccurate or false information. For this activity, however, we are concerned with understanding the difference between those statements which appear to be factual and those which appear to be based primarily on opinion.

Most of the following statements are taken from the viewpoints in this chapter. Consider each statement carefully. *Mark O for any statement you believe is an opinion or interpretation of facts. Mark F for any statement you believe is a fact. Mark I for any statement you believe is impossible to judge.*

If you are doing this activity as a member of a class or group, compare your answers with those of other class or group members. Be able to defend your answers. You may discover that others will come to different conclusions than you. Listening to the reasons others present for their answers may give you valuable insights in distinguishing between fact and opinion.

> O = *opinion*
> F = *fact*
> I = *impossible to judge*

1. The "Just Say No" slogan was coined by the Advertising Council in 1983.
2. Gateway drugs like alcohol, tobacco, and marijuana invariably lead to hard drugs like cocaine, acid, and heroin.
3. "Just Say No" is much more than a slogan.
4. The drug issue can tear families apart.
5. Adults should limit their consumption of chemical substances to appropriate times and places.
6. With adolescents, the "Just Say No" approach is totally misdirected.
7. Since the early 1970s, educators have been brainwashed to believe that using scare tactics and facts about drugs does not work to discourage drug use.
8. Five million Americans regularly use cocaine and about one million are addicts.
9. A massive supply of drugs has slipped into our midst during the past two decades.
10. If America's school kids stop using drugs, the demand for drugs will shrivel.
11. Drug education programs have little or no impact on actual drug use or sales.
12. According to research, illegal drug use is an activity of the young. Few adults over thirty-five use drugs.
13. The average age at which children first try alcohol or marijuana is twelve.
14. If parents let their kids do what they want, the children will end up using drugs.
15. Marijuana today has four to ten times more of the active ingredient THC than marijuana of ten years ago.
16. A California study showed that over 50 percent of high school juniors cited peer pressure as the reason they started using drugs.
17. Fighting peer pressure in some inner-city neighborhoods can be almost impossible.
18. Children with little parental supervision at home are doomed to become chemical abusers.

Periodical Bibliography

The following articles have been selected to supplement the diverse views presented in this chapter.

Joseph Adelson	"Drugs and Youth," *Commentary*, May 1989.
James N. Baker	"Programs That Can Make a Difference," *Newsweek*, September 11, 1989.
Ken Barun and Philip Bashe	"How to Keep Your Kids Off Drugs," *Reader's Digest*, September 1988.
Richard L. Berke	"Survey Shows Use of Drugs by Students Fell Last Year," *The New York Times*, February 14, 1990.
Joan France	"A 'Caretaker' Generation?" *Newsweek*, January 29, 1990.
Ingrid Groller	"Parents vs. Drugs," *Parents*, May 1987.
Jesse Jackson	"Down with Dope, Up with Hope," *Ebony*, August 1988.
William F. Jasper	"Some Kids Are Taught to Just Say Yes," *The New American*, November 7, 1988.
Kenneth E. John	"Higher Percentages of High School Students Just Say No to Cocaine," *The Washington Post National Weekly Edition*, January 25-31, 1988.
Paul Krantz	"Is Your Child Hooked on Drugs or Alcohol?" *Better Homes and Gardens*, February 1990.
Jacob V. Lamar	"Kids Who Sell Crack," *Time*, May 9, 1988.
Chris Lutes	"Positive Peer Pressure: A New Weapon Against Drugs," *Christianity Today*, February 20, 1987.
Ed Magnuson	"Bright Kids, Bad Business," *Time*, September 11, 1989.
Mark Miller	"Teaching Kids to Say No," *Newsweek*, June 5, 1989.
Walter Shapiro	"Feeling Low Over Old Highs," *Time*, September 18, 1989.
Rick Telander	"A Dubious Call to Arms," *Sports Illustrated*, June 5, 1989.
Valerie Wilson Wesley	"Raising Kids Strong," *Essence*, December 1989.
Geraldine Youcha and Judith S. Seixas	"Drinking, Drugs, and Children," *Parents*, March 1989.

Can the U.S. Stop International Drug Cartels?

Chapter Preface

The international drug trade has become a huge and profitable business. Since America's $50 billion-a-year drug habit cannot be satisfied by domestic production alone, many drugs are imported. The U.S. Drug Enforcement Administration estimates that seventy tons of cocaine come into the U.S. annually from the coca fields of South America. Mexican drug crops account for most of America's marijuana and heroin supply. Additional heroin, hashish, and opium come from the Golden Triangle region of Burma, Laos, and Thailand and the Golden Crescent area of Afghanistan, Iran, and Pakistan.

The impact of the drug trade in the impoverished drug-producing countries is staggering. Drug profits enable thousands of farmers, pilots, and drug lords to earn a living. The incredible profits for growing and transporting drugs have corrupted police officers, soldiers, customs agents, and other public officials. Thus, ending the production and distribution of drugs in these countries is a formidable task.

Most political and social commentators agree that something must be done to combat the worldwide drug trade. Few agree, however, on the best plan of action for defeating this underworld business. The viewpoints in this chapter reflect these disagreements.

"[The Administration's] primary goal is to attack and dismantle the drug trafficking organizations themselves."

The U.S. Fight Against International Drug Cartels Is Sincere

James A. Baker III

James A. Baker III is the U.S. secretary of state. The following viewpoint is taken from a speech Baker delivered to the Forum Club in Houston. In it, Baker argues that the U.S. government has implemented a strategy to help South American countries defeat drug traffickers. The strategy provides $2 billion in American aid to drug-producing nations like Colombia, Bolivia, and Peru. According to Baker, the money will finance military, economic, and law enforcement assistance to fight the war on drugs in South American countries.

As you read, consider the following questions:

1. What are the three points of the Andean plan, as outlined by Baker?
2. Why does Baker maintain that American drug users are responsible for supporting drug kingpins?

James A. Baker III, "Democracy, Diplomacy, and the War Against Drugs," a speech given at the Forum Club, Houston, Texas, November 22, 1989.

International drug trafficking is a threat to our national security. That is no exaggeration.

According to a survey taken in late September 1989, over half of the American people named illicit drug use as the most important problem facing the country today. Illegal drug use in this country crosses the entire spectrum of our society. It affects people from all walks of life, all age groups, all backgrounds, and all levels of income. And while some regard narcotics as an urban phenomenon, this big-city problem is also a major problem for rural America.

I am sad to say that this native city of mine [Houston], and our state of Texas are no exceptions. Houston is one of the four major narcotics distribution centers in the country. It has a significant cocaine problem. In east Texas, the Sheriff's Office of Gregg County reports that between 1987 and 1988, there was an 80% increase in the number of crack cases. Also during that period, robberies rose by 70%. Four years ago, crack cocaine was pretty much nonexistent in the town of Tyler, Texas. Today, Tyler has crack houses and "shooting galleries." Indeed, well over 80% of the crime in Tyler is crack related.

Close to Home

Drugs hit close to home—my home and that of another Houstonian, George Bush; your home and the homes of our neighbors. That is why the President and I are personally committed to the struggle against drugs. That is why I have made the narcotics issue a top foreign policy priority. I have instructed our ambassadors worldwide and the Department of State's assistant secretaries to ensure that narcotics control issues are fully integrated into our diplomatic efforts. To my mind, there is no foreign policy issue short of war or peace which has a more direct bearing on the well-being of the American people.

As I see it, the survival of democracy at home and abroad is perhaps our most fundamental national interest. And drugs are mortal enemies of democracy. Let me tell you why.

Democracy speaks to the dignity of every individual. Every person is considered a free and responsible citizen whose vote and say in public affairs is essential. An individual caught in the drug habit soon becomes a slave of that habit—no longer a free person or a responsible citizen. And in a similar way, what can happen to the individual can happen to a nation. The drug pirates and profiteers attack the central nervous system and vital organs of democracy: the administration of justice; the integrity of government; the right of free speech.

Ultimately, the illegal narcotics trade robs dignity and freedom not only from the individual but from entire nations. Malaysia was one of the first nations to declare that drug traffickers threatened its sovereignty. Pakistan, Thailand, Jamaica, and Mexico—all have come to the alarming conclusion that drug abuse is eroding their hopes for the future, and they are taking action to combat this insidious enemy.

Look at Colombia. No other nation has so bravely confronted the drug lords. No other nation can afford to be indifferent to Colombia's fate. We applaud Colombia's courageous decision to extradite traffickers and money launderers to this country. Time and again, President Virgilio Barco has put his own life on the line for his nation and for the cause of democracy everywhere.

In Colombia, the Medellin and Cali traffickers consider themselves a country and a law unto themselves. They operate just like the pariah states that export terrorism. They have bought banking systems to store their wealth and mercenaries to attack their adversaries. And who are their enemies: public figures, judges, journalists, and innocent bystanders, whom they murder in broad daylight.

A High Priority

The personal diplomacy of U.S. Government officials such as the Secretary of State and the Attorney General who both traveled to Latin America during 1988 reinforced the priority that the Administration places on the narcotics issue as a major foreign policy concern.

Ann B. Wrobleski, statement before the Senate Subcommittee on Terrorism, Narcotics, and International Communication, April 5, 1989.

It is hard for Americans to comprehend the scale of such violence and intimidation. Let me try to put it into perspective. Imagine one day that a hit squad attacks the U.S. Supreme Court and murders half of the justices. Imagine our Attorney General being assassinated by organized crime figures. And imagine a criminal organization declaring "absolute and total war" on our government after assassinating a leading presidential candidate.

This is what has happened in Colombia in one short and brutal decade: the traffickers have killed over 1,000 public officials, 12 Supreme Court justices, over two dozen journalists, and more than 200 judges and judicial personnel.

The Andean Strategy

President Bush has come to Colombia's aid by authorizing $65 million in emergency military assistance. Canada, Norway, United Kingdom, Italy, Spain, and Portugal have also pledged their help to Colombia's effort.

Moreover, this Administration has proposed a bold, compre-

146

hensive strategy to address the cocaine problem in the hemisphere. We call it "the Andean strategy." This strategy is nothing less than a multiyear, $2-billion American plan to provide military, economic, and law enforcement assistance to help the Andean governments as they fight cocaine. Our primary goal is to attack and dismantle the drug trafficking organizations themselves. In short, to put them out of business. We are going directly to the source. And that is the Andes, where we will support the governments of the region in a three-part plan:

First, to isolate and disrupt coca production by interdicting air, road, and river traffic in drugs and chemicals essential to drug production;

Second, to eradicate coca when and where possible and effective; and

Third, to develop income alternatives to the illicit drug industry by strengthening the legitimate economies of Andean countries.

This is not a strategy for massive and unilateral U.S. intervention in the Andes. The Andean countries want and need our assistance. But we know we won't be effective unless we attack the demand for drugs as well as the supply. . . .

American Demand

We realize that as long as American demand for drugs continues, we face an endless, uphill battle to halt supply. That is why the President decided that reducing the demand for drugs must be at the center of our antidrug policy. America's demand drives the spiraling cycles of production and trafficking, consumption, and addiction. Profits from every kilo of cocaine buy the bullets which rob Colombia of its dignity and freedom and threaten Bolivia and Peru.

I want every user of drugs in the United States to face a fact: Their actions are not just a personal indulgence. They act as paymasters to organized murderers whose victims are defenders of democracy and the rule of law. They are accessories to criminals who poison children and babies. And users by their habits also contribute to the murder of the land. Coca farmers have destroyed countless acres of forest; cocaine traffickers have dumped millions of gallons of chemicals into water supplies.

Above all, we must be honest with ourselves. There is nothing glorious or admirable or honorable in the so-called drug lords and kingpins. They are just criminals—criminals of uncommon power and uncommon brutality. No amount of laundering can wash the blood off money stained by drugs.

Narcotics has become a big business, a very big business. In Los Angeles, agents seized 20 tons of warehoused cocaine. If all these kilos were stacked, one on top of the other, the pile would

147

be a mile and a half high—half the height of Mount Whitney, the tallest mountain in the continental United States. It was estimated that this cocaine had a street value of $6.7 billion. That exceeds the individual gross national products of well over 100 nations. And this was just one warehouse. Imagine the mountain of misery that represents.

I want to say a few more words now about the international dimension of the drug problem and what we are doing about it. Narcotics use, production, and trafficking are urgent problems not only for our hemisphere but worldwide. So we are going to be taking some important actions that will give teeth to our campaign against the illegal drug trade. The central idea behind our efforts is to attack these merchants of death from every angle—production, distribution, finance, and use. Let me give you just a few examples.

Military Aid

Several years ago Bolivia asked sister countries in Latin America to help. They couldn't, so Bolivia asked the United States to provide logistical support. We sent our military helicopters to Bolivia for a limited operation to show them how they could work effectively. We left six helicopters with them, and our agents continue to work with Bolivian troops in destroying refineries in that country.

John Lawn, *American Legion Magazine*, April 1989.

One, we are working with the Senate to promote ratification of the UN [United Nations] Convention Against Illicit Traffic in Narcotic Drugs and Psychotropic Substances, and we will encourage other governments to ratify as well.

Two, over the next few years you will see an intensified effort to enlist our allies and friends in a common effort to fight drugs. We and our Summit Seven partners have established a financial action task force against money laundering. We have already launched an initiative to encourage our European allies to play a larger role in this and in other areas, such as approaching major drug countries such as Burma, Laos, and Iran—where U.S. influence is limited.

And three, we signed an agreement in Paris with the Soviets which permits us to share information on narcotics issues. Since then, Foreign Minister [Eduard] Shevardnadze and I agreed in Wyoming to expand our cooperation and, to follow through, the Attorney General has traveled to the U.S.S.R. . . .

These are only a few instances of how, working together with traditional allies, friends and adversaries alike, we are beginning to attack the multinational drug empires on every front. These actions, of course, are all part of the larger strategy announced by the President and which is being coordinated by Bill Bennett [director of the Office of National Drug Control Policy]. As Secretary of State, I pledge that we will hold to account nations that grant safehavens to drug profiteers, who actively permit the laundering of money, and who turn a blind eye to drug shipments.

When I began this speech, I called our war on drugs a struggle. Our struggle against narcotics is being fought abroad in the deep jungles and mountain valleys where coca and poppies are grown. It is being fought at home in the urban jungles ruled by corruption and cruelty. It is being fought in shadowy backrooms where drug-stained money is laundered. And, above all, it is a struggle of will and of conscience—one that is fought by each of us, often in the dark recesses of the soul.

"It is clear . . .that Bush's War on Drugs is nothing more than a disinformation campaign."

The U.S. Fight Against International Drug Cartels Is Insincere

Bruce McGraw

Investigators at the Christic Institute, a religious public-action group, have accused the U.S. government of using drug runners and drug money to supply the Nicaraguan contras with weapons in 1986. The Christic Institute asserts that U.S. government leaders, including then Vice President George Bush, knew that the contra suppliers were also shipping drugs into the U.S. In the following viewpoint, free-lance journalist Bruce McGraw argues that the war on drugs is a public relations ploy to cover up the government's support of drug trafficking. McGraw writes that the war on drugs is designed to make the public falsely believe the problem is being solved.

As you read, consider the following questions:

1. What proof does the author present that U.S. leaders knew of illegal arms shipments to the contras?
2. Why does McGraw think military aid sent to South America will be wasted?
3. According to the author, why were certain drug investigations ended prematurely.

Bruce McGraw, "Bush's Fraudulent Drug War: The Contra-Drug Connection," *The Truth Seeker*, September/October 1989. Reprinted with permission.

"The War on Drugs is a complete and unabrogated fraud," so says Daniel Sheehan, chief counsel and co-founder of the Christic Institute, an interfaith center for law and national policy in the public interest. "It is a knowing and willful act of disinformation and he knows it," continues Sheehan.

Daniel Sheehan, is a Harvard Law School graduate who has worked in the law office of F. Lee Bailey, on Wall Street for the ACLU [American Civil Liberties Union] and on such cases as the "Pentagon Papers" case, the Wounded Knee Trials, and the Attica Prison suit.

In case people don't believe President Bush is capable of such behavior, Sheehan lists a number of instances where Bush has lied. President Bush maintained he knew nothing about the illegal shipment of weapons to the Contras. However, during the Oliver North Trial the Government issued 42 pages of admissions that proved that Vice President George Bush not only knew of illegal shipments of weapons to the Contras but actively participated in them. The documents showed that Bush traveled to Honduras to meet with the President of Honduras to set up an illegal Quid Pro Quo arrangement. Honduras would provide additional weapons to the Contras in return for increased U.S. aid.

Contra Shipments

Donald Gregg, then Vice President George Bush's National Security Advisor, sent ex-Bay of Pigs veteran and Christic Defendant Felix Rodriguez to Illopango—El Salvador's main air base—to oversee the Contra-resupply operation. It was at a time when all aid to the Contras had been banned by the Boland Amendment. It was also the time when Rodriguez talked to Gregg and Col. Sam Watson, another top Bush aide, seventeen times and Bush three times. One memo setting the agenda for a meeting with Bush said the purpose of the meeting was discuss "resupply of the Contras." Col. Watson said the memo was typed wrong, but the secretary who typed it said she typed what Watson dictated.

It was also interesting to note that the first person Felix Rodriguez called when Eugene Hassenfus' plane went down in Nicaragua in October of 1986 was Col. Sam Watson.

Bush swore he knew nothing of the Iranian arms deal. But when he was confronted by Dan Rather on national T.V. he admitted he did know something, but that all he was trying to do was to get CIA [Central Intelligence Agency] station chief William Buckley out of captivity. . . .

The Christic Institute discovered that the drugs were shipped through John Hull's ranch in Costa Rica and then transported to Frigorificios de Puntarenas, a major frozen shrimp company in

Costa Rica owned by Dagoberto Nunez. From there the drugs were shipped to the Ocean Hunter Seafood Co. in Miami owned by Paco Chanes. The cocaine was then distributed and a portion of the profits were used to purchase weapons for the Contras by Ronald Joseph Martin, owner of the Tamiami gun shop in Miami. His partner Mario Delamico ran the Honduran branch of the operation.

Abe Blashko/*People's Daily World.*

The sources for the Christic Institute information are: Ramon Milian Rodriguez, the chief bookkeeper for the Medellin Drug Cartel, Jose Blandon, chief of Intelligence for Manuel Noriega in

Panama, George Morales, the chief pilot of the cartel, other drug pilots like Michael Tolivar, Gary Betzner, and Gerado Duran gave tail numbers of their planes and details and dates of their flights and Jack Terrel who worked with the Civilian Military Assistance group of Christic defendant Tom Posey.

The Christic Institute's information was confirmed when Christic defendant John Hull was indicted in Costa Rica for massive cocaine smuggling out of Costa Rica. He has since fled Costa Rica and is now a federal fugitive. A Costa Rican legislative assembly has filed a major report not only saying Hull's citizenship should be withdrawn from Costa Rica, but also recommended that he be declared "personna nongrata." They also recommended declaration of "personna nongrata" for cocaine smuggling for Richard Secord; Oliver North; Jose Fernandez, former CIA station chief of Costa Rica; Lewis Tambs, former U.S. Ambassador to Costa Rica; and Elliot Abrams, former Assistant Secretary of State for Latin America.

U.S. Foreign Policy

In July 1983 Christic defendant John Hull traveled to Washington and met with Sen. Dan Quayle of Indiana. There Hull was introduced to Quayle's legislative assistant, Christic defendant Rob Owen. Owen then introduced Hull to Oliver North. Later Own served as North's liaison to the Contras and the private aid network during the congressional ban on Contra aid.

Sen. Kerry's Senate Foreign Relations Subcommittee report also confirms many of the Contra-drug allegations made by the Christic Institute.

The report states,

> (U.S.) Foreign policy priorities toward such countries as Honduras, Nicaragua and Panama have halted or significantly interfered with U.S. law enforcement efforts to keep narcotics out of the U.S. Within the U.S. the drug traffickers have successfully manipulated the U.S. justice system by providing certain services in support of U.S. foreign policy. U.S. officials involved in Central America have failed to address the drug issue for fear of jeopardizing their war effort against the country of Nicaragua . . .There is substantial evidence of drug smuggling on the part of the Contras, Contra suppliers, Contra pilots, mercenaries who worked for the Contras and Contra supporters throughout the region.

The report also quotes Gen. Paul Gorman, head of the U.S. military command in Panama as saying, "If you want to move arms and munitions in Latin America, the established networks are owned by the Drug Cartel."

Finally, the report found that the State Department paid over $800,000 in Contra "humanitarian" aid to companies which were either run by indicted drug traffickers or were under investigation by the DEA.

The report, Sheehan states, shows "that a fundamental compromise has struck the heart of the law enforcement program in our country against cocaine importation because of an alliance between those who are engaged in drug smuggling and those who are charged with enforcing the law in our country. It is a campaign in a coalition of virulent anticommunism and that is the fundamental problem that we have to deal with.

Bush's Flawed Plan

Keeping all of the above in mind it is interesting to take a look at Bush's new drug plan of September 5th, 1989. First he called for tougher penalties; more prisons, more jails and more prosecutors. This in spite of Sen. Kerry's report that cites a study of the criminal justice section of the American Bar Association that states this: "The major problem reported by all criminal Justice participants is the inability of our Justice System to control the drug problem through simple law enforcement of the criminal law." It goes on to state, "The narcotics problem in our country is instead a problem of national security and foreign policy," i.e., the Reagan-Bush Administration believed it was more important to support the Contras than to stem the flow of cocaine into the U.S. In fact, the Contras were supported, in part, by monies from the massive smuggling of cocaine into America which was orchestrated by "super-patriots" within the Reagan-Bush Administration.

Dirty Work

The real deal behind the U.S. "antidrug operation" in Peru is not about stopping drug trafficking. It's well known that the world-class gangsters who sit in the halls of power in Washington work with big drug kingpins in Latin America to finance the U.S.'s secret wars—like the Contras in Nicaragua—and other dirty work all over the hemisphere. These criminals are stepping up attacks on oppressed people in America's inner cities in the name of the so-called "war on drugs," and they are using the same excuse to push their imperialist interests in Latin America.

Revolutionary Worker, July 3, 1989.

The second aspect of Bush's drug plan is to send $250 million to the military of Colombia, Peru and Bolivia. This in spite of a report in *The Washington Post* of August 31, 1989. The article entitled, "In Colombia the Military is Part of the Problem," states this: "the Cartel simply could not impose their reign of Terror

154

on the Colombians without direct cooperation of their military authorities . . . . The drug dealers have determined to wipe out left and progressive forces to insure the perpetuation of the regressive social order." The report suggests that, "President Virgilio Barcos should focus on the links between the drug lords and the military. That link originates in a shared ideology of virulent anti-communism. Military aid sent by the U.S. will be wasted on this unholy alliance." In other words, any military aid sent to these countries will not be used to fight the drug cartels, but rather to fight leftist-insurgency, e.g., peasant groups.

A Public Relations Ploy

And thirdly it is designed to attack the casual user.

Sheehan says, "It is clear that this (Bush's) plan is not designed to stop or deter the flow of cocaine, but rather to focus on the middle class so they get the impression that something is being done. This plan is nothing more than a public relations ploy."

The Christic Institute testified before Rep. Charles Rangel's (D-NY) House Select Committee on Narcotics that the source of the problem was the Operational Directorate of the CIA and this group of men, Christic defendants Ted Shakley, Tom Clines, and Richard Secord who were fired from the CIA by President Carter and CIA Director Stansfield Turner. These were men, Sheehan says, who set-up the off-the-shelf government and forged the links with the leaders of the drug cartels so that when charges were brought against these drug men and their operations the prosecutors were ordered to "stand down." Consider just a few examples:

1. The "Frogman" case in San Francisco where $36,020 was seized in a drug bust. The money was ordered turned back over to the defendants when they said it was for the "Contras."

2. In the book *The Underground Empire* by James Mills, Dennis Dale of the DEA said he quit his job because every time he was ready to close in on a major drug smuggler he was ordered off the case by the CIA for national security reasons.

3. the district attorneys from Arkansas to Florida have been ordered to stand down from investigations. In Mena, Arkansas a major cocaine operation was underway headed by Barry Seal. The investigation was topped because Seal was working for the CIA.

4. Leon Kellner, U.S. District Attorney in Miami, was obstructing drug investigations so the Christic Institute filed a formal complaint to Judge King who would not do anything about it. Kellner, however, resigned and Ed Meese replaced him with Dexter Lehtinen, one of the attorneys for Christic defendant Jack Singlaub. Dexter Lehtinen is also the husband of Ileana

Ros-Lehtinen who won the runoff for Claude Pepper's old house seat in Florida. Ros-Lehtinen is an outspoken supporter of the anti-Castro Cuban terrorist Orlando Bosch. Both Bush and Quayle made last minute trips to Florida to campaign for Ros-Lehtinen.

And why were these investigations stopped? Because, according to Sheehan, these drug lords were providing the CIA with (a) intelligence about left-wing organizations throughout Latin America—peasant groups, co-ops, land reform groups etc. and (b) money to run these covert operations when Congress won't fund them and (c) men to help fight these covert wars.

It is clear from the above that Bush's War on Drugs is nothing more than a disinformation campaign. It is not meant to stop the flow of cocaine into this country and never was. It is designed to focus attention on the drug consumer, thereby diverting attention away from the Reagan-Bush Administrations' complicity with the drug producers and traffickers that served their own political agenda.

"The United States must come to grips with this threat [of international drug trafficking] and attack it at every level."

U.S. Intervention Can Stop International Drug Cartels

Michael H. Abbott

Michael H. Abbott, a colonel in the U.S. Army, is the director of evaluation and standardization at the U.S. Army Aviation School at Ft. Rucker, Alabama. Abbott was an aviation battalion commander during Operation Blast Furnace in Bolivia. This operation marked the first time U.S. troops were used to help destroy cocaine production labs. In the following viewpoint, Abbott writes that the powerful drug cartels pose a threat to national security and must therefore be eliminated by U.S. military forces.

As you read, consider the following questions:

1. According to the author, why has drug trafficking become a threat to national security?
2. What area of drug interdiction does Abbott want to leave to civilian law enforcement agencies? Why?
3. In the author's opinion, how can international cooperation help defeat the drug cartels?

Reprinted from "The Army and the Drug War: Politics or National Security?" by Michael H. Abbott, *Parameters*, December 1988.

On 15 July 1986, six US Army Blackhawk helicopters from the 210th Combat Aviation Battalion, 193d Infantry Brigade (Panama), deployed to Bolivia to conduct an operation never before attempted on a large scale by a US Army combat unit. Called Task Force Janus, the unit's mission was to provide air transportation, at the direction of representatives of the US Drug Enforcement Administration (DEA) contingent stationed with the US Embassy in La Paz, to Bolivian counterdrug police forces as they sought to locate and destroy cocaine production laboratories. The US Ambassador to Bolivia retained overall responsibility for US involvement in the operation. This Joint Chiefs of Staff-directed operation, called Operation Blast Furnace, came just three months after President Reagan had announced that his Administration was declaring a "war on drugs."

Task Force Janus returned home in November of the same year amid public accolades for a successful operation. But while 22 cocaine labs had been discovered, no cocaine of any significance was seized and no arrests were made. Illicit drug production in Bolivia was severely disrupted while the US military was in country, but it quickly returned to a near-normal output once the Americans had gone home.

Tough Questions

Only a few days after the task force departed Bolivia, a political cartoon appeared in one of the major US newspapers. It showed the sky filled with US helicopters leaving Bolivia, while the caption between two of the pilots read, "This reminds me of Vietnam. We go in with a large force, accomplish almost nothing, declare victory, then go home." For me, that cartoon was the catalyst for more than a year's worth of wrestling with a number of questions. Did Operation Blast Furnace have any real significance? How do you define success in a counterdrug operation? Did Blast Furnace have any connection to our own national security or was it just an inconsequential move on a political chessboard? Should the Army be involved in counterdrug operations in the future or should that remain the domain of civilian law enforcement agencies? Since I was the aviation battalion commander who deployed assets to Bolivia to conduct Operation Blast Furnace, these questions hit close to home.

By way of answering these questions, this article will look at the magnitude of the drug problem and its relationship to national security, at the actions that led to the decision to launch Blast Furnace, and at some key lessons learned during the operation. Finally, it offers recommendations for a future US Army role in the war on drugs. In addition to my personal experience with that operation, the article is based on numerous interviews

158

conducted with key personnel in the drug policy arenas of the Office of the Vice President, Justice Department, Department of Defense, State Department, DEA, and the US Embassy, La Paz.

When we use the term war, we usually think of combat forces, either regular or irregular, engaged in a shooting competition directly related to the national security of one or more participants. Just what is the war on international drug trafficking, and is there a threat to national security?

Destroy Production

The only thing that will work is force. I see [the fight against drugs] as a war. It's a threat to our national security at the same level as a military threat from another nation or a group of nations. Internationalize a strike force. Arrest the major traffickers. Put them in jails where they would stay. I would destroy their means of production, the millions of dollars' worth of chemicals that they have around their laboratories and factories. I would burn their houses down, is what I would do.

Clarence Edgar Mervin, quoted in *The Atlantic Monthly*, May 1987.

We need to start by looking at some facts about drug trafficking and the magnitude of this multibillion-dollar business. First, how bad is the use of illicit drugs in the United States?

• In March 1987, the State Department presented these estimates of the number of users or addicts in the United States: marijuana, 20 million; cocaine, 4 to 5 million; heroin, 500,000.

• In terms of the dollar value of illegal drugs brought into the United States each year (some $70 billion), narcotics rank second to petroleum as the largest import. (And you thought our trade deficit was bad enough already!)

• US consumption of cocaine is estimated at well over 70 tons annually, and DEA is seizing about 35 to 40 metric tons per year.

• The number of cocaine users is estimated to increase at a rate of ten percent annually.

• The US resources dedicated to combating international drug trafficking are substantial: $60.2 million in 1986; $118.5 million in 1987; and a projected $98.7 million in 1988 (reduced because of budget cuts).

Second, where are these drugs coming from?

• 100 percent—every gram—of the cocaine and heroin and 85 percent of the marijuana consumed in the United States are imported.

• There are several principal sources of the three major categories of illegal drugs imported into the United States. Most of the cocaine comes from Peru, Bolivia, and Colombia. Heroin and opium are imported from Mexico, Burma, Thailand, Laos, Pakistan, Iran, and Afghanistan. And most marijuana comes from Colombia, Jamaica, Belize, and Mexico. Some 15 percent of the marijuana consumed in the United States is grown domestically. In addition to the nations listed, many non-producing countries sanction the active transshipment of illegal drugs through their country or are involved in drug money laundering activities.

Cocaine and Heroin

• Forty percent of the cocaine smuggled into the United States comes from Bolivia.

• The primary single supplier to the United States of both heroin and marijuana is Mexico.

• Gross production of coca leaves (the raw product from which cocaine is extracted) in both Peru and Bolivia is estimated to have increased at an annual rate of five to ten percent during this decade.

• Much of the marijuana grown in the United States is grown in our national parks, making identification of the grower difficult. The growers have even placed dangerous boobytraps in some of these public lands.

Third, the relationship between drug traffickers and terrorists or insurgent groups is a key factor linking drugs to national security. It is not an easy task to identify just how these groups are related or how strong are their bonds. In Colombia, the insurgent organizations M19 and FARC (Revolutionary Armed Forces of Colombia) have provided physical security to drug traffickers at their production facilities (cocaine laboratories, airfields, growing sites for coca and marijuana in addition to being their trigger men to carry out reprisals against the government for their efforts to fight drug trafficking. Similar links are believed to exist between terrorists and traffickers in Peru and other countries. . . .

It Is a War

It is clear that a war is going on, and the trafficker continues to hold the upper hand. And guess who funds *both* sides of this war? The US government spends in the vicinity of $100 million annually to fight against the traffickers and to help some 100 countries to counter the threat. Meanwhile, the US public spends some $70 billion annually to support the international drug network as consumers smoke, snort, and shoot themselves into oblivion.

In consideration of the threat, on 11 April 1986 President Reagan signed a National Security Decision Directive on Narcotics and National Security. He directed a number of important actions, four of which are key to this discussion:

- Full consideration of drug control activities in our foreign assistance planning.
- An expanded role for US military forces in supporting counternarcotics efforts.
- Additional emphasis on narcotics as a national security issue in discussions with other nations.
- Greater participation by the US intelligence community in supporting efforts to counter drug trafficking. . . .

Army Support

The Department of Defense continues to emphasize its support role in the counterdrug arena, and in fact that role has shown some increases. Six additional UH-1s have been offered to the State Department, to be distributed equally to Peru, Colombia, and Ecuador, along with pilot training to be conducted by the US Army Aviation School at Ft. Rucker. The Army has been operating two to three UH-60s in the Bahamas, carrying Bahamian police and DEA agents to arrest traffickers as they land at remote airstrips. The Georgia National Guard has conducted photo and visual reconnaissance flights with OV-1 aircraft. Air defense Hawk radars from Ft. Bliss, Texas, have deployed along the Mexican border from time to time as well as Army engineer units. Some Army National Guard units have entered the fray.

Full Military Power

Drug trafficking is—without question—the No. 1 security threat in this hemisphere. The enormous profits generated in the underground economy of the international drug trafficking market allow the major kingpins to hire and equip armies, buy elections and intimidate foreign governments. The full diplomatic, economic and military power of the United States must be marshalled in response.

Joseph Biden, comments made on the U.S. Senate floor, September 28, 1989.

Each of these efforts pales against the magnitude of the international drug trade. It is time to propose some better suggestions for DOD and, more specifically, Army involvement that could lead to significant long-term victories in the drug war.

Two areas provide opportunities for DOD interaction with other government drug agencies: interdiction on the air, land, and sea borders, and of course elimination of production means in the countries of origin.

A look at the various conveyances used to smuggle illegal drugs into the United States further helps to refine the DOD role in interdiction. The following table reflects those conveyances in terms of percent of volume of drugs actually seized in 1986:

	Cocaine(%)	Marijuana(%)	Heroin(%)
General Aviation	48	5	—
Commercial Air	11	2	5
Commercial Sea Vessels	13	4	87
Non-Commercial Sea Vessels	23	83	—
Land Transportation	5	6	8

For each of the three major drugs, land transportation accounts for a very small volume seized and should be left to the appropriate civilian agencies (Border Patrol, DEA, Immigration, and Customs). Commercial air and sea conveyances account for a fourth of the cocaine and most of the heroin imports. Again, civilian law enforcement agencies are appropriate. Non-commercial watercraft and general aviation account for nearly three-fourths of the cocaine and marijuana imports. This arena is most suitable to Coast Guard, Navy, and Air Force participation with civilian law enforcement agencies. The surveillance, early warning, and intercept requirements of an air and sea drug-interdiction program are aligned with wartime missions and capabilities of these services and present a training opportunity for them.

The elimination of the means of production is the arena where the Army can most appropriately contribute. However, that does not necessarily mean the encroachment of combat units upon the sovereignty of a foreign country, as was arguably the case in Bolivia.

A Matter of Security

The drug infrastructure in a major producing country must not be thought of as a criminal problem affecting private citizens, thus falling to the responsibility of police forces alone. Rather, it must be viewed as an insurgency, targeting the very security of the nation itself, for which the government, police, and military forces must accept combined responsibility. The corruptive influence on the government, coupled with the real physical threat against the government, fully justifies the development of a counterinsurgency-type approach. Colombia is fighting a losing battle against drug trafficking because of the drug-related terrorist activity directed against every element of its government. Bolivia is fighting a losing battle because of the financial influence the traffickers maintain over the peasant growers and the infiltration of drug corruption throughout various levels of the government. The drug infrastructure is an insurgent, not a criminal, problem.

The US Army's participation in the war on drugs must be in

162

the security assistance role. There are, of course, obstacles to this approach. One is the nightmare of the Vietnam experience, which "seems to loom large in the national subconscious, making the public nervous about any future commitments," [according to William J. Olson, *Military Review*, January 1988]. The security assistance program established in El Salvador still evokes the spectre of Vietnam in the minds of many people today.

A second and closely related obstacle is the reluctance of the American people, if not the government itself, to get entangled in a long-term problem, one that cannot be solved overnight by throwing a single-appropriation lump sum of money at it. Eradication of drug production will require staying for the long haul. Anything less than total commitment will simply result in short-term suppression, not elimination.

Money Needed

A third obstacle is cost. Security assistance programs throughout Latin America have been declining. Only three countries receive any security assistance in all of Latin America: El Salvador, Honduras, and Guatemala. An effective counterdrug security assistance program would require that big bucks be programmed within the Military Assistance Program, the International Military Education and Training Program, and the Economic Support Fund. . . .

The type of security assistance program to be developed requires imagination and should not be bound by traditional thinking. Colonel Richard H. Taylor has correctly reminded us that "military operations short of war do not mean business as usual." This statement is equally applicable to the development of a counterdrug security assistance program. It must be built upon an interagency community unlike any other organization, incorporating military, police, intelligence, investigative, agricultural, political, civil affairs, information media, and PSYOPS [Psychological Operations] organizations, all with a common purpose: to destroy the drug infrastructure and its means of producing illicit drugs while substituting other means of livelihood for the affected peasant growers. . . .

The intelligence community, both military and government, can play a significant role in breaking up a drug infrastructure. John Stewart's comment concerning the importance of military intelligence in a low-intensity conflict environment is also valid in counterdrug security assistance:

> In [low-intensity conflict], where the enemy avoids direct confrontation and where he may be trying to avoid US forces altogether by waiting out their withdrawal, [military intelligence] becomes a key means for maintaining momentum. By seeking out key insurgent leaders and agitators and identifying supply points and base areas, [military intelligence] is the key

to keeping the enemy off balance and preempting his plan of action.

The security assistance program must include training programs for both police (unauthorized under US laws) and military forces alike. Both military and civilian equipment may have to be provided, such as aircraft, riverine boats, secure communications, radars, night vision devices, etc. . . .

International Cooperation

Periodic combined joint military training exercises—as are now conducted in Ecuador and Bolivia, and have been conducted in the past in Panama and Colombia—could be planned in countries where counterdrug security assistance programs are indicated. The exercises could be built around a counterdrug scenario and include combined operations against production means for a two-week duration. . . .

The security assistance approach need not and should not be limited to a US initiative. The drug trade is an international cancer that knows no boundaries. There are a number of organizations within the United Nations that work in the narcotics area: the UN Fund for Drug Abuse Control, the International Narcotics Control Board, the International Criminal Police Organization (Interpol), and the Division on Narcotics Drugs. These organizations should be encouraged to work with the United States in creating international counterdrug security assistance programs.

The influence of the international drug traffickers, along with their terrorist supporters, is clearly a threat to the national security interests of producing, supporting, and recipient countries alike. It breeds corruption at every level of government and society; it crosses every ethnic, social, and financial boundary without preference.

The solutions are not easy, but the alternative of indifference or passivity is unacceptable. The United States must come to grips with this threat and attack it at every level. An economy-of-force approach in dollars and people will never make a difference. Commitment to the long-haul solution, with the necessary funding, cannot be avoided. US military forces have the potential to contribute much more to the fight than they presently are. Service participation should be viewed as an opportunity to enhance training, not as an enforced diversion which degrades readiness. Blast Furnace, perhaps derived out of the frustration of watching the drug trade continue to increase in spite of other government efforts to curb it, was at least an effort to do something. It was only a short-lived success, but it did generate a lot of thought across interagency boundaries concerning future counterattacks in the US war on drugs.

"Attacking peasants in South America is not the answer."

U.S. Intervention Cannot Stop International Drug Cartels

Michael T. Klare

Michael T. Klare is an associate professor of Peace and World Security Studies at Hampshire College in Amherst, Massachusetts. He is also the defense correspondent for the magazine *The Nation*. In the following viewpoint, Klare argues that the U.S. should not use military troops to combat drug trafficking in Latin America. Klare fears that sending troops to drug-producing nations could lead to an unwinnable war like that fought in Vietnam.

As you read, consider the following questions:

1. What similarities does the author see between U.S. military action in Latin America and the Vietnam War?
2. Why does Klare fear an escalation in the military tactics used against drug traffickers?
3. What motivation does the author believe the Pentagon has for fighting the war on drugs?

Michael T. Klare, "Fighting Drugs with the Military," *The Nation*, March 19, 1990, © The Nation Company, Inc. Reprinted with permission.

Slowly but surely the U.S. armed forces are edging to the brink of full-scale military involvement in the Latin American drug wars. With the mounting pressure on President Bush to "do something" against the illegal drug trade, it is only a matter of time before U.S. soldiers will be sent into combat against Latin American cocaine traffickers and their armed protectors. While such action would undoubtedly start out as a limited, small-scale operation, it is highly unlikely that such a piecemeal effort would make a significant dent in the drug trade. Thus demands will increase for larger and more aggressive military ventures—a process that could lead, as in Vietnam, to a major U.S. military commitment.

The first step in this process occurred on September 18, 1989 when Secretary of Defense Dick Cheney issued a directive to all U.S. military commanders, ordering them to develop plans for a major campaign against illegal drug trafficking. "Detecting and countering the production and trafficking of illegal drugs is a high priority national security mission," Cheney declared.

Going to the Source

In support of its antinarcotics mission, the Defense Department has already assumed significant responsibility for the monitoring of air and sea traffic into the southern United States and for the interception of illegal narcotics at the borders. These border interdiction efforts will be supplemented by intensified military operations aimed at the growing and processing countries themselves. "The Department of Defense will assist in the attack on production of illegal drugs *at the source*," Cheney affirmed in the guidelines issued to commanders. [Emphasis added.]

When asked if U.S. military personnel will be ordered to engage in direct combat against Latin American drug traffickers, Cheney and other Administration officials have repeatedly said no—while nevertheless leaving the door open for such action in the future. "I would say that we should not absolutely rule it off the table," William Bennett, the nation's antidrug chieftain, observed on September 8, 1989. "A sovereign government shouldn't do that." As evidence of a growing U.S. commitment to military action, in November 1989 the Navy announced that beginning in 1990 it will deploy permanently an aircraft carrier battle group off the coast of Colombia.

This is not to suggest that the U.S. military is itching for a fight. In fact, most senior officers recoil at the prospect of "another Vietnam" in the Andean jungles—an analogy that is often made in the military press. Not, of course, that we're likely to see 550,000 U.S. soldiers in South America. Still, there are important similarities. The "enemy" in Latin America, like that confronted in South Vietnam, constitutes a well-entrenched underground that cannot be easily distinguished from the urban poor and rural peasantry, and, as in Saigon, key government agencies in the drug-producing Andean countries are hopelessly corrupt, or have been compromised by enemy penetration.

Henry Payne. Reprinted by permission of UFS, Inc.

Perhaps the greatest similarity to the Vietnam War is the impressive capacity of opposition forces to resist or evade government attack, even in those cases where U.S. personnel provide the tactical leadership. The power and resilience of the drug syndicates are evident in the two principal U.S.-managed antidrug campaigns in South America, Operation Blast Furnace in Bolivia and Operation Snowcap in Bolivia and Peru.

Operation Blast Furnace

Operation Blast Furnace involved the deployment of 170 U.S. military personnel and six UH-60 Blackhawk helicopters to the Chaparé region of Bolivia for a four-month period in 1986 to support raids against suspected cocaine laboratories by Bolivian antidrug forces (the Leopards) and agents of the U.S. Drug Enforcement Agency (D.E.A.). The operation, hailed as a major U.S. initiative in the war against cocaine, produced a temporary decline in production but failed to net any significant suspects or supplies of cocaine. Michael Abbott, who commanded Army aviation personnel during the operation, wrote in 1988, "As soon as the U.S. military pulled out of Bolivia" the major traffickers came out of hiding and the price of coca leaves—the raw material for cocaine—"climbed to a level just short of its pre-Blast Furnace price."

Operation Snowcap was launched in 1988 to provide a permanent U.S. antidrug presence in the coca-growing regions of Bolivia and Peru. Like Blast Furnace, it entails U.S. support for helicopter strikes against drug laboratories by D.E.A. agents and host-nation forces. Snowcap also involves a training program for host-nation forces in counterinsurgency and small-unit tactics, provided by handpicked teams of U.S. Special Forces personnel. As of October 1989, there were approximately 100 U.S. civilians working in Peru and Bolivia under Snowcap, plus some fifty Green Beret training officers.

The Snowcap operations in Peru reveal the problems faced by Washington in attempting to suppress the drug traffic at the source. In the Upper Huallaga Valley, where the coca for an estimated 60 percent of the cocaine smuggled into the United States is grown, U.S. agents face not only the organized opposition of local farmers but also armed resistance by Sendero Luminoso ("Shining Path") guerrillas. In early 1989, Snowcap had to be suspended temporarily when Peruvian forces could no longer guarantee the safety of U.S. personnel. The operation was not resumed until September, following the construction of a fortified encampment at Santa Lucia.

A Small Dent

Although U.S. officials report a steady increase in the number of drug laboratories destroyed and acres of coca eradicated under Snowcap, nobody really believes that the operation is making a significant dent in the cocaine trade. In 1988 Peruvian forces managed to eradicate 5,130 hectares of coca—a mere 4 percent of the 115,630 hectares reportedly under cultivation at that time. Many experts believe, moreover, that total coca cultivation in Peru has risen to 200,000 hectares, with more fields being added all the time. Meanwhile, the Sendero guerrillas have steadily increased their control over the coca-growing regions, forcing the Peruvian government to abandon its plans to spray these areas with herbicides out of fear that such action will drive the coca farmers into the arms of the guerrillas.

The obstacles faced by Snowcap operatives in Peru and Bolivia exist throughout the drug-producing areas of Latin America. Coca cultivation and cocaine processing have become an essential way of life for hundreds of thousands of poor farmers who cannot earn a decent living from any other crop. An estimated 300,000 Peruvians are directly involved in coca production, and many more subsist on related activities; in Bolivia the numbers are roughly comparable.

Given these conditions, U.S. efforts to mobilize host-nation forces in the struggle against drug cultivation will inevitably produce hostility and resistance from the peasants, thus threatening the stability of the very governments upon whose assistance Washington has come to rely. As suggested by the Congressional Research Service of the Library of Congress, U.S.-backed eradication campaigns "portend real economic and political dangers for the governments of nations with marginal economic growth."

To complicate the picture further, the Peruvian *campesinos*, attacked by government antinarcotics forces on one side and exploited by Colombian drug traffickers on the other, have turned to the Senderistas for protection. And, although fiercely puritanical themselves when it comes to alcohol and drug use, the Senderistas have accepted drug money for their protective services in the coca-growing areas. Having obtained ample armaments with their newly acquired narcotics income, and enjoying widespread support from the rural population, the Senderistas have become formidable opponents of the Peruvian authorities.

Vietnam in the Andes

A Congress that balked at direct U.S. military intervention in Nicaragua has no qualms about seeing DEA [Drug Enforcement Administration] hardware on tarmacs in Colombia, Bolivia and Peru, and does not lose sleep asking whether the taxpayers' money is being spent in a war on drugs or on left-wing guerrillas.

As others have remarked, U.S. government policy on drugs adds up as a prison state for black America and a Vietnam war in the Andes.

Alexander Cockburn, *The Wall Street Journal*, September 7, 1989.

Ultimately, any major effort to suppress coca production in the Upper Huallaga Valley will require a full-scale counter-insurgency campaign of the sort attempted by the United States in Southeast Asia. And just as government forces in Vietnam proved incapable of sustaining such an arduous task on their own and eventually had to be buttressed by American troops, so it is likely that sustained counterinsurgency warfare in Peru will also exceed Lima's capabilities and thus invite full-scale U.S. military involvement.

An equally bleak outlook confronts U.S. antidrug officials in Colombia, the source of approximately 80 percent of the illicit cocaine now flowing into the United States. Drug trafficking brings an estimated $4 billion per year into the Colombian economy—about three times the amount generated by coffee exports, the leading legal crop—and as many as 1 million Colombians are directly involved in trafficking or benefit indirectly from the wealth acquired thereby. Moreover, the Colombian *narcotraficantes* have been able to corrupt important sectors of the military, the police and the judiciary and to win friends among the poor through conspicuous public works projects.

Issues of race and class also intrude into the Colombian narcotics picture. While Colombia's governing elite is made up largely of white entrepreneurs (many of whom are connected to the coffee industry), the drug syndicates are made up of poor blacks and mestizos from the slums of Medellín and Cali who feel no loyalty to the government in Bogotá. "With narcotics," says Medellín City Council member Mario Arango, "the mestizos, the mulattoes and blacks . . . have had the opportunities to enter consumer society and gain substantial wealth." It is no wonder, therefore, that the poor of Medellín have shown no enthusiasm for the current antidrug crackdown, and that no one has rushed forward with news of the whereabouts of the major traffickers sought by U.S. and Colombian authorities.

Supply or Demand?

Given this assessment of the narco-battlefield in Latin America, it appears that the Bush Administration has two choices if it is determined to wage a war on drugs: It can change its basic approach to the drug problem by switching from a strategy aimed at choking off supplies to one aimed at reducing domestic demand, or it can assume increased responsibility for the antidrug military campaign in Latin America.

Focusing on the demand side would, in the view of many U.S. specialists, prove more effective over the long run, but would also require extensive Federal spending on drug education, treatment services and social welfare in inner-city neighborhoods—a price that Bush does not appear to be willing to pay. Instead, the Administration has chosen to emphasize a punitive approach, entailing increased arrest and imprisonment of traffickers in the United States and stepped-up military action against suppliers abroad. For this approach to make any progress, however, the war against growers (and peasants) will have to escalate—and since the capacity of the military in the cocaine-producing countries has pretty much been stretched to the limit, increased involvement by U.S. forces appears inevitable.

Such involvement, once approved, could take several forms:

hit-and-run attacks by U.S. Rangers or Special Forces personnel against major drug laboratories and storage sites, participation (with host-nation forces) in periodic "search and destroy" missions aimed at crippling coca production in such areas as the Chaparé or the Upper Huallaga Valley, full-scale counterinsurgency warfare against the Sendero Luminoso and drug-connected guerrilla groups in Colombia, and military assaults on the headquarters of the drug barons and their major allies.

Major military action of this sort would undoubtedly damage the syndicates' supply operations in Latin America and possibly would demolish some of the major drug rings. It would be the height of folly, however, to assume that such operations will succeed in shutting off the supply of drugs to the United States. Contrary to the U.S. perception of a highly organized cartel that controls the drug trade from a central headquarters in Medellín—one that could be neutralized in a single military sweep—the syndicates are loosely tied criminal organizations that can subdivide, disperse and reunite in new and unpredictable formations. Moreover, the syndicates have already begun coca production in new areas, including remote stretches of Brazil, that are beyond the reach of U.S. forces. Thus, the United States could find itself bogged down in a bloody struggle with well-armed insurgents and their peasant supporters.

A Convenient Excuse

The U.S. troops sent to "train" local forces in the Andes could become a tripwire for quickly expanding U.S. aggression in those countries. People who know a thing or two about how the U.S. imperialist gangsters operate around the world are on to their tactic of using "American casualties" as an excuse for direct military intervention. Many people remember how the U.S. war in Vietnam started with the sending of a few "advisers."

Revolutionary Worker, September 25, 1989.

Given the risk of military entanglement in another jungle quagmire, many senior Pentagon officials have warned against the use of U.S. combat troops in Latin American drug wars. "Gringos must not shoot Latins," observed one general, warning that such action would precipitate an anti-U.S. backlash of tremendous proportions. Other officials have expressed unease at the Pentagon's assumption of what is seen as a law-enforcement function. "That is not the function of the military," Secretary of Defense Frank Carlucci declared in 1988. "We are not the frontline agency in the war on drugs."

There are, however, contrary pressures acting on and within the military. Most prominent, of course, are the voices in Congress that are calling for more vigorous action from the Bush Administration. The Administration's antinarcotics plan "is not tough enough, bold enough, or imaginative enough to meet the crisis at hand," proclaimed Joseph Biden, the Democratic leader of the Senate Judiciary Committee, on September 5, 1989. "The President says he wants to wage a war on drugs, but if that's true what we need is another D-Day, not another Vietnam, not a limited war, fought on the cheap, and destined for stalemate and human tragedy." Such language is being used with increasing fervor by Democrats on Capitol Hill, putting pressure on Bush to demonstrate his "toughness" through some sort of military action.

Such action is also being advocated by counterinsurgency enthusiasts in the Defense Department, who view antidrug operations as a legitimate form of "low-intensity conflict." Among the adherents to this position are Army Col. John Waghelstein, former commander of U.S. military advisers in El Salvador. Charging that Marxist guerrillas have forged an alliance with Latin American drug traffickers, Waghelstein called for vigorous Pentagon action "to counter the guerrilla/ narcotics terrorists in this hemisphere." Such action, he contended, would provide the Pentagon with an "unassailable moral position" from which to counter the "church and academic groups" that have resisted U.S. intervention in Central America.

Defense Spending

Some military officers perceive another compelling reason for taking on the drug war: increased defense spending. With fears of the "Soviet threat" in decline and concern over the Federal deficit on the rise, the Pentagon has begun to brace itself for significant cutbacks. However, the one area where Congress seeks to raise funds is the antidrug campaign. "In a time when there will be increasing demands for fiscal constraints and selective spending, Congress has already demonstrated that it is willing to provide funding for counternarcotics programs," Maj. Susan Flores wrote in *Marine Corps Gazette*. Because such funds could be used to acquire a wide variety of hardware sought by the military, "before the Marine Corps says 'no' to [fighting] drugs, it should think seriously about what is to be gained."

With such arguments and pressures, the Pentagon is being pushed closer and closer to the brink of direct intervention in Latin America. It is not a task that senior officers look forward to with relish but one that they will eventually be forced to assume when the political pressures become strong enough—and there is no doubt that President Bush, who has declared a full-scale war on drugs and has yet to achieve any notable victories, is feeling the heat.

Undoubtedly, a dramatic effort to solve the drug problem with machine-gun fire in South America will generate a fair amount of applause in the United States, especially in the first few weeks after an initial Army or Marine Corps assault. It will give President Bush an opportunity to demonstrate some machismo and distract attention from other problems at home. But the only sure results of such action will be an upsurge of anti-imperialism in Latin America and only a temporary dip in drug production. Eventually, the production sites will be moved while drug prices rise in the United States and, in reaction, the severity of urban violence will increase.

The Wrong Answer

Halting the devastation of our inner cities and the poisoning of our urban youth is a vital national priority. But attacking peasants in South America is not the answer. Not only would such action risk U.S. entanglement in a debilitating and inconclusive jungle war; it would also drive the cultivators into new (and more inaccessible) areas. Ultimately, the only sure method for reducing the traffic in narcotics is to curb the appetite for these substances through education, treatment and urban economic renewal. As Lieut. Gen. Stephen Olmstead declared at a Congressional hearing, "interdiction is not the answer to the drug war. Demand-reduction is."

*"The most important thing now is to provide
resources for crop substitution in the zones
where marijuana and coca are being produced."*

Economic Aid Could Stop Drug Production

Michael Massing

The average citizen in Colombia makes $1,586 a year. In Peru
the figure is $900. In poor countries like this, growing the
prized coca leaves from which cocaine is extracted provides an
alluring alternative to growing traditional crops. In the following
viewpoint, free-lance writer Michael Massing argues that until
South American peasants can make a living growing legal crops,
the drug problem will continue. Massing writes that military solutions are not the answer to an economic problem. He believes
financial aid to coca growers could help them switch to other
crops.

As you read, consider the following questions:

1. In the author's opinion, what effect has the war on drugs
   had on drug smuggling?
2. According to Massing, what must South American governments do to stop farmers from cultivating coca?
3. How much money does Massing contend is spent each year
   for crop substitution? How much on coca and marijuana
   eradication?

Michael Massing, "The War on Cocaine," *The New York Review of Books,* December 22,
1988. Reprinted with permission.

With each passing month, the "war on drugs" looks increasingly like the war in Vietnam. The more money and manpower we pour into it, the more the enemy seems to advance. Since 1983, the budget of the Drug Enforcement Administration (DEA) has almost doubled, to more than half a billion dollars. Over the same period, the staff of the US Customs Service has grown from 12,000 to 16,000. To detect smugglers, the Reagan administration set up a national interdiction center in El Paso, Texas, installed radar-bearing blimps on the Mexican border, and sent sophisticated AWACS [airborne warning and control system] planes over the Caribbean. In Latin America, CIA [Central Intelligence Agency] agents are gathering intelligence on cocaine producers, the State Department is deploying expensive Huey helicopters, and the Green Berets are instructing local policemen in the art of paramilitary war.

Despite all this, narcotics continue to flow into the country with the same ease with which Viet Cong troops slipped down the Ho Chi Minh Trail. Cocaine from the Andean nations of South America, heroin from the Golden Triangle in Southeast Asia, marijuana from Mexico, Colombia, and Jamaica—all cross our borders like a silent invading army. As many as fifty countries are involved in the production, processing, and transporting of narcotics, forming an international network aimed at indulging American consumers. Every year, Americans spend between $50 billion and $100 billion on drugs. And that sum does not begin to measure the real cost to the nation—the crime, the accidents, the lost work days, not to speak of the destroyed lives. The toll is so great that drugs have surpassed even communism as a subject of national concern.

Cocaine's Damage

No substance causes as much damage as cocaine. An estimated 6 million Americans regularly use the drug. It has wrecked promising athletic careers, sparked violent gang wars, turned children into dealers, and, in the ubiquitous and relatively cheap form of crack, laid waste to our inner cities. For years now, the government has made cocaine its primary target. Nevertheless, more of the drug is entering the United States than ever before, causing a free fall in its price. Every April, the government issues a National Narcotics Intelligence Consumers Committee Report, considered the most reliable source on domestic drug consumption. For cocaine in 1987, it stated, wholesale prices during the year were the lowest ever reported, and the purity remained at high levels, reflecting widespread availability. In 1980, a kilogram of wholesale cocaine sold in Miami for $60,000; today, it goes for $14,000.

As in Vietnam, the lack of results in the drug war has prompted calls for escalation. The new anti-narcotics law, passed by Congress in October 1988, provides for a multinational task force designed to strike at trafficking organizations around the world. Mayor Ed Koch of New York has suggested that the United States send tanks and bombers to level Medellín, seat of the infamous Colombian cartel, which is made up of the largest traders in cocaine. "I am beginning to think that the normal, acceptable methods no longer apply," Representative Lawrence Smith (Democrat of Florida) observed during a House hearing. "If we do not begin to come up with creative, effective solutions to these problems, this war is going to be lost."

The Essential Ingredient

The United States could make a major contribution by helping to provide programs for crop-and-income substitution to drug farmers in economically depressed Latin American nations. Similarly, new economic opportunities could be made available by the simple lowering of import barriers on legitimate Latin American exports—textiles, sugar, coffee, flowers, and so forth—and by extending the Caribbean Basin Initiative (CBI) system to those South American governments which undertake serious anti-drug campaigns. The United States could also aid Latin American economic development by taking the lead in alleviating the crushing burden of Latin American debt, now inhibiting that development, perhaps by devising new formulas for debt relief. Unquestionably, renewed economic development in the region will be an essential ingredient in any successful, long-term effort to reduce the drug traffic.

Bruce Michael Bagley, *Journal of Interamerican Studies and World Affairs*, Spring 1988.

Is there any solution? Seeking an answer, I paid a visit to Colombia, the source of about 80 percent of the cocaine entering the United States. After talking with officials in Bogotá, touring the drug districts of Medellín, and visiting Colombia's coca heartland, I came away convinced that the failures of US drug policy spring from a fundamental misreading of how the drug trade works. I found, in fact, that the cocaine business is undergoing some important changes, offering a rare opportunity to do something about it. That, however, would require a sharp reversal of the mistaken policies of the [Reagan administration]. . . .

San José

In San José de Guaviare, a rough river town in the Colombian jungle, the main street is lined with pool halls, video shops, cheap hotels, discos, and unisex beauty parlors. In the mornings, people sit in fly-infested cafés drinking cups of black coffee, called *tintos*. At night they gather in the town's many bars—boisterous places where the *ranchero* music is always played at full blast. The drinking lasts only until 11 o'clock, when San José's generators are turned off and the town suddenly goes dark.

I came to San José to see the region where coca is grown and to learn what the government was doing about it. Everywhere the talk was about the crisis in coca production. During the boom, people said, the main bars in town had a few hundred prostitutes each; today, they're lucky if they have a dozen. Then, peasant farmers ordered bottles of eighteen-year-old Chivas Regal; now they take *aguardiente*, a nasty local brew that tastes like cheap ouzo. The town's airport used to have three hundred flights daily; today it rarely gets forty.

An hour's plane ride southeast of Bogotá, San José is the capital of the Guaviare, a lush, untamed region that accounts for 80 percent of Colombia's coca. In 1978, Colombia produced no coca, and San José had only a few thousand residents. Today, Colombia produces 30,000 hectares, and San José is a busy little town of 25,000 people. . . .

The Guerrillas

The guerrillas came, too. The lure of money and the absence of government made the Guaviare an irresistible target, and in the early 1980s the FARC [Colombian Revolutionary Armed Forces]—the country's largest and most orthodox guerrilla group—moved in. The FARC never got much involved in production; rather, it levied taxes on both farmers and traffickers (about 10 percent in each case). The organization grew very rich, using its revenues to buy arms and extend its control. Gradually, the FARC took over the functions of the state in the Guaviare, imposing its own draconian system of justice. This included a remarkably effective technique for stamping out drug addiction: any peasant found consuming bazuco (a local form of crack) was given several warnings; if he persisted, he was taken into a field and shot.

The boom began to fade in 1983. With the price of cocaine tumbling, many peasants went into debt, and the traffickers hired *sicarios* to settle scores. Shootouts became a nightly affair, claiming five, ten, even fifteen victims at a time. With the massacres mounting and the guerrillas grown rich off coca, the government eventually decided to retake the region. In December 1987, it sent hundreds of heavily armed troops sweeping into the Guaviare's remote settlements. The guerrillas did not put up much resistance, preferring instead to disappear into the bush.

For the government to maintain control of the region, it had to win the support of the peasants, and to that end it began build-

177

ing public works. Maintaining control also meant denying the guerrillas their chief source of income, which was coca. So the government set about to eliminate it. A large detachment of antinarcotics police was assigned to San José. By helicopter they fanned out over the jungle, looking for coca fields and setting fire to them. However, it was clear that such a strategy could never destroy more than a fraction of the crop—the region was simply too vast and inaccessible. Clearly a less coercive program was needed.

Weaned from Drugs

Eradication programs could be made more effective, not primarily by spending more to uproot crops, but by investing more in rural areas to create new jobs and income for peasant farmers and others who currently derive their livelihood from narcotics. Ultimately, sustained economic development is what is required to wean drug-producing regions from their dependence on drug crops.

Sol M. Linowitz, *Foreign Affairs*, Winter 1988/1989.

The key factor in planning that program was the depressed price of coca. With world markets glutted, coca paste was earning one fifth or less of what it had during the boom; at such a level, the plant was barely profitable. To make it even less so, the government clamped down on the sale of the materials used in the production process. Gasoline, cement, plastic, chemicals—anyone wanting to purchase these products had to obtain a license indicating that he would use them for legal purposes. Prices for these goods immediately shot up.

Many Guaviare farmers now wanted to stop cultivating coca, but they needed something to grow in its place. "We can't tell the peasants to get out of coca without providing an alternative," the *comisario* told me during our interview.

Enter the PNR [National Rehabilitation Plan]. It offered the peasants loans to buy the seeds, fertilizer, and other materials needed for new crops. There was one major obstacle, however. "The state is very poor," *Comisario* José Francisco Gómez explained. "People tell me that they want to leave coca, but we don't have enough money to help them."

When I asked him whether the United States had offered any assistance, Gómez said no and began to speak loudly: "Instead of spending millions of dollars trying to stop the flow of cocaine into the United States, you should help us build up the infrastructure and make loans to the farmers. Instead of spending all this money in Florida on interdiction, send it here, to the source.

This is the best place to fight the war against cocaine."

The chief preoccupation of the officials in the region was finding a way to allow peasants to get their food crops to market. For a close look at the problem the PNR had arranged for me to visit Calamar, a major trafficking center fifty miles to the south. The road there was terrible, so Jaime, the PNR representative, and Juan Carlos, his aide, an agronomist, had reserved a four-seat air taxi. Throughout the flight the pilot kept the plane very low—no more than eight hundred feet—so that we could get a good glimpse at the landscape below. Ten minutes out of San José, we flew over a small patch of land whose bright green color stood out from the surrounding vegetation: coca. Four or five times during the trip, Jaime pointed out similar splotches—many fewer, he assured me, than before the army's occupation, which had encouraged the planting of other crops. But the San José-Calamar road, which stretched out below us, was, he said, "a terrible road and the peasants can't get their crops to market." As we glided along, I could make out slowly moving packs of mules and, occasionally, trucks trying to navigate mammoth potholes.

The Colombian Coca Problem

Twenty-five minutes out of San José, Calamar came into view. The dirt runway, too, had large potholes. We took a mule-drawn cut into town, getting off at the Danubio restaurant, on Calamar's unpaved and badly rutted main strip. Nearby were greasy food kiosks, sour smelling bars, and tawdry shops selling used clothes. Soldiers carrying submachine guns ambled along, paying no notice to the Communist party posters plastered on the walls (a reminder of the FARC's popularity).

Calamar has no telephones. When somebody is wanted, his name is broadcast MASH-like over loudspeakers manned from the Danubio. We asked for the mayor, and a few minutes later he materialized. I explained my interest in the coca problem. The seventy-year-old mayor, Vincente Ferrer Londoño, began describing Calamar's many woes. "Coca is dying," he said. "It's no longer profitable. The only people who keep growing it are those who can't find any other work." Most traffickers had long since stopped coming.

The government's assistance program was not doing well, he said. He was particularly unhappy about the state of the road system. "Farmers here can grow a lot of corn and rice," Ferrer said. "But how are they going to sell it if there aren't any roads?" If the government paved the road from Calamar to San José—the gateway to the national market—"coca would completely disappear."

Sitting in Calamar's bars, with the heat breaking in waves and

179

names crackling over the loudspeaker, I felt that I had somehow arrived at the source of the cocaine entering the United States. The message from everyone was virtually identical: the dramatic fall in the price of coca was forcing farmers to move into food crops. But they could do so only if they had sufficient credit and, more importantly, good roads. Everyone agreed that enabling the peasants to get their crops to market was the key to any anticoca program. Certainly "repressive" methods would never get the job done.

Earning a Living

The U.S. must provide source nations with the economic aid and expertise which will rebuild their economies and rejuvenate their citizens. The farmers who grow the coca leaves do so not because they want gold necklaces or fancy boats and cars, but because they want to feed and clothe their families; because they want to survive from one day to the next. While the money that they get from growing coca leaves is not a great sum, it is still more than they could hope to get raising more acceptable crops or pursuing other ways of making a living.

L. Douglas Wilder, *TransAfrica Forum*, Spring/Summer 1989.

Back in San José, I talked to the head of the anti-narcotics police. Captain Omar Humberto Díaz is only twenty-six, but he commands a 120-man force that is responsible for all eradication efforts in the region. For once I found someone willing to defend the DEA. "Without the DEA, we wouldn't be able to get anything done," Captain Díaz told me. The agency's most important contribution, he said, was the helicopters it provided: "When the helicopters are here, we can do a lot to find coca fields and burn them." Unfortunately, he added, the copters came only every two or three weeks and stayed for a few days before flying off to other districts. When I mentioned my trip to Calamar, and the farmer's pleas for help, Díaz made it clear he knew what I was talking about. "I need more helicopters in my work," Díaz said, "but it's also important to give the peasant the means to replace his coca with other crops." I noted that the United States these days had very limited resources to spend abroad. "If you had to choose between getting a new helicopter and giving farmers more credit," I asked, "which would you take?" "The credits," he said without pausing. . . .

From peasants to professors, police captains to politicians, I found a consensus about how best to fight the cocaine trade. Even the attorney general, Horacio Serpa, one of the country's top law enforcement officials, told me: "The most important thing now is to provide resources for crop substitution in the zones where marijuana and coca are being produced—to give the Colombian peasant, who is a victim of poverty and the voracity of the narcotraffickers, a chance to earn an income sufficient for a dignified life." . . .

The low price of coca offers an excellent opportunity to attack the drug problem at its source. We might begin by building a road between Calamar and San José de Guaviare. It would cost about 500 million Colombian pesos, or not quite $2 million—a bargain, given the blow it would strike at Colombia's coca production.

Of course, Calamar is hardly alone in needing better transportation facilities. Throughout the Guaviare, poor, remote settlements are clamoring for their own roads. And beyond the Guaviare are the vast coca regions of Peru and Bolivia. Building enough roads and extending enough loans to make a difference there would require a huge sum—$200 to $300 million, according to State Department estimates.

The Money Exists

At a time of soaring deficits and foreign aid cuts, such a price would seem out of the question. But the money already exists—in current anti-narcotics programs that aren't working. Year after year, we spend huge sums on tired schemes that have failed to show even the slightest results. Why not divert a portion of that money into a new approach, which holds out at least some hope? A good starting point would be to eliminate the State Department's eradication program, which is a demonstrable failure. Phasing it out would immediately save $45 million. Next, liquidating the State Department's air wing, a white elephant if there ever was one, could raise the available pool to $100 million.

The rest could come from the nation's interdiction budget. Between 1987 and 1988, the United States spent about $1 billion trying to intercept drugs at its borders. In the case of cocaine, we've probably interdicted no more than 10 percent of the total amount shipped here. No matter what technique we adopt, smugglers always manage to adapt. The US Customs Service is lining the Mexican border with huge radar-equipped blimps. . . . Since the first dirigible was installed early in 1988, Customs has failed to capture a single smuggler; nevertheless, it plans to install fifteen more blimps at a cost of up to $1 billion. Imagine what that sum could accomplish if it were invested in the coca regions of South America.

181

"Political, economic, and law enforcement conditions do not warrant massive infusions of U.S. aid [to fight the war on drugs]."

Economic Aid Could Not Stop Drug Production

Rensselaer W. Lee III

Rensselaer W. Lee III is an associate scholar at the Foreign Policy Research Institute in Philadelphia and is the president of Global Advisory Services, an international development consulting firm. The following viewpoint is taken from Lee's book, *The White Labyrinth: Cocaine and Political Power*. In it, Lee argues that the profitability of cocaine would overwhelm any U.S. effort to send aid to drug-producing countries. He writes that Latin American countries are dependent on the $3 to $5 billion dollars per year that drug trafficking brings into their economies. U.S. economic aid to end coca production, Lee believes, would be wasted unless the American demand for drugs can be cut.

As you read, consider the following questions:

1. Why does Lee argue that, even with significant U.S. help, the Andean governments cannot control cocaine production?
2. What point does the author make by comparing the annual income of cocaine dealers with the amount of aid the U.S. gives Latin America to fight drugs?

In recent years, the abuse and control of illicit narcotics have come to pervade U.S. relations with the Third World. The drug issue is a source of conflict and mutual recrimination between North and South. The main consumer countries are rich and industrialized; the main drug-producing countries are poor and predominantly agricultural. The drug trade generates an annual transfer of billions of dollars from North to South and has gained a powerful economic foothold in some Third World countries. Producing countries and consuming countries blame each other for the accelerating drug traffic and advocate, respectively, demand-side and supply-side solution. U.S. programs to control drug cultivation and production overseas often engender nationalist resentment. Moreover, political elites in some Third World countries view antidrug crusades as imposing significant economic and social costs and as creating new and formidable political challenges.

The cocaine traffic in the Western Hemisphere constitutes a particularly severe manifestation of the North-South conflict over drugs. U.S. concerns over cocaine are fairly clear-cut. Although U.S. imports of heroin and marijuana remained roughly stable from 1977 to 1987, imports of cocaine apparently increased five- to ten-fold during that time. Traffickers are "literally just throwing it at our shores," in the words of the U.S. Commissioner of Customs. Abuse of cocaine and its derivative "crack"—a highly toxic and addictive substance—has become a fairly serious U.S. public health problem. According to data from the Drug Abuse Warning Network, cocaine overdoses were the main cause of 46,331 hospital emergency cases and 1,696 deaths in 1987; in contrast, in 1980, the corresponding figures were, respectively, 4,154 and 250. "Cocaine wars" among rival gangs of dealers have raised the murder rate and lowered the quality of life in Washington, New York, Miami, and other U.S. cities.

Funding and Foreign Aid

The United States expends considerable diplomatic energy on pressing Colombia, Bolivia, and Peru—the major countries producing cocaine—to curb illicit drug cultivation and refining. The United States also provides funding, technical assistance, and personnel for narcotics control programs in the three countries; such arrangements total about $50-$60 million annually. In addition, since 1983, the U.S. Congress has increasingly linked foreign aid to performance in narcotics control. Countries that do not take adequate steps to control illicit drug production, trafficking, and money laundering can lose certain specified economic and military assistance and trade preferences, such as sugar quotas or Caribbean Initiative benefits.

Supply-side approaches, however, have obviously failed to stem the flow of cocaine into U.S. markets. Latin American governments lack the resources to counter the traffic: There is no correspondence between the resources available to cocaine traffickers and the resources available to combat them. Perhaps more important, however, governments and important constituencies in the main producing countries do not give the war against cocaine their unconditional support. This is true even though the cocaine traffic in many respects damages the source countries—rampant corruption, rising numbers of drug addicts, escalating levels of violence, declining moral standards, and a deteriorating national image are among the more obvious consequences. The reasons for this Latin American reticence are complex. Several points, however, deserve mention at the outset.

A Pound of Bananas

Some advocates of curbing production believe that the wisest course is to back up crop substitution programs with economic support from the consumer countries. But the problem will remain one of supply and demand. On the day that a pound of bananas is worth more than pound of cocaine, there will be no South American coca farmers.

J. Martinez Vera, *World Press Review*, May 1988.

First, moving against the cocaine traffic entails serious economic and political costs. Narco-dollars have represented a relatively important source of foreign exchange for Andean countries, as traditional sources—foreign investment, bank loans, and earnings from Andean exports such as oil, gas, copper, and fishmeal—have contracted. The cocaine industry is an important source of jobs and income in regions characterized by desperate poverty and widespread unemployment. An estimated 500,000 to one million people are employed directly in the upstream and downstream phases of the industry—cultivation, initial processing, refining, and smuggling. Coca farmers receive less than one percent of the final street value of their crop—that is, the equivalent value of refined cocaine sold to consumers in industrialized countries—yet, they typically earn several times the income they would receive from growing alternative crops such as cacao, oranges, and coffee. All along the cocaine production-logistics chain, people receive substantially higher wages than they would in the licit economy.

Second, the cocaine industry as a whole has accumulated significant political clout. Coca farmers are numerous and well organized; in Bolivia, national labor and campesino organizations provide direct political support to farmers. Cocaine traffickers play the role of power brokers and are a major source of funding for political campaigns. Traffickers also have penetrated and corrupted nearly every important national institution: police forces, military establishments, legislatures, key government ministries, the judiciary, the church, and the news media. Some cocaine traffickers exhibit a rudimentary sense of social responsibility—a critically important development that enabled them to build a popular following by sponsoring public works and welfare projects that benefit the urban and rural poor.

Third, the war on cocaine is not especially popular in South America—it is perceived as a program imposed on South America by the United States. Certain U.S.-initiated measures—such as extradition, the spraying of illicit crops, U.S. military intervention against cocaine laboratories, and economic sanctions against cocaine-exporting countries—have provoked considerable anti-Yankee sentiment. Furthermore, most Latin American leaders see the supply-side approach to drug control as fundamentally flawed: In the Latin American view, demand, not supply, drives the international drug traffic. Says Peru's Alan García: "I have always thought of drug trafficking as the final stage of capitalist consumerism. The problem does not lie in the fact that a poor town produces coca leaves in the Peruvian jungle. The basic problem lies in the world's big consumer markets consisting of the richest societies."

This is not to say that the drug war in South America is totally useless. It at least limits the inroads that traffickers can make into the political system. It is significantly harder than it was in the early 1980's for cocaine dealers to run for political office, to form "nationalist" political parties, and to occupy cabinet-level positions. Yet, limiting the more outrageous political manifestations of the cocaine trade is not the same as curbing exports of cocaine from South America. On this count, U.S. programs and those of the Andean countries themselves have largely failed. . . .

A Dependence on Drug Money

The research and interviews conducted by the author and subsequent analyses lead inevitably to several conclusions that advocates of supply-side programs will find discouraging. First, the cocaine trade has altered irrevocably the economic and political landscape of the Andean countries. Cocaine traffickers constitute an interest group with extensive resources and political connections, just like the coffee barons in Colombia or the mining elites in Peru and Bolivia. Indeed, studies of these countries' development patterns, decision-making processes, and relations with other countries are no longer possible without reference to coca and cocaine.

185

Second, the drug war in South American source countries presents difficult if not unmanageable problems for both South American governments and the U.S. government. The drug war requires that Andean countries address a host of obstacles, such as national economic dependence on drugs, powerful narcotics lobbies, indifferent or hostile publics, weak political structures, and porous systems of criminal justice. In addition, other compelling U.S. interests in the region—such as promoting economic stability, preserving democracy, or preventing the emergence of Marxist regimes—are not necessarily compatible with aggressive drug control programs.

"For today's 'Lifestyles of the Rich and Famous,' we take you to the home of one of Colombia's leading drug barons. . . ."

Third, even with significant U.S. help, Andean governments will make little progress in controlling cocaine production. Eradication campaigns, occasional large drug busts, and a few major arrests (like the highly publicized arrests of Carlos Lehder in Colombia and Roberto Suarez in Bolivia) will continue in the Andean countries. Nonetheless, the basic structure of the cocaine industry—its agricultural base, manufacturing infrastructure, leadership, smuggling networks, and so on—will remain more or less intact. The corollary: Victory in the war against cocaine cannot be won in the jungles, shanty towns, and trafficking capitals of South American countries; only when Americans decide that they will no longer be the drug lords' customers will the industry collapse. . . .

Aid and Drug Control

U.S. foreign policy toward Latin America during the 1980s can genuinely be characterized as drug diplomacy. Once an issue far out of the diplomatic mainstream, narcotics control has become a vital component of U.S. relations with countries such as Bolivia, Peru, Colombia, Mexico, Jamaica, and Panama. Controlling drug production and exports officially carries the highest U.S. diplomatic priority in Colombia and one of the top two or three such priorities in Bolivia and Peru. The United States allocates economic aid accordingly: Narcotics-related assistance rose from 30 percent of all U.S. aid to Colombia in fiscal year 1984 (FY 1984) to more than 90 percent in FY 1988. Moreover, Congress now ties foreign aid to measurements of recipient countries' drug control efforts. For instance, in 1986 and 1987, the United States withheld $17.4 million in aid from Bolivia, primarily because coca crop-eradication targets were not met.

Drug diplomacy, however, is largely a region-specific tool: The United States never seriously threatened to cut off economic and military aid to Pakistan (the world's largest heroin producer) or to stop supplying Stinger missiles to the Afghan freedom fighters (who cultivate opium extensively). The United States can pressure Latin America more intensely about drug policies in part because the region does not abut the major communist powers. A more important reason is that Latin America supplies most of the marijuana, about 40 percent of the heroin, and all of the cocaine entering U.S. markets. Cocaine represents the biggest concern—the war against cocaine now consumes the bulk of the federal government's drug-fighting resources. Public and Congressional outrage over the U.S. cocaine epidemic —there are an estimated six million regular users of the toxic and highly addictive drug—has prompted Congress to expand its role in foreign policymaking and has altered, perhaps irrevocably, the shape of American diplomacy in the Western Hemisphere. Replying to criticism that the United States was scapegoating the region, a member of the House Committee on Foreign Affairs staff notes, "We have focused more on Latin America, because cocaine has been more of an issue." . . .

The Industry's Power

The industry is a powerful antagonist—largely because it has cultivated extensive ties with the existing power structures in the Andean countries. Several conclusions are highlighted below.
- Although an inefficient engine of economic growth, the co-

187

caine industry serves as an important source of jobs, income, and foreign exchange. The industry compensates for the failings of formal economies, especially in Peru and Bolivia.

• Powerful and politically articulate constituencies have developed around the cocaine industry in both its upstream (agricultural) and downstream (processing and distribution) phases. Coca farmers are blocking eradication programs in Peru and Bolivia, and cocaine syndicates are using their massive financial and logistical resources to undermine criminal justice systems and to buy a share of political power.

No Deal

The United States' push-and-pull approach to the Bolivian Government had included a proposal to pay $800 per acre to plow under the coca and substitute another crop. But neither Government officials nor the people are foolish: $800 per acre for 175,000 acres gives the country only $140 million. Each year the country receives $500 million in laundered cocaine money. Oranges, coffee and bananas cannot compare with cocaine when the latest Miami street price of $16,000 a kilo reflects a 15-percent increase in three months—the bottom-line explanation of why more than 400,000 Bolivians work in some phase of cocaine production. The shadow economy of drugs offers no incentive for change to any Bolivian government.

Michael J. Gillgannon, *America*, October 29, 1988.

• In its higher value-added stages, the cocaine industry has little in common with the revolutionary left. Marxist insurgents have gained a foothold among the coca-growing peasantry, but large trafficking organizations remain generally hostile to guerrillas and to the left. Indeed, informal anticommunist alliances have developed among cocaine dealers, right-wing military officers, and large landowners, especially in Colombia.

• Andean governments cannot muster the resources, strategic reach, and political clout to confront the cocaine industry. Furthermore, governments do not view the industry as a serious threat to their own survival. In Colombia and Peru, left-wing guerrillas are the principal enemy, and the war against drugs conflicts in part with counterinsurgency efforts. Andean leaders also fear that a successful crackdown on drugs would destabilize the economy and breed new and lethal political changes.

Wasted Aid

Three policy implications follow from the above conclusions. First, U.S. interests in cutting the supply of cocaine are not necessarily compatible with the interests of the producer nations.

Second, U.S. drug diplomacy as currently practiced probably will exacerbate tensions in U.S.-Latin American relations. Third, the marginal impact of expanding supply-side programs is likely to be low. U.S. narcotics assistance programs are admittedly poorly funded—the $50-$60 million that the United States spends annually in Colombia, Peru, and Bolivia compares rather unfavorably with the $5-$6 billion that South American cocaine dealers earn each year. However, political, economic, and law enforcement conditions do not warrant massive infusions of U.S. aid, which probably would be wasted. (Moreover, given current U.S. budget deficits, Congress would be unlikely to allocate the additional funds.) The solution, if there is one, lies not in the Andean jungles but in the United States: The six million people who now consume cocaine must be persuaded to change their habits and preferences.

a critical thinking activity

Evaluating Sources of Information

When historians study and interpret past events, they use two kinds of sources: primary and secondary. Primary sources are eyewitness accounts. For example, the diary of a Peruvian peasant who describes life in rural Latin America in the 1950s would be a primary source. A book about Latin American peasants by an author who used the peasant's diary would be a secondary source. Primary and secondary sources may be decades or even hundreds of years old, and often historians find that the sources offer conflicting and contradictory information. To fully evaluate documents and assess their accuracy, historians analyze the credibility of the documents' authors and, in the case of secondary sources, analyze the credibility of the information the authors used.

Historians are not the only people who encounter conflicting information, however. Anyone who reads a daily newspaper, watches television, or just talks to different people will encounter many different views. Writers and speakers use sources of information to support their own statements. Thus, critical thinkers, just like historians, must question the writer's or speaker's sources of information as well as the writer or speaker.

While there are many criteria that can be applied to assess the accuracy of a primary or secondary source, for this activity you will be asked to apply three. For each source listed on the following page, ask yourself the following questions: First, did the person actually see or participate in the event he or she is reporting? This will help you determine the credibility of the information—an eyewitness to an event is an extremely valuable source. Second, does the person have a vested interest in the report? Assessing the person's social status, professional affiliations, nationality, and religious or political beliefs will be helpful in considering this question. By evaluating this you will be able to determine how objective the person's report may be. Third, how qualified is the author to be making the statements he or she is making? Consider what the person's profession is and how he or she might know about the event. Someone who has spent years being involved with or studying the issue may be able to offer more information than someone who simply is offering an uneducated opinion; for example, a politician or layperson.

Keeping the above criteria in mind, imagine you are writing a paper on how drug cartels have affected Latin America. You decide to cite an equal number of primary and secondary sources. Listed below are several sources which may be useful for your research. *Place a P next to those descriptions you believe are primary sources. Place an S next to those descriptions you believe are secondary sources.* Next, based on the above criteria, *rank the primary sources assigning the number (1) to what appears to be the most valuable, (2) to the source likely to be the second-most valuable, and so on, until all the primary sources are ranked. Then rank the secondary sources, again using the above criteria.*

P or S		Rank in Importance
_____	1. A book by a former newspaper editor entitled *How the Media Distorts the International War on Drugs.*	_____
_____	2. A report analyzing the effectiveness of "Spike," an herbicide sprayed on drug crops. The report was written by a company that produces the herbicide.	_____
_____	3. Person-in-the-street interviews asking Colombians what they believe their government should do to stop the drug cartels.	_____
_____	4. An editorial written by a columnist claiming the U.S. government helps drug smugglers in certain situations.	_____
_____	5. The transcripts from a drug trafficking trial describing how the drug operation worked.	_____
_____	6. A historian's perspective on drug use in the last century and the crime it has created.	_____
_____	7. President Bush's speech on American efforts to eliminate the illegal drug trade.	_____
_____	8. A documentary on the lives of Colombian peasants who process coca into cocaine.	_____
_____	9. Viewpoint 3 in this chapter.	_____
_____	10. An article in *Time* describing the illegal drug trade's effect on the economies of Bolivia, Peru, Colombia, Laos, and Thailand.	_____
_____	11. A lab analysis on the relative purity of cocaine in 1990 compared to 1980.	_____

Periodical Bibliography

The following articles have been selected to supplement the diverse views presented in this chapter.

Peter Andreas	"Drug War Zone," *The Nation,* December 11, 1989.
Bruce Michael Bagley	"Dateline Drug Wars: Colombia: The Wrong Strategy," *Foreign Policy,* Winter 1989/1990.
Ric Dolphin	"A Global Struggle: Drug Police Are Fighting the Odds," *Maclean's,* April 3, 1989.
Brian Duffy	"Now, for the Real Drug War," *U.S. News & World Report,* September 11, 1989.
Paula Dwyer	"Can the Drug Lords Be Dethroned?" *Business Week,* September 11, 1989.
Fabio Gastillo	"The Drug Economy," *The Economist,* April 2, 1988.
Gustavo A. Gorriti	"How to Fight the Drug War," *The Atlantic Monthly,* July 1989.
Louis Kraar	"The Drug Trade," *Fortune,* June 20, 1988.
Penny Lernoux	"Playing Golf While Drugs Flow," *The Nation,* February 13, 1989.
Mary Jo McConahay and Robin Kirk	"Over There," *Mother Jones,* February/March 1989.
Ed Magnuson	"More and More, a Real War," *Time,* January 22, 1990.
Paul Mann	"Congress Pressures Military to Assume Direct Antidrug Role," *Aviation Week & Space Technology,* May 23, 1988.
Eliot Marshall	"A War on Drugs with Real Troops?" *Science,* July 1, 1988.
Michael Massing	"Coke Dusters: The Air War on Drugs," *The New Republic,* January 30, 1989.
Tom Morganthau	"A Mission to Nowhere?" *Newsweek,* February 19, 1990.
Tina Rosenberg	"A Mess in the Andes: Colombia's Government-by-Cocaine," *The New Republic,* September 18, 1989.
Hobart Rowen	"The Heart of the Drug Problem," *The Washington Post National Weekly Edition,* September 18-24, 1989.
Elaine Shannon	"Attacking the Source," *Time,* August 28, 1989.
James Traub	"The Law and the Prophet," *Mother Jones,* February/March 1988.

CHAPTER 5

How Can the War on Drugs Be Won?

Chapter Preface

The war on drugs is waged in numerous ways. Media campaigns with themes like "Speed Kills" and "Just Say No" attempt to convince people to stay away from drugs. Increased border patrols and customs screening prevent vast quantities of illegal drugs from crossing U.S. borders. Police sweeps through crack neighborhoods send many drug dealers to jail every year. Yet these programs have not been able to end, or even to noticeably curtail, the tremendous influx of drugs into the country and their attendant problems.

Many law-and-order advocates recommend tougher sentencing for drug dealers, increased border patrols to catch smugglers, and the use of the U.S. military to cut off the supply of drugs. Jeffrey Eisenach, a visiting fellow at The Heritage Foundation, writes, "Our greatest single failure in the war on drugs is directly attributable to the lack of sufficient effort to enforce existing state laws against drug possession and even drug dealing." Eisenach, among others, believes that a stronger antidrug message must be sent to drug producers, smugglers, dealers, and users.

Many critics believe that focusing so intensely on law enforcement can actually worsen the drug problem. Programs to treat addicts have been underfunded because too much money has been spent on law enforcement, these critics argue. An editorial in the *Los Angeles Times* stated, "Police can help stop drug abuse, but treatment costs less and does more good." The editorial admits that although an effective residential treatment program may be expensive—$14,000 per person per year in a nonprofit treatment center—the money spent is well worth it: "Users can develop the will to resist drugs and master the secrets of staying clean." In addition, the *Times* contends, "Drug rehabilitation is expensive, but not as expensive as building new prisons and running them at double the capacity."

The viewpoints in the following chapter are written by government officials, journalists, educators, and concerned citizens. Each presents a distinctive view on how the war on drugs can be won.

"We must isolate the enemy, attack with every means at our disposal . . . [drug] production, distribution, and financial supply lines."

The Supply of Drugs Must Be Cut

Richard W. Fisher

American military forces have ventured into the jungles of Colombia to destroy cocaine production labs. Coast Guard crews and customs officials board and search the boats and aircraft of drug smugglers. Supporters of such actions say these programs must be increased to win the war on drugs. In the following viewpoint, Richard W. Fisher, a chairperson of the Institute of the Americas, writes that drug production must be attacked at the source. He advocates a wide-ranging effort to halt the growth, production, and importation of illegal drugs.

As you read, consider the following questions:

1. Why does the author consider drugs a national security threat?
2. According to Fisher, how can U.S. intelligence officers and diplomats be used to combat drugs?
3. In the author's opinion, how can military cooperation between the U.S. and Latin America help cut the supply of drugs?

Richard W. Fisher, "Rhetoric Won't Win the Drug War," report entered into the Congressional Record on November 21, 1989.

We have been bombarded with some remarkable assertions regarding the Latin American drug cartels. Testimony before the Senate has revealed that the narco barons have considered using submarines to smuggle cocaine into the United States. Jack Anderson has reported that narco terrorists are plotting attacks against U.S. nuclear power plants in retaliation for Washington's anti-drug campaign. The president's children have been placed under Secret Service protection. The governor of Florida is rumored to be on the Medellin Cartel's hit list.

Many of these allegations have a chilling ring of plausibility, however lunatic. Others are no doubt evidence of nothing more than panic and fear of the unknown. Yet all are manifestations of a sudden recognition that the Latin narco powers pose a real and dreadful threat to our collective well-being.

There is a pathetic irony in all this. After 40 years and countless billions spent fighting the Soviet threat, we find our national security under frontal attack from an entirely different quarter. On the eve of our victory in the Cold War, we have suddenly realized that we are at risk of losing the Drug War.

Our Newfound Enemy

To be sure, our newfound enemy does not possess the capacity for nuclear attack. It does not have troops massed along our frontier. Yet it is nonetheless threatening. Indeed, it already has accomplished what the Soviets and the Nazis before them never accomplished. It has invaded our territory, placed armed agents on our soil, taken hundreds of thousands of Americans prisoner and set in motion a frightful challenge to the American way of life.

The president and Congress are close to agreement on a program to combat the narco threat. Much is being made of its domestic components. Little has been focused on its foreign policy content. We cannot expect to overcome this threat by depending alone on "kinder and gentler" approaches to education and treatment and a "tough love" approach to law enforcement and interdiction. Severe measures must be taken on the supply side. We must isolate the enemy, attack with every means at our disposal its production, distribution and financial supply lines, and destroy it outright.

We might start by tightening up some diplomatic initiatives. The United Nations adopted the Convention Against Illicit Traffic in Narcotic Drugs and Psychotropic Substances in December of 1988. The convention calls for "criminalization of the production, cultivation, transport and trafficking of cocaine, heroin, marijuana and other danger drugs." It also lays the groundwork for criminalization of money laundering and trafficking in chemicals used to refine drugs, and provides for seizure of assets, extradition of traffickers and transnational transfer of criminal proceedings.

The Senate has yet to ratify the convention. Nor has it ratified the mutual legal assistance treaties that would enable U.S. law enforcement authorities to obtain evidence abroad for admission in U.S. courts and facilitate extradition agreements and strong asset seizure measures. Both should be ratified immediately, as is being urged by the president.

Don Wright/*The Palm Beach Post.* Reprinted with permission.

On the trade front, an export control mechanism must be developed by Washington along the lines of that which we have used to control potential strategically harmful exports to the Warsaw Pact [nations]. The Chemical Diversion and Trafficking Act of 1988 establishes a system for controlling chemical shipments which might be diverted to the illegal drug trade. But it needs to be strengthened and expanded. Most of the cocaine smuggled into the U.S. continues to be processed with chemicals exported by U.S. companies. Most of the automatic weapons used by the narco thugs to wage war against their governments are of U.S. manufacture. Their export must be stopped. An international agreement must then be forged to prevent others from filling the gap.

The U.S. intelligence agencies must become fully engaged in this war. At home, drug traffickers must be sought out with the same intensity as foreign spies. And, as with foreign agents caught in acts of espionage, drug traffickers, once caught, must be tried with dispatch and subjected to swift and certain punishment. Abroad, the intelligence mechanisms of the U.S. government and international agencies such as Interpol must be enhanced.

Bilateral diplomatic initiatives to enhance military cooperation in Latin America also must be pursued, in order to contain the geographic reach of the narco producers. Already, a narcopact exists between the illegitimate forces of four countries. The Colombia drug lords, who control 80 percent of the refined cocaine business draw their raw materials from their Peruvian and Bolivian colleagues. Gen. Manuel Noriega, in turn, provides transhipment facilities in Panama for export of refined dope and imports of chemicals for Colombian refineries, and also provides money and arms laundering facilities for his Peruvian, Bolivian and Colombian partners.

Repair Relationships

Inevitably, the narcopact will seek to expand its territorial reach into Brazil, Argentina, Venezuela, Paraguay and other neighboring countries where, for various reasons, the United States does not currently enjoy extensive military and diplomatic solidarity. These relationships must be repaired. In Brazil, for example, the U.S. military has been restricted in information sharing and joint training by strictures imposed by the U.S. Senate due to Brazil's refusal to sign the Nuclear Non-proliferation Treaty. In Argentina, our military liaison efforts were cut back by President Reagan in an effort to appease Mrs. Thatcher after the Falklands War.

It is time to rebuild military cooperation in Latin American nations within the context of the narco threat. We must move quickly, both bilaterally and multilaterally, to form a united containment force employing the military and national police forces of the neighboring Latin nations. Doing so will likely require a change in U.S. foreign aid, conventions which generally prohibit foreign governments from spending U.S. aid on police and internal security forces.

Powerful Drug Lords

Like any Latin Americanist, I would prefer that legitimate governments corral the traffickers on their own. The delicate sensitivity about American intervention which pervades interhemispheric relations must always be borne in mind by U.S. policymakers. But we must acknowledge reality. One-half of Bolivia's gross national product is under the influence of the coca producers. The power of the drug lords in Peru threatens to supersede that of the government. The Medellin and Cali cartels exert de facto civil control of Colombia. We must spare no effort in assisting the legitimate governments of these countries to destroy the drug producers. For should they fail, we may have no choice but to take matters into our own powerful hands.The United States does not want to use its armed forces overseas, except by invitation. But there may be circumstances which warrant unilateral action. Such a grave step should be taken only in very restricted circumstances, such as when governments lose control of areas where major drug processing takes place, or refuse, as in Gen. Noriega's Panama, to take action.

For example, according to Deputy Secretary of State Lawrence Eagleburger's testimony before the Organization of American States, the Colombian cartels have begun to erect alternative refinery facilities in the Darien province of Panama. We should request that the Panamanian government destroy those facilities. If it does not, we should consider doing it ourselves.

The Narcopact

Adopting new foreign policy measures to complement demand management in fighting an effective war against the gangster powers of the narcopact will seriously complicate the U.S. relationship with the region's legitimate governments. It will require a dramatic change in our diplomatic effort in all of Latin America.

The region always has been the neglected stepchild of the U.S. foreign policy community, which focuses almost myopically on Europe as the front line of our defense against external threat. If the president and the State Department had spent one one-hundredth of the time, effort and money developing with Latin American governments the kind of relationship we enjoy with our North Atlantic Treaty Organization partners, we might not today be fighting the Drug War. If Washington does not reorient itself now, we will seriously jeopardize our ability to defeat the narcopowers. We will be condemned to fighting a war without allies, a war we cannot win.

"Any new fiscal firepower should be targeted at reducing demand [for drugs] in the U.S."

The Demand for Drugs Must Be Cut

Louis Kraar

Though scores of people are caught smuggling illegal drugs across America's borders each year, the staggering U.S. demand for drugs keeps the flow alive. Critics of America's get-tough policy on drug smuggling say government officials are fighting the wrong battle. In the following viewpoint, Louis Kraar, a reporter for *Fortune* magazine, argues that the U.S. must spend more money to curb its demand for drugs instead of trying to cut the supply. Kraar maintains that cutting demand through education and treatment programs is the most effective method of solving the drug problem.

As you read, consider the following questions:

1. What programs would Kraar institute to help drug addicts?
2. How would the author change drug education programs in America's schools?
3. According to Kraar, how could television be used to battle drug abuse?

America's so-called war on drugs is looking more and more like the real thing. Troops invade Panama in part to bring Manuel Noriega to justice for his alleged crimes as a drug trafficker. On the Mexican front, U.S. Marines, deployed for the first time in border patrols, engage marijuana smugglers in a firefight. And in mid-February 1990, President Bush flies to Cartagena, Colombia, for an unprecedented antidrug summit aimed at rallying the governments of Colombia, Bolivia, and Peru to escalate their military struggle with the powerful cocaine cartels.

Will all this saber rattling make much of a difference? Don't bet on it. Despite record seizures, the supply of cocaine on America's mean streets—as well as the many not-so-mean ones —has never been more available or less expensive. In a persuasive study conducted for the Defense Department, Peter Reuter of RAND Corp. concludes that even a vastly more stringent interdiction program would at best reduce U.S. cocaine consumption by a mere 5%. Admits Jack Lawn, chief of the federal government's Drug Enforcement Administration (DEA): "Our enforcement efforts will continue to build statistics and fill prisons, but they won't turn around America's love affair with drugs."

The Wrong Answer

Is the answer, then, to raise the white flag and legalize the stuff? Yes, say a small but influential number of professors and politicians, and at least one big-city judge. They argue that legalization would reduce violent crime and divert money from crooks to the government.

But they're probably wrong. The drugs popular today are so cheap to produce—a vial of crack cocaine selling for as little as $3 costs just 35 cents to import and manufacture—that a black market would continue to thrive alongside the legal one. Nor would legalization stop addicts from stealing to support their habits. What it would surely do is swell the use of substances far more dangerous than alcohol. While 10% of drinkers become alcohol abusers, 20% to 30% of cocaine users wind up addicted. Since 1986 at least 100,000 infants have been born to drug abusers. The intensive care they require is costing several billion dollars a year.

Moreover, not all the battles in the drug war have been losing ones. Heroin use, which in the early 1970s threatened to become epidemic, has stabilized at roughly half a million addicts and attracts relatively few new recruits. Casual use of marijuana and cocaine also seems to be declining. The number of Americans who acknowledge using illicit drugs declined 37% between 1985 and 1988, according to household surveys conducted by the government's National Institute on Drug Abuse.

The main reason the U.S. is experiencing what federal drug czar William Bennett describes as "the worst epidemic of illegal drug use in its history" is crack, the new plague.

The U.S. *can* gain further ground in the 1990s—but only by waging a more effective fight against illegal drugs at home. That doesn't mean policymakers ought to abandon longstanding efforts to curb the supply from abroad. But it does mean acknowledging that any new fiscal firepower should be targeted at reducing demand in the U.S.

Engine of Demand

For our part, the best thing the United States can do is to begin to work on our problem—demand. It does no good to blame us for causing Colombia's troubles; however the scourge arrived, it is now Colombia's problem and thoughtful Colombians recognize that fact. It is fair, though, to observe that until the engine of American demand is slowed, cocaine will afflict both the United States and Latin America.

Gregory F. Treverton, *Los Angeles Times*, September 1, 1989.

Under President Bush, annual federal spending on the anti-drug fight will have climbed 68%, to $10.6 billion, in two years. In a welcome reversal from the Reagan era cutbacks, Bush is increasing spending on prevention and treatment. But he still devotes only 30% of the budget to attacking the demand side of the problem. Instead, Bush is pouring $2.4 billion—a billion dollars more than Reagan—into the effort to interdict drugs before or as they enter the U.S., mainly by relying more on the armed forces.

Fortune would reverse those priorities. We would also invest a few billion dollars more in the struggle than the White House has proposed, though most of that new money will have to come from states and cities on the front line. Treating every one of the country's drug abusers, for instance, would cost $5.6 billion a year—more than half Washington's total spending on the drug war. Happily, much can also be achieved by simply spending and reacting smarter. Here's what we suggest:

Treatment

Provide more medical help for addicts. The toughest challenge is curing the roughly four million Americans who are serious substance abusers. Only about 20% currently get medical help. Many shun it, but most cannot find it. While expensive private treatment centers have plenty of room, public centers—the only ones most addicts can afford—typically have long waiting lists.

Says Robert Stutman, a veteran DEA agent in New York: "Imagine if I had cholera and walked into a city hospital and the doctor said, 'Come back in seven months.' It would be a scandal, but that's exactly what happens every day to addicts seeking help."

Though it has increased spending in this area, the Bush Administration is hardly acting like a government faced with an epidemic. Bennett's strategy, shaped more by budgetary constraints than hard evidence, is to focus on the half of the four million addicts whom he deems most capable of being helped. Another million, he argues, can help themselves. The remaining million are "hard-core addicts or career criminals" whom existing methods of treatment can't change much.

Doing better requires new medical techniques as well as more money. Only about half of cocaine addicts stay drug free for up to two years after treatment. Part of the problem is that some 70% of drug users also have an alcohol or mental disorder. Says Dr. Frederick Goodwin, head of the federal government's Alcohol, Drug Abuse, and Mental Health Administration: "We need more effective matching of individuals with particular treatments." A centralized registry of programs and openings in them would be an inexpensive first step.

Drug addiction can be cured, as successful treatment centers such as Phoenix House demonstrate. Says Frank Gough, a former heroin addict and director of an adult treatment center for Daytop Village in New York State: "We return to society productive, responsible people." The big problem is getting those whose judgment has been spiked by drugs to enter and stay in treatment. Most are pushed into it by their family or the threat of imprisonment. . . .

Prevention

Do more to equip children to resist drugs. Surprisingly, only about half the nation's public schools provide comprehensive substance-abuse education. Less surprisingly, since the key is building character, it's a struggle to find methods that work. Merely providing information in a classroom does little to curb demand and may even stimulate curiosity to try drugs.

Kansas City has proved that mobilizing parents and the community can make drug education more effective. Starting with sixth- and seventh-graders, schools discourage the use of cigarettes, alcohol, and marijuana, widely considered the path to more dangerous substances. Students get classroom training in skills for resisting drug use, involve parents in discussion sessions, and see their efforts covered in the local media. The result: These youngsters show only half the drug use typical among their age group.

Bringing local police into the classroom helps too. The Drug Abuse Resistance Education program that Los Angeles started in 1983 uses specially trained officers as instructors for fifth- and sixth-graders. By appearing in full uniform, the teachers in blue immediately command attention. They maintain it by dealing with the real world of adolescents, presenting a course that aims at building self-esteem and teaches how to say no without losing friends. The L.A. cops' promising technique has spread to some 2,000 communities in 49 states.

Education

Do more to spot drug use early. Many public schools require a health examination for new students, an ideal checkpoint. The Los Angeles County district attorney's office focuses heavily on truancy, an early sign of drug use, and gets families into fighting it.

Tom Toles © 1988 *The Buffalo News.* Reprinted with permission of Universal Press Syndicate. All rights reserved.

Shout louder from the most bully pulpit around. The nonprofit Partnership for a Drug-Free America has created a starkly emotional series of ads on TV all across the U.S. In one, a young woman snorts cocaine in the privacy of her home, while an off-stage voice notes that one out of five users gets hooked, then asks, "But that's not your problem. Or is it?" In the last scene, she reappears driving a school bus. Space for this $150-million-a-year campaign is donated by newspapers, magazines, and TV. Surveys suggest that the ads do reduce consumption of marijuana and cocaine, particularly in markets that run them frequently. By slightly more than doubling the reach of its ads, the Partnership hopes to expose every American to an antidrug message at least once a day.

Companies should join the drug war. Already, federal law requires those in fields such as transportation, nuclear power, and defense to maintain a drug-free workplace. With good reason. In 1987 a Conrail train ran through a restricted switch into the path of a high-speed Amtrak train, killing 16 people and injuring 174. The "probable cause," according to the National Transportation Safety Board's report: The Conrail engineer was suffering from marijuana "impairment."

Now other corporations are getting interested in drug testing as a way to cut health insurance costs and productivity losses. According to a study by the Bureau of Labor Statistics, some 9% of corporate America's employees show up for work with illegal substances in their systems. The cost to the economy: an estimated $60 billion a year.

IBM has a model program that protects both the company and its employees from drug abuse. Since 1984 every job applicant has had to undergo a urine test for illegal drugs. Any employee caught bringing drugs into IBM, including its parking lots, gets fired. Employees who act strangely or perform erratically can be referred to the company's medical department, but are not required to take a drug test unless their job is safety sensitive. Those who admit to having a drug problem, however, get counseling and medical attention. Says Dr. Glenn E. Haughie, the company's director of corporate health and safety: "IBM considers drug use a treatable disease." Among his success stories is a manager who ran up big bills on a company credit card before admitting to a decade-long cocaine habit. After treatment the manager is back at work and drug free. . . .

Patience

In the struggle against drugs, what can we expect to achieve by the year 2000? Drug czar Bennett's goal is to reduce drug use in the U.S. by 55% in ten years. Sounds terrific, until you realize that's about what the U.S. has done since 1985. And who feels better off today? Moreover, who knows what cheap, new designer drug could come along to fuel the epidemic? Use of a smokable form of methamphetamine called ice, which gets users high for up to eight hours vs. 20 minutes for crack, could spread rapidly. Says Robert W. Burgreen, police chief in San Diego: "Anyone with a chemistry book and the ability to experiment can make meth."

Still, that's no reason to despair, as some do, that this fight is destined to prove another Vietnam. To the extent that it implies the U.S. can win a reasonably swift and clear-cut victory, as it did in World War II, today's drug war rhetoric is misleading. Think instead of another struggle that offered no quick fix but instead required patience, vast resources, bipartisan and international cooperation, but which America saw through successfully—the cold war. Policies based on containment may not stir the blood. Pursued long enough, though, they can ultimately prevail.

3

VIEWPOINT

"Law enforcement represents the best hope of beating cocaine."

Tougher Law Enforcement Will Win the War on Drugs

Tom Morganthau and Mark Miller

The advent of crack, a highly addictive and inexpensive form of cocaine, has significantly changed the nation's drug problem. Many people can afford to use crack, thus creating a lucrative market that has encouraged other people to sell the drug. The violence associated with this drug trade has led to calls for stricter law enforcement. In the following viewpoint, Tom Morganthau and Mark Miller, reporters for *Newsweek*, argue that laws against drugs must be strengthened and enforced. Arrests, interdiction, and prison terms will stop drug abuse more quickly and effectively than treatment programs or education, the authors believe.

As you read, consider the following questions:

1. Why do the authors think the drug epidemic will persist?
2. What evidence do Morganthau and Miller present to show that law enforcement works?
3. Which drug traffickers should drug agents target, in the authors' view?

Cocaine is the Third World's atomic bomb.
—Carlos Lehder Rivas, in a 1985 interview

Lehder, the flamboyant Colombian drug smuggler who is now serving life plus 135 years in the U.S. penitentiary at Marion, Ill., was half right, anyway. Cocaine, crack and drug-related crime—*la bomba atómica*—pose a devastating threat to U.S. society. But the analogy to nuclear war is imprecise: America's struggle against cocaine is much more like the war in Vietnam. As in Vietnam, the United States is fighting an adversary that is adept at concealing itself among the civilian population and operates from safe haven across international borders. As in Vietnam, the United States has misspent billions, botched both strategy and tactics, and consistently underestimated the enemy. And as in Vietnam, America is slowly losing the war. There is one vital difference, of course: this time the United States cannot pull out. Cocaine and crack are among the most addictive substances known to modern science, and they have already ruined the lives of millions of Americans. Their presence in truly astonishing quantities on the street of American cities and towns has created a level of criminal mayhem that dwarfs the gang wars of the Prohibition era. Behind it all is a network of so-called drug cartels based in Colombia—underworld syndicates that must be regarded as among the best-organized, most lucrative and most violent criminal enterprises of modern times. Asked whether Americans should be concerned about the Mafia breaking into the cocaine trade, a ranking federal lawman simply laughed. "Don't worry about it," he said. "The Colombians would blow 'em out.". . .

No "Magic Bullet"

What is the best way to combat the rise of cocaine abuse—and how much effort should be expended on law enforcement, prevention and treatment? Is there any one strategy, or even some combination of strategies, that guarantees victory? The answer to the latter question is probably no: there is no "magic bullet" solution. Total victory—an America that is truly cocaine-free—is almost certainly beyond reach. But real progress is achievable so long as the public and its elected representatives are prepared to think clearly, spend wisely and recognize that cocaine is a long-term threat to the nation. Unfortunately, the ongoing national debate over America's drug war has often been shallow and misinformed. In part, that is because cocaine abuse exploded so recently as a major social and law-enforcement problem. Public attitudes have lurched from indifference (cocaine is safe and trendy) to shock (is crack *really* that addictive?) to something approaching panic (they've got Uzis and they're *everywhere*). Congress, responding to rising voter concern, has spent $16 billion on the drug war since 1981, but victory is still not in sight. As a result, the new chic among the war's armchair strategists is pessimism: nothing works, every solution leads to an even more intractable problem, and it is therefore time to give up hope—or legalize, which is the same thing.

Beef Up Enforcement

The inadequacy of current law enforcement resources has resulted in the *de facto* decriminalization of drug possession and, to a lesser extent, of drug dealing as well. States have a moral as well as legal responsibility to see that laws are enforced and that those committing drug crimes are punished appropriately. States and localities thus need to beef up resources devoted to police, prosecutors, the courts and the prisons to see that this responsibility is met.

Jeffrey A. Eisenach, *The Heritage Foundation State Backgrounder*, July 7, 1989.

Much of the current confusion about drug strategy rests on a single misjudgment about the nature of the problem. That misjudgment—call it a misdiagnosis—is the widely held assumption that the U.S. cocaine epidemic is primarily *demand-driven*. It is not, although there is no question that U.S. consumption of the drug is higher than ever before. Cocaine and crack abuse could not possibly have reached epidemic levels in this country if the Colombian drug cartels had not been successful in expanding coca-leaf production in Colombia, Peru and Bolivia. (Coca production has doubled since 1982, according to U.S. government estimates.) Given that gusher of white powder—and given the power of the Colombian cartels—it is imprudent to assume that the current epidemic will somehow fade away of its own accord. Cocaine and crack abuse will not disappear—and probably will not decline significantly—as along as supplies are abundant and prices are low.

Prevention Failures

Nevertheless, many critics, policymakers and even law-enforcement officials seem to believe that the solution to America's cocaine problem will ultimately be found on the "demand side"—by some combination of prevention, treatment and deterrence aimed at the cocaine-consuming public. That hope, which is probably fueled by frustration at law enforcement's lack of speedy results, will almost certainly prove illusory. While it is vitally important that government at all levels continue the attempt to quell demand, demand-side strategies will not win the drug war.

Prevention, for example, works—but only up to a point. New

research on the in-school prevention programs suggests that the good ones succeed with 50 to 60 percent of the children who take part. That's not bad, but the other 40 percent is more than enough to stoke the drug crisis. Nancy Reagan's "Just Say No" campaign has not prevented large numbers of young adults from dabbling with cocaine, and school programs have not kept thousands of inner-city kids from selling and using crack. Treatment works—but it is very expensive, and its success rate under the best conditions is no higher than 50 percent. Deterrence strategies, such as jailing users, have hardly been tried, and, given the high cost of "Just Say Jail," they probably never will be. The bottom line, in broadbrush terms, is that demand-side strategies may help slow the growth of cocaine and crack abuse—but they are unlikely to succeed in bringing U.S. cocaine consumption down very much for the foreseeable future.

Cocaine Dependency

How much larger can the cocaine problem grow? Barring the possibility of legalization, the "at risk" population is usually estimated at 12 percent of the U.S. population, or about 29 million people. As of 1985, some 22 million Americans admitted using cocaine at least once, which could suggest that the cocaine epidemic is nearing its upper limit. Unfortunately, the issue is more complicated than that. What worries epidemiologists is how many current users are becoming addicted—progressing, if that is the word, from casual use to true dependency. By that standard, the cocaine problem has plenty of room for growth. In 1985, 5.8 million Americans said they used cocaine regularly, and experts believe that more than a third of this group was addicted. How many more have become addicted since 1985, given the craze for crack? No one really knows, but the available evidence is disturbing. According to reports from hospital emergency rooms around the nation, cocaine-overdose complaints have soared more than 700 percent since 1983. (Crack complaints rose fifteenfold between 1984 and 1987.) Although there is no sure way to estimate the increase in addiction from such statistics, health experts say the emergency-room trend is a clear sign that cocaine dependency is taking hold.

Can't we just end the war by legalizing cocaine? Yes—but Americans must be prepared to pay the price. Advocates of legalization say the main benefit of decriminalizing cocaine would be a reduction in the social and economic costs of drug-related crime and law enforcement. They claim that the level of cocaine addiction will not rise significantly, or that if it does, the percentage of addicted people in U.S. society will ultimately be no higher than it is now—about 7 percent, counting both drug addicts and alcoholics. Finally, legalizers argue that the money now spent on drug-war law enforcement could be redirected to treating and preventing addiction.

The Gamble

But legalization is an enormous social gamble—and it is a policy that is at least partly rooted in indifference toward the addicted. Opponents are unanimous in predicting that the increase in addiction, over time, would be very large. A worst-case scenario assumes that legalized cocaine could eventually become as widely used as alcohol, which could create as many as 20 million new addicts. The cost of treatment for those addicts would be impossibly high: treating the 2 million Americans who are already addicted to coke would cost between $8 billion to $30 billion a year, depending on the number who needed long-term care. But the real issue is moral. Should the United States adopt a policy that guarantees severe injury to millions of its citizens? So far, at least, Americans seem to be saying no.

Cutting Demand

Critics complain that there is too much law, not enough persuasion, in drug czar William Bennett's plan. It retains the traditional 70-30 split in drug expenditures: 70 percent for law enforcement and 30 percent for education, prevention and treatment. But those who complain that this skews spending to the "supply" rather than the "demand" side of the drug problem make the false assumption that law enforcement has no effect on demand.

Of course it does. Millions of Americans who might otherwise have an occasional joint don't—because it is illegal. The threat that an $80 ounce of marijuana will cost $10,000 in fines will do more to dampen demand than "education" programs appealing to people's higher selves to turn down the pleasures of drugs.

Charles Krauthammer, *Los Angeles Times*, September, 10, 1989.

If legalization is undesirable and demand-side strategies pose the risk of stalemate, law enforcement represents the best hope of beating cocaine. There are sound reasons for emphasizing a supply-side offensive. One is the fact that cocaine-related crime— gang murders, street violence and corruption—is what concerns voters and policymakers most. A second is that America's cocaine problem in fact has been caused by the Colombian cartels and their U.S.-based accomplices: attacking the enemy high command is good strategy. No one thinks a concerted attack on trafficking will reduce the supply to zero, but aggressive law enforcement can significantly disrupt the flow. Indeed, there is at least some evidence that the much-maligned federal effort is beginning to pay off. Cocaine seizures, for example, have risen dramatically—from about 45 tons in 1986 to 71 tons in 1987.

The Solution

Taking the offensive against cocaine will take time and cost more money. It will require a more cohesive effort on the part of federal, state and local governments and solid support from the public. The major components of U.S. policy should include:

Diplomacy: The U.S. government has failed to make the drug war a diplomatic priority with the countries—Colombia, Mexico, Peru and Bolivia—that are most implicated in cocaine production and trafficking. It must now do so. Granted, foreign policy is a complex business, and stemming the flow of drugs is not America's only goal in Latin America. Still, the United States can and should increase diplomatic pressure on South American governments to attack the cocaine industry, which clearly threatens the stability of the region. Extraditing or prosecuting major traffickers is the primary objective; Since 1983, only 16 drug suspects have been turned over to U.S. authorities, and the Colombian courts have overturned that country's extradition treaty with the United States. Destroying cocaine-processing laboratories and warehouses is another major objective, along with eradicating the coca crop. (Progress in both areas has been minuscule.) Cutting off foreign aid has limited value, since few nations in the region get much assistance from Washington. But economic pressure, including trade sanctions, should be used as a bargaining tool.

Interdiction: Much criticized, but worth every kilo it stops. Radar surveillance along the Gulf Coast and the Mexican border is improving, and smuggling flights are being deterred. The new threat is bulk shipments of cocaine concealed in air freight and seaborne cargo. The U.S. Customs Service has asked for 500 additional inspectors (at a cost of $25 million a year), and it needs them. Port-of-entry inspections will always be selective. But with more agents, Customs could adopt pressure-point tactics, inspecting *all* shipments in a particular airport or harbor on a short-term basis.

Go for the Head

Targeting traffickers: Top priority. To make it work, the Drug Enforcement Administration needs at least 2,500 more agents at a cost, in round figures, of $1 billion over five years. (DEA now has almost 3,000 agents. The FBI [Federal Bureau of Investigation] has 1,200 agents assigned to drugs.) The Feds should emphasize a "decapitation" strategy aimed at busting major American dealers and key players in the Colombian cartels. The cartels have scores of "sales managers" in the United States, and these traffickers are highly skilled at evading police. Investigation is labor-intensive and expensive: a typical stakeout, assisted by electronic surveillance, requires 25 to 30 agents. There is no choice if big-time smugglers are to be brought to justice.

Coordination: Boring but essential. The federal effort involves at least 30 separate agencies and seven cabinet departments: bureaucratic rivalries, turf wars and policy conflicts are perennial problems. The appointment of a drug czar may help, but many veterans of the drug war are skeptical; the czar's reign may be bumpy. (The 1988 drug bill, which created the job, also seems to have made Dan Quayle ineligible. The bill stipulates that the czar can hold no other job in government.) Supporting state and local police agencies with money and training is probably even more important, since they are stuck with the massive task of shutting down retail-level trafficking. The consensus verdict on local law enforcement's performance against drugs: only a few cities are really doing the job.

The demand side: Prevention would be one of the least expensive items in a drug-war strategy, since it would cost no more than $5 per child per year. The only problem is that many school districts aren't doing it, or aren't doing it well enough: federal leadership is needed. Treatment is expensive—outpatient slots cost $4,000 a year, residential slots $15,000 a year—but the United States needs to do much more. Every addict who stops using becomes a walking advertisement for abstinence, which is why treatment is regarded as "secondary prevention."

Recreational Use

The tricky part of drug prevention is deterring recreational use. The Partnership for a Drug-Free America, a privately funded consortium, is justifiably praised for its efforts to educate employers and provide public-service advertising against cocaine. For adult users, at least, tougher propaganda may be valuable: even casual cokeheads are supporting an industry that commits murder, destabilizes governments and corrupts society. The new drug bill includes a provision to fine users up to $10,000, which is one way of discouraging middle-class users. Hard-liners want jail terms as well, but there is no space in America's overcrowded prisons. . . .

Stemming the flood tide of cocaine will take time, and few law enforcement experts believe the drug can ever be eliminated completely. But America has no choice: it must begin to fight back.

4

"I'm not ashamed to tell you that law enforcement is not the answer to our [drug] problem."

Tougher Law Enforcement Will Not Win the War on Drugs

Stanley Meisler

Stanley Meisler writes for the Washington bureau of the *Los Angeles Times*. In the following viewpoint, Meisler quotes many law enforcement officers who no longer believe they can win the war on drugs. Meisler writes that police and military efforts to cut the drug supply have resulted only in higher drug prices, more violence, and disillusionment with law enforcement. In Meisler's view, treatment and education programs for drug users would be more effective.

As you read, consider the following questions:

1. Why does the author think drug seizures have been counter-productive?
2. According to Meisler, why has enforcement raised violence within the drug trade?
3. Why does the author foresee a societal split over the war on drugs?

James A. Van Horn Jr. sits at a table in the spacious Congressional Room of the Capital Hilton in Washington, listening as a parade of federal bureaucrats prescribe their latest remedies for America's drug problem. The husky, heavily, bearded mayor of Artesia doesn't need to be reminded of the facts that brought him here: The county of Los Angeles has 80,000 known gang members. That's the equivalent of four Army divisions, he'll tell you. They control the streets and franchise the drug trade. The police are outmanned and outgunned.

So far, there have only been a few murders, only one drug-dealing gang in Van Horn's predominantly working-class, industrial community. But, as he likes to say: "The hoodlums of Los Angeles don't know any boundaries."

So heavily does the problem of drugs weigh on the spirits of Van Horn and most American mayors that in 1989 they changed the name of their annual "National Conference on Crime" in Washington to "National Conference on Crime and Drugs." And most invoke the imagery of war when they call on the federal government to help them eliminate the scourge of drugs. "The country doesn't need a federal narcotics czar. It needs a supreme allied commander," Van Horn tells the mayors. He envisions that commander leading an army with a single-minded mission: to squelch the drug hoodlums and wipe out the supply of drugs.

But what he hears from the experts he'd hope to count on to lead the war against drugs drives him to fury. Some of the federal bureaucrats in the forefront of the war are urging the mayors to focus on cutting the demand for drugs, not the supply.

The Wrong Answer

"I've been in law enforcement for 24 years," Thomas C. Kelly, the smiling, smooth-shaven deputy administrator of the federal government's Drug Enforcement Administration, tells the mayors, "but I'm not ashamed to tell you that law enforcement is not the answer to our problem."

On hearing that, Van Horn steps up to a microphone near his table and bellows into it angrily. "You see, guys, the Viet Cong is abroad in our society," he shouts. "We have guerrillas in the street armed with AK assault rifles. Our job now is to get our streets back." The mayor demands that the United States recall its troops from Europe, where, he says, they are unwanted anyway, and enlist them in the fight against drugs. All the money saved from closing bases overseas could then fund more police. "What we don't need," he says to a reporter later, "are bureaucrats who sit in Washington and pontificate about demand. I'm sick of it."

The meeting of the nation's mayors reflects a bitter truth

about the nature of the country's fearsome drug problem: While public pressure mounts and politicians sound ever-more-strident calls for a renewed war on drugs, a deep sense of pessimism pervades the ranks of the specialists who deal most directly with narcotics and narcotics addicts. They've been thwarted, they say, at every turn.

Peter Reuter is an Australian researcher for the RAND Corp. whose work is highly regarded by specialists on all sides of the narcotics field. "At the moment," he says, sitting in his book-lined office in Washington, "the conventional wisdom is [that] nothing works. It's a view that comes out of despair."

A Dismal View

Reuter does not share this despair completely, but he contributed to it with a pair of reports crammed with statistical evidence indicating that the much-publicized patrolling of borders and policing of the streets since 1981 have failed to damage the drug trade significantly.

The Wrong Solution

City, county, state, and federal responses have been too reliant on law-enforcement solutions to the drug problem. Law enforcement solutions seek to preserve the status quo and are aimed at *social control*. We can never expect to make real progress in the fight against drugs if the primary vehicle through which the fight is waged is the agency of social control.

Mark Ridley-Thomas, *Christianity and Crisis*, September 11, 1989.

President Bush is not ready to accept this dismal view. He and federal drug czar William J. Bennett often invoke furious allusions to war when they talk about drugs. In April, 1989, in his first dramatic act as director of the White House Office of National Drug Control Policy, Bennett excoriated the Washington drug scene as being "out of control," scorned the leaders of the city and sent a task force of federal agents into the battle. Bennett's tone was so belligerent that Rep. Lawrence J. Smith (D-Fla.) mocked him for trying to act like "a supercop with a red cape and blue suit."

Despite all the rhetoric, however, Bush and his officials acknowledge that the paramilitary approach so dear to the hearts of many politicians falls short of a complete answer. And there is little doubt that Bennett, as he develops the national drug-control strategy he's required to outline under the 1988 law that created his job, will underscore the more soft-spoken themes already voiced by the DEA's Kelly and by the President

Bush proclaimed in a Feb. 10, 1989 address to a joint session of Congress that "the scourge of drugs must be stopped." He asked for almost a billion dollars more in spending "to escalate the war against drugs . . . on all fronts." He said the money should be spent on border controls, tough law enforcement, education and research.

"But for all we do in law enforcement, in interdiction and treatment," Bush went on, "we will never win this war on drugs unless we stop the demand for drugs." The President was echoing a prevalent view in the federal government these days that sounds like an answer to a sphinx's riddle: If you can't cut the demand for drugs, it's a hopeless task trying to cut off the supply; if you can cut the demand, it won't matter what happens to the supply.

Even as Washington prepares to pour millions of new dollars into the nation's struggle, the people closest to the problem —from front-line police officers to doctors and scientists probing the roots of drug use—admit that they have little confidence in anything they've tried so far.

Increasing Drug Prices

The Reagan Administration put most of its faith and resources in the paramilitary approach to fighting drugs. Treatment and education were neglected while federal narcotics agents, customs officers, Coast Guardsmen, border guards, local police, prosecutors and judges concentrated on fighting the system that supplies the drugs. The statistics seemed impressive: Seizures of cocaine and heroin, numbers of arrests, length of jail terms all increased dramatically. But so did the supply of drugs.

The value of such policing was directly challenged in the depressing reports done by research teams working under Reuter at the RAND Corp., the prestigious research institute that often prepares studies for the Department of Defense.

In the first report, requested by the Pentagon, the RAND team concluded that the U.S. government, despite having spent more than $700 million a year on trying to stop cocaine from crossing the borders, had accomplished little more than increasing the earnings of producers in Colombia, Peru and Bolivia. Whenever cocaine is seized, smugglers simply buy more from the producers and try again to slip it into the United States. The total seized by the Coast Guard and Customs Bureau increased from 1.7 metric tons of cocaine in 1981 to 27.2 metric tons in 1986. (One metric ton is about 2,205 pounds.)

But the researchers insisted that these enormous seizures —usually ballyhooed as battlefield victories—only reflect the increase in the amount of cocaine entering the United States. Citing official surveys, the RAND report estimated that cocaine imports jumped from between 38 tons and 68 tons in 1981 to between 111 tons and 153 tons in 1985. The cost of cocaine in the United States, according to the Department of Justice, dropped from $60,000 a kilogram in 1981 to $35,000 a kilogram in 1986, another sign that, despite the war, cocaine was more—not less plentiful in the United States.

Another Discouraging Report

"If . . . the United States wished to prevent the smuggling of Japanese-manufactured automobiles, it could probably succeed with relatively little effort," Reuter wrote. ". . .Cocaine represents almost the opposite kind of target. . . . A single cargo plane, fully loaded, could supply the nation's current demand for a year."

Wasted Money

The rhetoric of drug policy has changed. Political figures, from the head of the Drug Enforcement Administration to local police chiefs, have agreed that enforcement of drug prohibitions has clear limits in its ability to reduce drug use. The call now is for so-called "demand-side" measures, particularly prevention programs. Nonetheless, America continues to commit its resources, if not its spirit, almost entirely to enforcement. In the 1988 fiscal year, 75 percent of the federal "drug-war" budget was devoted to enforcement; total expenditures reached almost $4 billion.

Peter Reuter, *The Public Interest,* Summer 1988.

The second RAND report—an analysis of the war on drugs in Washington prepared for the Greater Washington Research Center—was even more discouraging for police and narcotics agents. Despite all the abuse heaped upon Washington these days as a glaring failure in law enforcement, many politicians and drug experts were praising it just a couple of years ago as a grand success. Specialists had looked on the capital as a model city in terms of its attempt to wipe out the drug trade through tough enforcement. Washington police had organized sweeps of drug markets without letup. In six years, the number of arrests for drug trafficking increased more than 12 times, from 408 in 1981 to 5,274 in 1986. Prosecutors indicted a heavy percentage of those arrested, juries convicted them, and judges doubled the average length of prison sentences.

Yet the researchers could find no evidence that law enforcement had hurt the drug trade. Police raids of markets often did little more than drive these markets to other streets. The street price of drugs even declined. The percentage of arrested Washingtonians testing positive for cocaine increased from 15% in March, 1984, to 60% in December, 1987. Studying results from these tests and from polls of the rest of the population, Reuter wrote: "The available drug-use indicators show no decline. Indeed they point to growing use for more dangerous drugs"—mainly crack, a cheaper and smokable form of cocaine.

"More disturbing," the report went on, "is the possibility that the intensified enforcement has raised the violence of the drug trade, simply because the participants feel more threatened. . . . Dealers threatened with a high probability of a lengthy prison sentence following arrest have strong incentives for resistance."

As crack dealers fought over territory in a new market, murders increased steadily in Washington, reaching a record of 372 in 1988.

Fix the Dike

In this climate of escalating violence, the federal narcotics czar allocated most of the $70 million to $80 million to be poured into the city's "drug emergency assistance program" into more law-enforcement measures: a task force of 57 federal agents to wipe out the city's open-air drug markets, a new detention center and a new prison. He also assigned 25 FBI [Federal Bureau of Investigation] agents and 10 U.S. military lawyers to augment the task force's investigations.

But, following the latest strategy, Bennett did not ignore treatment and education, promising to build three new clinics to treat a total of 300 outpatients and to increase federal spending for drug-prevention programs in the Washington schools to $1.4 million.

Still, the Bennett program evokes little enthusiasm from most specialists. Says James Fyfe, a tall, baggy-sweatered former New York City policeman who is now a professor of criminal justice at American University in Washington: "it's like little Peter putting his finger in the dike. He can't keep his finger in there forever. Someday you have to fix the dike." Fyfe insists that Washington will never solve the inner-city problems of drugs and crime until American society faces up to the root causes of poverty and racial discrimination that spawn the problems. . . .

It's no coincidence, some observers believe, that the government's fierce crackdown on drug users is occurring when the user population has shifted from being largely white to largely non-white. Statistics indicate that the decline in use of cocaine by middle-class whites has been paralleled by an increase in the use of cocaine—in the form of crack—among poor blacks. Mark Gold, who runs a New Jersey telephone hot-line service on cocaine problems, reported that, in 1983, 50% of the calls came from college-educated cocaine users, a figure that dropped to 16% in 1987. At the same time, the percentage of calls from unemployed cocaine users increased from 16% to more than 50%.

Heavily financed education and treatment programs could further widen this gap, feeding speculation that the drug problem could be perceived as a black problem in a few years.

"If this war heats up," said Harvard University psychiatrist Norman E. Zinberg just before his death April 2, 1989, "it will not be just a war on drugs but a war mobilized by the reigning cultural majority, the franchised and employed, against a minority—an essentially disenfranchised and deeply alienated segment of our society."

Endorsing this theory, David F. Musto of Yale University, a prominent historian of American drug policy, insists that "a two-tier system" is developing in American attitudes toward drugs. Middle-class whites, according to Musto, are realizing that drug use "is damaging to their long-term interests." But "these restraints don't exist in the inner city," he says. As a result, there is continued and even growing drug use among poor blacks, who feel they do not have jobs or educational opportunities to lose, he says. And middle-class whites who give up drugs "become very intolerant" and look on drug users "as beyond the pale." . . .

Fear and Hostility

As the Bush Administration formulates its own version of the war on drugs, the nation seems to be in for a good deal more anger and frustration—much like the dramatic outburst of Mayor Van Horn of Artesia at the mayors' conference. And that, some scholars fear, could leave the country with problems even more damaging than drugs.

"What will happen to the enormous fear and hostility that are building up on drugs?" Musto asks philosophically. "People can get so angry at the drug use in the inner city that they will believe everyone there is a drug user." As a result, the historian warns, most Americans could lose the patience to invest the time and money needed to create the schools, jobs and community spirit that could drive drugs from the inner cities in the long run.

"You don't want to have public policies that cause more harm than good," he says.

"The Department of Defense has a crucial role in defending the United States from the scourge of illegal drugs."

Using the Military Will Win the War on Drugs

Richard B. Cheney

Richard B. Cheney is the U.S. secretary of defense. The following viewpoint is taken from a speech before the U.S. Senate detailing the Department of Defense's plan to implement President Bush's national drug control strategy. In it, Cheney says that U.S. forces can help cut both the supply and demand of illegal drugs. He also supports using military advisers to help local drug enforcement agencies as part of a national effort to eradicate drug production, smuggling, and abuse.

As you read, consider the following questions:

1. Why does Cheney consider the war on drugs a security mission for the Department of Defense?
2. According to the author, what are the three lines of defense against drugs?
3. How does Cheney think the army can help law enforcement agencies in the war on drugs?

Richard B. Cheney, "Department of Defense Guidance for Implementation of the President's National Drug Control Strategy," a speech given before the U.S. Senate, September 18, 1989.

The supply of illicit drugs to the United States from abroad, the associated violence and international instability, and the use of illegal drugs within the country pose a direct threat to the sovereignty and security of the country. The threat of illicit drugs strikes at the heart of the Nation's values. It inflicts increased crime and violence on our society and attacks the well-being and productivity of our citizenry. One of the principal foreign policy objectives of this Administration is to reduce, and if possible to eliminate, the flow of illegal narcotic substances to the United States. Also, the Congress has by statute assigned to the Department the duty to serve as the single lead agency of the Federal Government for the detection and monitoring of aerial and maritime transit of illegal drugs to the United States. For these reasons, the detection and countering of the production, trafficking and use of illegal drugs is a high priority national security mission of the Department of Defense.

The Nation ultimately will be rid of the scourge of illegal drugs only through the sustained application of the energy, courage and determination of the American people. As the President's strategy reflects, the Nation must seek to eliminate both the demand and the supply for illegal drugs, for the Nation will conquer neither if the other is left unchecked.

The Department of Defense

The Department of Defense, with the Department of State and U.S. law enforcement agencies, will help lead the attack on the supply of illegal drugs from abroad under the President's strategy. The efforts of the Department of Defense will complement those of other U.S. agencies and cooperating foreign countries. The Department of Defense will work to advance substantially the national objective of reducing the flow of illegal drugs into the United States through the effective application of available resources consistent with our national values and legal framework.

An effective attack on the flow of illegal drugs depends upon action at every phase of the flow: (1) in the countries that are the sources of the drugs, (2) in transit from the source countries to the United States, and (3) in distribution in the United States. The United States Armed Forces can assist in the attack on the supply of drugs in each of these phases.

The Department of Defense will assist in the attack on production of illegal drugs at the source. The production of illegal drugs is a complex criminal enterprise. The criminal enterprise requires illicit labor, capital, entrepreneurship and a substantial infrastructure to grow the plants that are the raw materials for illegal drugs and to refine and manufacture the illegal drugs. Reducing the availability of these elements of illegal drug production in the countries from which illegal drugs originate would reduce the flow of illegal drugs to the United States.

The Department of Defense can assist in the three elements of an effective attack on the supply of drugs in source countries: (1) assistance for nation-building, (2) operational support to host-country forces, and (3) cooperation with host-country forces to prevent drug exports. Pursuant to the National Drug Control Strategy near-term efforts will focus on the Andean nations from which most cocaine entering the United States originates. A key requirement for the success of U.S. efforts directed at the supply of illegal drugs, and in particular U.S. counternarcotics operations, will be the cooperation of the foreign countries involved.

Military Action

The United States has a material incentive as well as moral motive to stop the commerce in drugs across its borders. We have the moral authority to designate it as piracy, and we have the power to act on this designation. If we are at all serious about a "war on drugs," let's begin by taking appropriate military action.

Irving Kristol, *The Washington Post National Weekly Edition*, April 4-10, 1988.

As the National Drug Control Strategy indicates with respect to the Andean countries, a sustained, multi-year effort to provide economic, security, and law enforcement assistance is an essential element for a successful fight against illegal drugs abroad. Drug-producing criminal organizations control what amounts to private armies that challenge the law enforcement and military forces of their countries. Often such organizations are intertwined with insurgent forces that challenge directly the governments of their countries. The National Drug Control Strategy calls for the United States to reinforce the abilities of the governments of the countries cooperating in the fight against illegal drugs to combat drug-producing organizations. Security assistance will help enable such a government to protect itself from criminal drug enterprises and drug-related insurgencies, and to enforce its laws against drug producers and traffickers. Future economic assistance will help to strengthen the national economy and keep the labor, capital and entrepreneurship available in the country channeled toward useful production and away from drug production. Success in other efforts to attack the supply of illegal drugs depends in the long-run upon the establishment of healthy economies in drug-producing countries and the restoration of government authority in those countries. To assist in the implementation of this element of the

National Drug Control Strategy, the Department of Defense will execute security assistance programs in accordance with Presidential instructions and applicable law, and in coordination with the Department of State.

International Cooperation

Effective implementation of the National Drug Control Strategy requires that the Department of Defense be prepared to provide counternarcotics operational support to the forces of cooperating countries. The U.S. Armed Forces can provide foreign forces substantial assistance in training, reconnaissance, command and control, planning, logistics, medical support and civic action in connection with foreign forces' operations against the infrastructure of drug-producing criminal enterprises. Such U.S. military support would be designed to increase the effectiveness of foreign forces' efforts to destroy drug processing laboratories, disrupt drug-producing enterprises, and control the land, river and air routes by which the enterprises exfiltrate illegal drugs from the country.

In addition to assistance for nation-building and support for foreign forces' strikes on drug-producing enterprises, the U.S. can assist law enforcement agencies of cooperating foreign countries in combatting the export of drugs from those countries. The Department of Defense can assist with an improved intelligence collection effort, which will be essential not only to assist the governments of the source countries, but also for U.S. actions in the second line of defense—the attack on drugs in transit to the United States.

The Second Line

The substantially increased effort to attack drugs at their source in the drug-producing countries as a first line of defense should help reduce over time the export of illegal drugs to the U.S. Nevertheless, drug-producing criminal enterprises in those countries currently are so vast in scope that, even if U.S. efforts to attack drugs at the source are highly successful, the flow of drugs by sea, air, and land will continue. As the second line of defense against the flow of illegal drugs, the U.S. armed forces will implement the National Drug Control Strategy through substantial efforts to counter the flow of illegal drugs in transit to the United States, both outside the United States and at the Nation's borders and ports of entry. The Department's service pursuant to statutory direction as the single lead agency of the Federal Government for the detection and monitoring of aerial and maritime transit of illegal drugs to the United States will prove particularly important to the success of this effort.

Deployment of appropriate elements of the U.S. armed forces with the primary mission to interdict and deter the flow of drugs should over time help reduce the flow of illegal drugs into the U.S. At a minimum, deploying the armed forces with this mission should have the immediate effect of substantially complicating the logistical difficulties of criminal drug traffickers and increasing the costs and risks of their drug smuggling activities.

Use the Military

The hard cold fact is that we're up against highly sophisticated, well-organized industries whose sole service is the delivery of illicit drugs into our country. The profit is so great and the risk of detection and capture is relatively so small that our outmanned drug-stopping forces are falling further and further behind. . . .

Every fact tells us that we're fighting a war. We have the best military in the world. We need it on our side in this war, because we can't win without it.

John Bryant, *Congressional Record*, January 3, 1989.

As a high priority, United States military counternarcotics deployments will emphasize combatting the flow of drugs across the Caribbean Sea and across the southern border of the United States. The Department of Defense will proceed with planning to deploy a substantial Caribbean Counternarcotics Task Force, with appropriate air and maritime drug interdiction assets and aerial and maritime detection and monitoring assets, to combat the flow of illegal drugs from Latin America through the Caribbean Sea. The Department also will proceed with planning for other deployments of U.S. forces to complement the counternarcotics actions of U.S. law enforcement agencies and cooperating foreign governments.

In Transit

Success of the attack on drugs in transit will require sustained deployment of appropriately trained and equipped members of the U.S. armed forces and substantially improved cooperation between the armed forces and U.S. law enforcement agencies. The substantial increase in military participation in the attack on drugs in transit is intended to be in addition to, rather than in place of, Federal law enforcement agencies' efforts.

The success of interdiction and deterrence efforts will depend greatly upon the ability of the Department of Defense and law enforcement agencies to marshal effectively the myriad command, control, communications and intelligence resources they possess into an integrated counternarcotics network. The Department of Defense will serve as the single lead Federal agency for the detection and monitoring of aerial and maritime transit of illegal drugs and will be prepared, with the cooperation of U.S. enforcement agencies, to integrate expeditiously into an effective network of Federal command, control, communications, and technical intelligence assets that are dedicated to the mission of interdicting illegal drugs from abroad. The Department of Defense will seek to develop and employ when appropriate the capability to exercise tactical control of Federal detection and monitoring assets actively dedicated to counternarcotics operations outside the United States and in border areas.

To ensure that action to implement the President's National Drug Control Strategy begins immediately, the Commanders-in-Chief of all unified and specified combatant commands will be directed to elevate substantially the mission priority within their commands of actions to fight illegal drugs.

The Third Line

After the first and second lines of defense—actions directed at illegal drugs in source countries and in transit—the third line of defense against drugs will be in the United States itself. The role of the armed forces in the third line of defense includes both actions to reduce the supply of illegal drugs and actions to reduce the demand for those drugs.

Within the United Sates, to assist in reducing the supply of illegal drugs, the counternarcotics actions of the Department of Defense will emphasize support to Federal, State and local law enforcement agencies, and the National Guard in State status. The Department of Defense will assist requesting law enforcement agencies and the National Guard with training, reconnaissance, command and control planning, and logistics for counternarcotics operations. In appropriate cases, armed forces personnel and equipment will be detailed directly to law enforcement agencies to assist in the fight. The Department of Defense will ensure that its administrative and command structures permit rapid and effective response to appropriate requests for counternarcotics assistance from law enforcement agencies and the National Guard. The Department will continue to assist the Governors of the several States in employing the National Guard in the fight against illegal drugs.

With respect to reduction of demand for drugs within the United States, the Department of Defense bears an important responsibility to reduce the use of illegal drugs within the armed forces and among its civilian personnel. The Department of Defense has met with substantial success in its demand reduction efforts with armed forces personnel through aggressive drug abuse education and drug-testing programs—an 82%

reduction in drug abuse since 1980. The Department will step up its efforts to combat illegal drug use by departmental personnel and will make available to other large organizations its experience in reducing the demand for illegal drugs. The Department also will emphasize drug abuse awareness and prevention programs in the Department's school system, which educates over 190,000 of America's children

A Crucial Role

The Department of Defense will be prepared to assist the Department of Justice with its responsibilities for incarceration and rehabilitation of drug criminals, through means such as training Federal, State and local personnel in the conduct of rehabilitation-oriented training camps for first-offense drug abusers and providing overflow facilities for incarceration of those convicted of drug crimes.

The President's National Drug Control Strategy emphasizes a multi-national and multi-agency approach to reduction of the drug supply. The Department of Defense has a crucial role in defending the United States from the scourge of illegal drugs. The Department will employ the resources at its command to accomplish that mission effectively. Should it prove necessary in implementing the President's strategy effectively, any needed additional statutory authority will be sought. The men and women of America's armed forces will fight the production, trafficking and use of illegal drugs, as an important part of the national effort to secure for all Americans a drug-free America.

"I wish that requiring the military to seal the borders would cure the problem, but it will not."

Using the Military Will Not Win the War on Drugs

Frank Carlucci

The continental United States has 5,000 miles of ocean coastline and a 6,250 mile border with Canada and Mexico. Covering this area against drug smuggling would be prohibitively expensive, according to the author of the following viewpoint, Frank Carlucci. Carlucci, the former U.S. Secretary of Defense, also writes that military forces, besides being barred by the Constitution from law enforcement work, are ill-equipped to stop the flow of drugs.

As you read, consider the following questions:

1. According to Carlucci, how do defense budget cuts affect the military's ability to fight the war on drugs?
2. Why does the author contend that the military is barred from making searches, seizures, and arrests?
3. In Carlucci's opinion, how has Congress stifled the war on drugs?

Frank Carlucci, statement before a joint hearing of the U.S. House and Senate Armed Services Committees, June 15, 1988.

Drugs are entering our country at an alarming rate. Drug dealing is on the increase, and our streets are the scene of an ever-increasing number of drug-related crimes.

I fully agree that our Nation must increase its efforts. The toll in terms of the loss of life and reduced productivity is unacceptable.

The Department of Defense [DOD], though, is no stranger to fighting the evils of drug abuse. As a result of a comprehensive testing and education program, our troops are far more drug-free today than they were 8 years ago. We have told our soldiers that drugs will not be tolerated in the military, and reported drug use has decreased at least 67 percent since 1980. . . .

The Primary Role

Over this same period of time, we have also substantially increased our support for law enforcement agencies in their efforts to eradicate and interdict drugs.

I am sure you are aware of the 2,500 ship days the Navy provided to the Coast Guard in fiscal year 1987; the more than 16,000 flight hours provided by the Air Force and Navy to the interdiction effort, our contributions to operations in the Bahamas, Operation Blast Furnace in Bolivia, and Operation Alliance in the Southwestern United States; as well as more than $300 million worth of equipment we have on loan to law enforcement agencies.

I am proud of what the Department has done to date.

The primary role of the Department of Defense is to protect and defend this country from armed aggression. Nothing must stand in the way of our readiness or our preparedness to perform this task.

During the early 1980's, the administration requested and the Congress approved the resources to bring our troops and equipment to appoint where they can perform their responsibilities with an acceptable level of risk. However, dwindling defense resources during the past several years and the resulting increased level of risk are a matter of deep concern to me.

The defense budget has been reduced by over $50 billion in the last two budget cycles. Adding another mission at this time will come at the expense of the Department's primary mission, unless additional resources are made available.

Not a Lead Agency

The Department of Defense will continue its active support to the drug law enforcement agencies. This activity should remain in a support mode and not as lead agency. However, this suport role is not an inactive one, as some would assert.

But it does rely on the express needs and requests for support from those law enforcement agencies that are legally charged with a mission to interdict drugs.

It is also constrained by the Department's requirement to perform its primary mission under strict budgetary constraints.

There are those who say the answer to the drug problem is to use the military to seal the borders to prevent drugs from entering our country. Others would have the military seal a portion of the border and/or empower our troops with law enforcement authority. . . .

I suggest there is a real question whether these actions can be accomplished and, even if successful, whether they would only serve to trigger a significant increase in domestic production.

Independent studies by the GAO [General Accounting Office] and by the RAND Corporation reached strikingly similar conclusions. GAO reports that among law enforcement experts there is no agreement that increased Federal interdiction efforts, with or without increasing DOD assistance, will significantly reduce the amount of drugs entering the country.

Political Quicksand

This wave of public support for military participation in the drug war is fed by the widespread belief that the Army, Navy, Air Force and Marines will be able to do what the police haven't: stop crack-dealing gangs in the U.S. and knock out the "drug lords" in Latin America. But, as some administration and Pentagon officials admit, a military victory in the drug war would be neither quick nor certain. What's more, because the cocaine industry has become such a part of economic, social and political life in Latin America, further militarization of the drug war could pull the U.S. into conflicts that go far beyond drugs, including the guerrilla wars in Peru and Colombia.

Jo Ann Kawell, *In These Times*, October 25-31, 1989.

The RAND study strongly suggests that, "a major increase in military support is unlikely to reduce drug consumption in the United States."

None of the interdiction approaches in and of themselves will work. I believe that these are not solutions to the problem, but rather the result of our rising frustration and our inability to find a real solution.

Constitutional Principles

Aside from the practical problems involved in these proposals, there are more fundamental constitutional principles involved. I remain absolutely opposed to the assignment of a law enforcement mission to the Department of Defense.

And I am even more firmly opposed to any relaxation of the posse comitatus restrictions on the use of the military to search, seize, and arrest. I have discussed this matter with the President and other senior members of his Cabinet, and I can report that these views are shared throughout this administration.

The historical tradition which separates military and civilian authority in this country has served both to protect the civil liberties of our citizens and to keep our armed forces militarily focused at a high state of readiness. Further, our equipment assets are designed for war-fighting and not law enforcement. They are therefore of doubtful cost effectiveness in a law enforcement role.

An AWACS [airborne warning and control system] costs an estimated $4,200 an hour to fly. It requires a crew of 27 to operate fully. The total inventory of them worldwide is barely sufficient to meet current obligations.

The Navy's E-2C is a carrier-based airborne early warning aircraft, and in view of the wing crack problems we are now experiencing there are not enough of them to fulfill the Navy's existing requirements.

Serving the Taxpayer

When these assets are regularly diverted to a law enforcement mission, a mission which experience indicates they are not ideally suited for, the taxpayer is ill served and readiness for our war-fighting mission is degraded. Additional training demands and potential logistical complications attendant to any use of the military in a law enforcement function would likely cause additional degradation in readiness.

The law enforcement agencies currently charged with enforcing drug smuggling laws should remain the sole entities with the power to search, seize, and arrest; and they should be provided the resources they need to do the job. We must explore all possible avenues to halt the supply of illicit drugs.

However, all the eradication and interdiction programs in the world will not be effective as long as the demand for illegal drugs in this country is so great. I wish I had a magic answer, but I do not. And I wish that requiring the military to seal the borders would cure the problem, but it will not. . . .

Limited Resources

Any discussion of the expansion of the military's role must include careful consideration of the cost of such an expansion, cost in terms of both mission preparedness and dollars. The Defense Department can increase the level of support we provide to the Nation's anti-drug efforts, but we must be provided additional resources. Otherwise, our military readiness, which is already under pressure due to budget restrictions, will suffer even more.

The only answer to the demand problem that I can see is an extensive education campaign, backed up by stringent legal methods of dealing with those who sell and those who buy illegal drugs.

In this regard, I read with interest a proposal sponsored by several Members of the Senate for a drug-free America by 1995. This proposal focuses on the demand side of the drug problem, and it contains a number of constructive initiatives.

Dan Wasserman, © 1988, Los Angeles Times Syndicate. Reprinted with permission.

I believe that we can make some inroads into the supply problem if the executive and legislative branches can work together to interdict and eradicate drugs and raise the pressure on drug producers, drug dealers, and drug abusers.

While the Congress does have a role to play in this national effort by providing the necessary resources, my initial analysis suggests that the Congress has not fully lived up to this responsibility.

Reduced Budgets

Between 1984 and 1988, for example, the Congress has reduced the Coast Guard operating budget by $458 million, and their procurement budget by $396 million, for a total reduction of $854 million.

As a result, Coast Guard hulls are tied up at the dock for lack of fuel, and the helicopter decks on some of their vessels are empty due to a lack of helicopters. These reductions have a direct adverse impact on the Coast Guard's ability to support drug interdiction efforts.

In 1988 the House Appropriations Committee proposed transferring $475 million from DOD to the Coast Guard, while at the same time reducing the Coast Guard budget by a similar amount.

Such actions by the Congress undermine our drug interdiction efforts. I might note that they are also contrary to the budget summit agreement. We have lived up to our part of that agreement in good faith, and I would request that the Congress live up to its part of the agreement.

In addition to fully funding the Coast Guard, there are other actions the Congress could take to enhance our drug interdiction efforts.

These include increasing security assistance for Latin America and funding for the State Department's international narcotics matters, and the Drug Enforcement Agency's international programs.

Funding we provide to source countries through these programs has had a dramatic impact on joint efforts to address the drug threat.

Alternative Strategies

Fund the Navy's request for its relocatable over-the-horizon radar program, and fund the continuation of the Air Force over-the-horizon backscatter radar program.

If testing of the Custom's P-3 aircraft with the E-2C radar is successful, then more of these aircraft should be bought, to relieve pressures on the inadequate inventory of military airborne early warning assets.

I would urge you to consider requiring transponders and pre-filed flight plans along established mandatory air entry corridors for all aircraft entering our national territory, and transponders on selected categories of boat traffic entering our coastal waters.

The Department of Defense stands ready to do what is required to succeed in the crusade against illicit drugs. The Department of Defense can play a role, but it must be an appropriate one.

The Armed Forces should not become a police force, nor can we afford to degrade readiness by diverting badly needed resources from their assigned missions. We should certainly not make the age-old mistake of assigning the Department of Defense an additional mission without the appropriate resources necessary to carry it out.

233

"The only feasible solution to the supply side of that drug-abuse equation is the death penalty for kingpin drug traffickers."

The Death Penalty Will Help Win the War on Drugs

DeForest Z. Rathbone Jr.

Since the mid-1980's certain special interest groups have worked to strengthen drug laws and enforcement. Despite their efforts, however, illegal drugs remain a national problem. Some people, like DeForest Z. Rathbone Jr., think legal measures must go further to protect American citizens. In the following viewpoint, Rathbone argues that only the imposition of the death penalty on a large scale for drug traffickers will solve the drug crisis. Rathbone writes for the Committees of Correspondence, a Massachusetts group dedicated to ending drug abuse.

As you read, consider the following questions:

1. What social problems does the author blame on drug abuse?
2. Why does Rathbone not support the death penalty for small-time drug pushers?
3. In the author's view, how will the death penalty for drug dealers protect society?

"Drug Testing and the Death Penalty," by DeForest Z. Rathbone Jr., in *America Under Siege: The Drug Invasion,* by Tom J. Ilao and edited by The forWords Company, and published in 1989. Reprinted with permission.

Under the twin driving forces of human greed for wealth and human lust for instantaneous sensual pleasure, the drug holocaust rages out of control throughout much of America. After nearly two decades of a no-win "war on drugs," assured of its no-win status by all the corruption $500 billion in illegal revenues can generate, the problem remains firmly entrenched for the indefinite future.

Enormous social problems have either been directly caused by drugs or greatly aggravated by them. A fact that best describes the net human costs of the drug epidemic is this awful statistic: the only age group in America today which has an increasing death rate (all others are getting healthier and living longer) is the age group from 15 to 24, primarily due to their compulsive use of drugs. Tragically, recent statistics show that age group declining toward the 12 to 20 age bracket.

Social Ills

Somehow many of our citizens seem to have missed the obvious connection between the drug problem and the increase of those enormous social problems whose development has closely tracked that of the drug problem. While many suspect that the increase in driving accidents and street crime may be drug-related, few have attributed to drugs the inordinate increase in teen suicides, teen pregnancies, sexual abuse of children, AIDS, the proliferation of "street people," murders of infants by parents and babysitters, murders of parents by children, school children murdering each other, commuters shooting each other over minor traffic incidents, and the increase in fatal plane, train, and bus crashes.

One shudders to think that the entire class of the 60's and 70's, constituting in large part the dope generation, is out there operating and maintaining our planes, trains and buses, building our atomic power plants, building and repairing our cars and homes, educating our children and, as we now see from the example of the dope-smoking Harvard law professor who became a Supreme Court nominee and as further evidenced by the resistance of some U.S. Justice Department attorneys to taking drug screening tests, entrenched throughout our judicial system as well.

Americans who have suffered through the drug epidemic of their children's generation are now facing the anguish of seeing this plague destroy the minds and lives of their grandchildren. And there is no end in sight!

Unless we are willing to use the legislative equivalent of atomic warfare on this "war on drugs," our children will continue to be sacrificed for the benefit of the wealthy dope merchants and their corrupt co-conspirators among public officials, lawyers, and business interests who profit so greatly from the continuation of this vile trade.

Just as Harry Truman's atomic bombs stopped World War II and saved many GI lives which otherwise would have been lost, so will the following legislative "atomic bombs" stop the drug-related slaughter of America's children. These vital weapons are the death penalty for kingpin drug traffickers and diagnostic drug testing for schoolchildren. . . .

The Only Solution

The only feasible solution to the supply side of that drug-abuse equation is the death penalty for kingpin drug traffickers. I wish to accentuate the term "Kingpin" which is defined in current federal legislation as "major drug trafficking organizational leaders" whose ill-gotten profits number in the millions of dollars. I also wish to accentuate that the death penalty is *not* appropriate for the small-time pusher who is often as much of a victim of the wealthy drug lords as are the hapless addicts.

Drastic Measures Needed

If anyone . . . still remains squeamish about the imposition of the death penalty in proper cases, I would refer him or her to the development in New York City where a drug law enforcement agent was cold-bloodedly killed at the hands of drug dealers. . . .When we consider the ever-increasing momentum of this war, we can stop at nothing, because the drug dealers themselves will stop at nothing. They will execute judges, they will shoot down drug law enforcement officers, potential witnesses, anyone who gets in the way of their criminal enterprises, and so we have taken this first proper step.

All we need now to do is to raise the consciousness of the American public as to the drastic measures required to win this war on drugs.

George W. Gekas, *Congressional Record,* March 1, 1989.

In addition to being responsible for the drug-related carnage among America's youth, kingpin drug traffickers have been responsible for the murder of a great number of public officials such as judges, legislators, prosecutors, DEA [Drug Enforcement Administration] agents, and police officers who are our first line of defense in combating their evil enterprise.

It is strongly suspected that the enormous profits of drug trafficking which are often used to corrupt public officials (or intimidate them through acts of violence) are a major driving force behind the refusal to date of politicians to enact the death penalty for kingpin traffickers. Many suspect that this same economic incentive is also the impetus behind the opposition to such legislation by lawyers who stand to profit so greatly from their share of the nearly $500 billion world-wide commerce in illegal drugs as defense attorneys, legal advisors, etc.

Opposition

Because of the enormity of this economic incentive, it is going to take massive political pressure by parents and other citizens to reverse that corruption-induced legalistic resistance to the death penlaty.

Those who oppose the death penalty on religious or moral grounds should consider that by protecting kingpin drug traffickers from the death penalty, we are in fact sentencing our own children to the death penalty imposed upon them by those traffickers. It would seem that as long as people are going to die anyway from the flourishing illegal drug trade, it would be better that those who die be the kingpin drug traffickers themselves rather than our own children and our honest public officials.

Whether America can enact such laws to protect our citizens from the ravages of drug abuse remains to be seen. Opposition from the liberal lawyers' lobby, the ACLU [American Civil Liberties Union], is virtually certain. And their influence is substantial. However, unless the American people can be persuaded that the health and safety of their kids, their family, their elderly, and their communities are more important than any slavish adherence to the ACLU's perverted view of the Constitution which presently favors the drug criminal over the ordinary citizen-victim and favors the drug culture over traditional civilized values, the drug holocaust among America's children will continue unabated.

Bite the Bullet

Millions of frustrated Americans are in for a continuation of the heart-breaking destruction of our kids by drugs unless we are willing to bite the bullet and make use of such effective weapons as will guarantee the end of this drug nightmare: drug testing and the death penalty.

Therefore, I propose adoption of such legislation at both the state and federal level without further damaging delay.

And I further propose that all concerned citizens join the effort to get these laws enacted as a major step needed to turn this continuing no-win war on drugs into an unconditional victory for our children and for our country.

"Even hundreds of executions per year would leave the drug markets virtually unchanged."

The Death Penalty Will Not Help Win the War on Drugs

Mark A.R. Kleiman

In the following viewpoint, Mark A.R. Kleiman writes that capital punishment for drug lords would have little effect on the drug trade. Any effect, he argues, would be minimal or even beneficial to dealers. Kleiman is an author and a professor at the John F. Kennedy School of Government at Harvard University in Cambridge, Massachusetts. He was a director in the Criminal Division of the U.S. Department of Justice from 1981 to 1983.

As you read, consider the following questions:

1. According to Kleiman, why would the death penalty raise drug prices?
2. Why does the author argue that the death penalty is not worth the effort?
3. In Kleiman's opinion, does drug dealing meet the rationale used to justify capital punishment? Why or why not?

Mark A. R. Kleiman, "Dead Wrong," *The New Republic,* September 26, 1988. Reprinted by permission of THE NEW REPUBLIC, © 1988, The New Republic, Inc.

Federal prisons are filling up with narcotics dealers. Convicting drug traffickers is turning out to be easier than finding cell space for them. Why not just give 'em a fair trial and hang 'em?

That question has been raised by George Bush, New York Mayor Ed Koch, and the Senate Republican Task Force on Drugs, among others. All have recommended capital punishment for drug dealers, though with some ambiguity about whether the ultimate sanction should be imposed for dealing or only for drug-related murders. . . .

A Question of Economics

It's easy, and accurate, to deride such plans as election-year demagoguery, but attacks on motives are no substitute for policy analysis. Would the death penalty help control drug abuse? More precisely, how many dealers would we have to execute every year to make a substantial dent in the drug problem?

Put that way, the question is largely one of economics. Illicit drugs are expensive because drug dealers face risks that tobacconists, for example, do not face. Drug dealers hazard both the penalties of the law—imprisonment and forfeiture—and the penalties of the lawless: violent death at the hands of competitors, dissatisfied customers, and thieves. (Many of the 20,000 or so annual murders in the United States arise from drug transactions.) Drug dealers' earnings reflect the extraordinary risks of the trade, just as the wages of stunt men and high-rise construction workers reflect the risks of their trades.

The death penalty, in effect, would raise the rate of fatal "industrial accidents" in the dope industry, thus raising the cost of doing business. As that cost, like all costs in competitive markets, is passed along to consumers, the result would be higher prices and reduced consumption. The size of the price increases would depend on the number of executions.

Total Wage Bill

Over the past decade W. Kip Viscusi and colleagues at Northwestern University, among other scholars, have studied the effects of industrial accident rates on wages. Each additional annual death in a job category seems to add between $1 million and $5 million to the total wage bill. That is, if there are two otherwise identical jobs, each with 10,000 workers, but Job A has one fatality per year and Job B two fatalities, annual earnings per worker in Job B will, on average, be $100 to $500 higher than in Job A.

Now assume that next year, and every year after that, we execute 100 drug dealers—more executions than have been carried out in the United States in the past ten years combined. And assume that the impact on wages is at the high end of Viscusi's range. If each execution adds $5 million to the drug industry's wage bill, 100 executions will impose new costs of $500 million.

Pointless Macho Talk

I don't care for people who sell crack. Truth be told, in my private moments I don't care a great deal about their civil rights. I spent a fair amount of time with a 17-year-old kid who'd been a crack addict for a couple years; it did not fill me with liberal warmth about people who deal with poverty by selling crack.

But this pointless, excessive macho/preppie talk about beheadings is really slimy. It's that elite assumption that there really is a common-sense solution to these problems if only we would *let the executioners be the executioners*. It's bureaucrats playing cowboy, talking tough on talk shows and then retreating to maximum security official buildings.

Jon Carroll, *San Francisco Chronicle*, June 28, 1989.

Annual sales in the illicit drug market are about $50 billion per year. So a $500 million cost increase passed through to consumers will generate a price increase of one percent. The resulting decrease in consumption is anybody's guess, but coffee, tobacco, and alcohol appear to have what economists call "relatively inelastic demand"; if illicit drug consumers are similarly committed to their habits, then a one percent price increase would lead to a consumption decrease of less than one percent, perhaps substantially less.

Little Effect

Of course, nothing says we have to stop with 100 executions a year. Five hundred, by these calculations, would increase the price of heroin, cocaine, and marijuana by five percent; a thousand, by ten percent. There are no limits to this game other than your imagination, the public's stomach, and the capacity of the courts to try the cases and hear the appeals. (The formula, remember, is "give 'em a fair trial and hang 'em"; the fair trial is not optional.)

In the case of cocaine, a ten percent increase in price would mean that a gram of pure cocaine would retail at $110 rather than $100. That's not much of a recovery from the cocaine price collapse of the 1980s; a pure gram cost $500 back in 1981.

"The mountain has labored, and brought forth a mouse." A $10 increase is a pretty small mouse to emerge from a mountain of a thousand corpses, especially when you consider that the Reign of Terror in post-revolutionary France involved no more than a thousand executions a year.

And these estimates may well overstate the bang-per-body. Indeed, if execution were reserved for drug-related murders, rather than being extended to all high-level drug dealing, it could end up defeating its purpose. After all, most drug-related murders involve the killing of drug dealers. If capital punishment cut down on such murders, the result might be *lower* drug prices due to *reduced* industrial hazards.

Unjustified Punishment

Lower drug prices might be a social cost worth bearing in return for fewer murders. But if the goal is preventing murder, what difference does it make whether the killing is drug-related? Is a drug murder more heinous, or easier to deter, than a domestic murder, a contract murder, a political murder, a rape-murder, a robbery-murder, or an arson-murder?

Punishments can be justified either by their effectiveness or their appropriateness. Execution is a morally appropriate penalty for crimes that deny their victims' humanity: premeditated murder, felony murder (killing, whether intended or not, in the course of a violent crime), and forcible rape. That justification holds good even if the actual effects of executions on the murder rate are too small to measure. Extending capital punishment to transactional crimes such as drug dealing has a somewhat more tenuous rationale. And doing so before making execution a common punishment for murder and rape seems almost inexplicable, unless executions would greatly reduce the volume of illicit transactions. The calculations above suggest that even hundreds of executions per year would leave the drug markets virtually unchanged.

Drug Policy Disaster

Killing people—publicly or privately—isn't something to take lightly. That's the whole point of reviving the custom of executions for murder: to reinforce the idea that killing a man is incommensurably more serious than lifting his wallet or cheating the tax collector.

When we talk of killing, we should do so with a decent solemnity, and with as much moral and intellectual seriousness as we can muster. It takes a special cynicism—or a desperate need to distract the public from eight years of drug policy disaster—to use "the death penalty for drug kingpins" as a cheap applause line in a speech.

Developing the Main Idea

The ability to write an essay in a clear and persuasive manner is an extremely valuable skill. Both in school and at work, you will have to be able to explain and defend many of your ideas, often in writing. The following activity can help you practice logical construction of a brief paper outlining and supporting a particular argument.

Below are eight statements. Each is related to the information you have read in this chapter. Choose one statement as the main idea of your essay. Then write an essay five to six paragraphs long, supporting and explaining your stand on the topic.

The first paragraph of your essay should state your topic and briefly discuss the stand you are taking on it. The middle paragraphs should each discuss one aspect of the main topic. The final paragraph should restate your thesis and summarize your position.

Each paragraph in your essay should have a clear topic sentence. The rest of the paragraph should explain the topic idea or give one or more examples illustrating it. Be sure you tell your readers *how* the examples illustrate your point.

Be sure you use transitions so that each paragraph is clearly related to the ones before and after it. Your reader should also understand how each paragraph relates to the main idea of your essay.

An outline will help you plan your essay in the most effective way. A sample outline is included at the end of this activity.

Main ideas: Write a brief, persuasive essay on one of these topics:

242

1. The U.S. Army is not prepared to fight the war on drugs.
2. To end the problem of drugs in America, the supply must be eliminated at the source.
3. Using the military is the only way to stop the flow of illegal drugs into the U.S.
4. When consumers no longer demand drugs, drug smuggling will cease to be a problem.
5. Police, prosecutors, judges, and lawmakers must strengthen existing laws to win the war on drugs.
6. The death penalty is an effective deterrent to drug trafficking
7. Tougher drug laws will only fill U.S. jails with small-time dealers and do little to reduce the drug problem.
8. The death penalty for drug dealers is not a just punishment.

Sample essay outline:

Topic idea: Establishing more treatment centers for drug abusers can help the nation win the war on drugs.

Paragraph 1: Introduction; state the topic idea.
    One of the most effective ways of solving the nation's drug problems is by treating and curing individual drug abusers. If there are fewer drug abusers, the demand for drugs will be reduced and drug sellers will go out of business. Establishing more treatment centers for drug abusers can help the nation win the war on drugs.

Paragraph 2: Topic sentence and support for it.
    Topic: Treatment centers help individual drug abusers get off drugs.

    Support:
    a) statement by Mitchell Rosenthal, director of the Phoenix House, a treatment center in New York City
    b) testimony by Ron, a former drug abuser who spent six months in treatment and now is cured

Paragraph 3: Topic sentence and support for it.
    Topic: There are not enough treatment centers now.
    Support:
    a) fact: the average wait to get into a drug abuse treatment program is eight weeks
    b) statement from research study showing that drug abusers who have to wait a long time lose their resolve and may never get treatment

Paragraph 4: Topic sentence and support for it.

Topic: Helping individual drug abusers is an effective way of solving the drug problem.

Support: example: facts about the positive impact on the school and surrounding community of a program in a St. Paul, Minnesota high school that mandated treatment programs for students caught abusing drugs.

Paragraph 5: Conclusion; restatement of main topic and summing up.

Thus if the nation establishes more treatment centers, we could help individual drug abusers. This will reduce the demand for drugs and reduce other drug-related problems, including crime and violence. Treating drug abusers can help the nation win the war on drugs.

Periodical Bibliography

The following articles have been selected to supplement the diverse views presented in this chapter.

Fred Barnes	"Dopey," *The New Republic,* May 23, 1988.
Ted Gest	"Soldiers Can't Beat Smugglers," *U.S. News & World Report,* May 30, 1988.
Howard Kurtz	"Getting Mad as Hell," *The Washington Post National Weekly Edition,* April 17-23, 1989.
Richard Lacayo	"On the Front Lines," *Time,* September 11, 1989.
William McGurn	"Drug Czar in Search of a Throne," *National Review,* June 16, 1989.
Ed Magnuson	"More and More, a Real War," *Time,* January 22, 1990.
Michael Massing	"The War on Cocaine," *The New York Review of Books,* December 22, 1988.
Tom Morganthau	"Losing the War?" *Newsweek,* March 14, 1988.
Mary Nemeth	"The Cocaine War," *Maclean's,* September 4, 1989.
P.J. O'Rourke	"Taking Drugs—Seriously," *Rolling Stone,* November 30, 1989.
Charles B. Rangel	"Drugs and the Death Penalty," *The Washington Post National Weekly Edition,* July 11-17, 1988.
Joseph P. Shapiro	"Community Action," *U.S. News & World Report,* September 11, 1989.
Herbert R. Temple Jr.	"The Nation's War on Drugs," *Vital Speeches of the Day,* June 15, 1989.
Lester C. Thurow	"U.S. Drug Policy: Colossal Ignorance," *The New York Times,* May 8, 1988.
Jarvis Tyner	"The Drug Epidemic: Cause, Effect, and Cure," *Political Affairs,* June 1989.
Kenneth T. Walsh	"The New Drug Vigilantes," *U.S. News & World Report,* May 9, 1988.
Caspar W. Weinberger	"Let's Keep the Military Out of the War on Drugs," *The Washington Post National Weekly Edition,* May 30-June 5, 1988.

Organizations to Contact

The editors have compiled the following list of organizations that are concerned with the issues debated in this book. All of them have publications available for interested readers. The descriptions are derived from materials provided by the organizations. The list was compiled upon the date of publication. Names and phone numbers of organizations are subject to change.

American Civil Liberties Union (ACLU)
132 W. 43rd St.
New York, NY 10036
(212) 944-4064

The ACLU champions the rights set forth in the Declaration of Independence and the Constitution. It objects to drug testing because it believes such testing violates the individual's right to privacy. The ACLU also objects to illegal searches and seizures in the course of narcotics investigations. It publishes a *Briefing Paper on Drug Testing* and also distributes a packet of materials on drug testing.

American Council for Drug Education
5820 Hubbard Dr.
Rockville, MD 20852
(301) 984-5700

The Council strives to educate the American public about the health hazards associated with the use of marijuana and other psychoactive substances. It believes that an informed public is the nation's best defense against drug abuse. It publishes *The Drug Educator*, quarterly, along with many pamphlets and books on drug abuse.

American Medical Association (AMA)
Department of Media and Information Services
1101 Vermont Ave. NW
Washington, DC 20005
(202) 789-7419

The AMA is a professional organization for people who work in the health care field. Many of the Association's members study and treat drug abuse. The AMA publishes two weeklies, *The Journal of the American Medical Association* and *American Medical News*.

CATO Institute
224 Second St. SE
Washington, DC 20003
(202) 546-0200

The Institute is a public policy research foundation dedicated to furthering policy debate, particularly as it relates to limiting the control of government, protecting individual liberty, and ensuring peace. The Institute believes the war on drugs threatens individual rights. It publishes *CATO Journal* three times a year, and the bimonthly *CATO Policy Report*.

Citizens in Defense of Civil Liberties (CDCL)
343 S. Dearborn St., #918
Chicago, IL 60604

CDCL works to defend civil liberties through educational programs and publications. It publishes several quarterly newsletters, including *Bulwark*, *Civil Rights and Public Misconduct*, and *The Public Eye*.

Coalition for 100% Drug Reform
Box 392, Canal St.
New York, NY 10013
(212) 677-4899

The Coalition, founded by Dana Beal, former Youth International Party (YIP) spokesperson, works to legalize all drugs. It believes a drug-free America is an unrealistic goal. Legalizing drugs will ensure that the drugs on the street are as safe as possible. It also endorses a boycott on crack and promotes marijuana as the safest of all illegal drugs.

Do It Now Foundation
2050 E. University Dr.
Phoenix, AZ 85034
(602) 257-0797

The Foundation, founded in 1968, offered one of the first drug-abuse hotlines in the country. It publishes pamphlets on chemical dependency, such as *Valium, Librium, and the Benzedrine Blues* and *Everyday Detox: A Guide to Living Without Chemicals.*

Drug Enforcement Administration (DEA)
1405 I St. NW
Washington, DC 20537
(202) 633-1000

The Drug Enforcement Administration is a branch of the federal government that is charged with enforcing the nation's drug laws. This agency concentrates on stopping high-level narcotics smuggling and distribution organizations in the United States and abroad. It publishes *Drug Enforcement Magazine*.

Drug Policy Foundation
4801 Massachusetts Ave. NW, #400
Washington, DC 20016-2078
(202) 895-1634

The Foundation supports legalizing many drugs. It also believes in reducing the demand for drugs, and thus advocates more treatment programs so addicts can overcome their habit. It distributes material on legislation regarding drug legalization. The Foundation's publications include the bimonthly *Drug Policy Letter*, and the books, *The Great Drug War* and *1989-1990, A Reformer's Catalogue*. It also distributes an annual compilation of newspaper articles on drug legalization issues called *Press Clips*.

Drugs and Crime Clearinghouse
1600 Research Blvd.
Rockville, MD 20850
(800) 666-3332

The Clearinghouse compiles and distributes material on drug-related crime. It gathers material from a wide range of sources and publishes *Drugs and Crime Facts* annually.

Families in Action
3845 N. Druid Hills Rd., Suite 300
Decatur, GA 30033
(404) 325-5799

Families in Action was the nation's first community-based parent group formed to prevent drug abuse among children. It has proposed bills to ban the sale of drug paraphernalia. It publishes *Drug Abuse Update*.

Fraternal Order of Police
National Headquarters
2100 Gardiner Lane
Louisville, KY 40205-2900
(800) 451-2711

The Order distributes material related to criminal justice and law enforcement issues. It supports employee drug testing and the right of law enforcement agencies to test their officers and applicants. The Order works to support national efforts in the war on drugs. It sends out copies of current periodical articles on drug laws and various police memos, including: "Drug Testing and Polygraphs" and "Law Enforcement Drug Screening Guidelines."

The Health Connection
Narcotics Education, Inc.
6830 Laurel St. NW
Washington, DC 20012-9979
(202) 722-6740

The organization distributes magazines, audiovisuals, and other materials that warn about the hazards of drug abuse. It publishes several magazines aimed at children, including *The Winner*, for ages nine through twelve, and *Listen*, for teenagers.

The Heritage Foundation
214 Massachusetts Ave. NE
Washington, DC 20002
(202) 546-4400

The Heritage Foundation publishes position papers on a broad range of topics, including legislation concerning illegal narcotics. The Foundation opposes the legalization of drugs and advocates strengthening law enforcement to stop drug abuse. It publishes the monthly *Policy Review*, the *Backgrounder* series of occasional papers, and the *Heritage Lecture* series, all of which sometimes address the war on drugs.

"Just Say No" International
1777 N. California Blvd., Suite 210
Walnut Creek, CA 94596
(415) 939-6666

The program provides positive peer pressure for a drug-free America. It created an anti-drug television program, "The Flintstones Kids 'Just Say No' Special," and coordinated a drive to get schoolchildren to take the "Just Say No" pledge. The organization advocates reducing the demand for drugs as a way to win the war on drugs.

Legal Action Center
153 Waverly Place
New York, NY 10014
(212) 243-1313

The Center is a nonprofit organization dedicated to preventing and combating discrimination on the basis of a person's history of drug or alcohol addiction. It has mounted test cases challenging many employment practices, including drug-screening programs. It publishes a bimonthly newsletter, *Of Substance*, and several books, including *Confidentiality*, about the federal regulations protecting the records of those treated for drug or alcohol additions.

Libertarian Party
1528 Pennsylvania Ave. SE
Washington, DC 20003
(202) 543-1988

The Libertarian Party's goal is to ensure respect for individual rights. It advocates the repeal of all laws prohibiting the production, sale, possession, or use of drugs. It believes law enforcement should stop violent crime against persons and property—not prosecute people with peaceful but unpopular personal lifestyles. It publishes *Libertarian Party News*, many books, and distributes a compilation of articles supporting drug legalization.

The Narcotic Educational Foundation of America
5055 Sunset Blvd.
Los Angeles, CA 90027
(213) 663-5171

The Foundation sends "drug educational-warning materials" to every sheriff's and police department in the country, as well as to all secondary schools and many colleges. Such materials include a handout for students entitled *A Very Potent Drug: Ethyl Alcohol* and a brochure, *Drugs and the Automotive Age*.

Narcotics Anonymous (NA)
PO Box 9999
Van Nuys, CA 91409
(818) 780-3951

NA is an organization of recovering drug addicts who meet regularly to help each other abstain from all drugs. It publishes *NA Way Magazine* and *Newsline* monthly.

National Association of Drug Abuse Problems (NADAP)
355 Lexington Ave.
New York, NY 10017
(212) 986-1170

The Association believes the fight against drug and substance abuse will only be won by further knowledge and education. The primary focus of the group is to rehabilitate former drug users and provide opportunities for them to re-enter the work force. NADAP publishes *Recent Developments Memo*, monthly, and *Report*, quarterly.

National Association of State Alcohol and Drug Abuse Directors
444 N. Capitol St. NW, Suite 530
Washington, DC 20001
(202) 783-6868

The Association coordinates comprehensive drug abuse education and prevention programs in every state. It publishes *Monthly Report* and *Special Report*.

National Clearinghouse for Alcohol and Drug Information
PO Box 2345
Rockville, MD 20852
(301) 468-2600

The Clearinghouse provides educational literature and a reference and referral service. It publishes a bimonthly newsletter, *Prevention Pipeline: An Alcohol and Drug Awareness Service,* to report the newest data on alcohol and drug abuse. The Clearinghouse also distributes pamphlets, booklets, posters, films, and videotapes.

National Drug Institute
112 Sladen St.
Dracut, MA 01826
(617) 957-4442

The Institute provides consultation and training to private industries, school systems, health care professionals, and others in the area of substance abuse prevention and education. It also provides reprints of articles on these topics.

National Federation of Parents for Drug-Free Youth
1423 N. Jefferson
Springfield, MO 65802
(417) 836-3709

The Federation began REACH, Responsible Educated Adolescents Can Help America Stop Drugs, to train high school students to help educate younger children. It also coordinates the Red Ribbon Campaign to increase public awareness. It publishes a quarterly newsletter as well as the *Parent Group Starter Kit, Press/Media Guidelines,* and the *Anti-Paraphernalia Kit.*

National Institute of Justice
PO Box 6000
Rockville, MD 20850
(800) 851-3420

The Institute serves as a clearing house for information on the causes, prevention, and control of crime. Among the publications available are *Research in Action* and the *Bureau of Justice Statistics Bulletin,* which include articles linking drug use to high crime rates and statistics on the number of illegal drug users in the U.S.

National Lawyers Guild
853 Broadway
New York, NY 10003
(212) 966-5000

The Guild is a progressive organization made up of lawyers, law students, and legal workers. It opposes government efforts to impose widespread drug testing. It publishes the monthly *Bulletin* and a biennial *Referral Directory.*

National Organization for the Reform of Marijuana Laws (NORML)
2001 S St. NW, Suite 640
Washington, DC 20009
(202) 483-5500

NORML fights to legalize marijuana and to help those who have been convicted and sentenced for possessing or selling marijuana. The Organization publishes a newsletter, *Marijuana Highpoints,* on the progress of legislation concerning marijuana throughout the country.

National Parent Resource Institute for Drug Education (PRIDE)
100 Edgewood Ave., Suite 1216
Atlanta, GA 30303
(800) 241-7946

PRIDE is committed to providing the most up-to-date information on drug abuse, its causes, and prevention. It organizes local parent groups to educate children about the dangers of abusing drugs. Its publications include a quarterly *Newsletter* and *Drug Conference Proceedings*.

The RAND Corporation
Publications Department
1700 Main St.
PO Box 2138
Santa Monica, CA 90406-2138
(213) 393-0411

The RAND Corporation is a private research institution. It publishes material on the costs, prevention, and treatment of smoking, alcoholism, and drug abuse. The Corporation believes the war on drugs is misdirected and must be refocused on reducing the demand for drugs. Its extensive list of publications includes the book *Sealing the Borders* by Peter Reuter.

Wisconsin Clearinghouse
1245 E. Washington Ave.
Madison, WI 53703
(608) 263-6884

The Clearinghouse provides publications and video tapes on drug and alcohol abuse. Titles include *Drugs and Drug Abuse: A Reference Text* and the *Making Prevention Work Kit*.

Bibliography of Books

Howard Abadinsky	*Drug Abuse: An Introduction.* Chicago: Nelson-Hall, 1989.
Shana Alexander	*The Pizza Connection: Lawyers, Money, Drugs, Mafia.* New York: Weidenfeld and Nicolson, 1988.
Ken Barun and Philip Bashe	*How to Keep the Children You Love Off Drugs.* New York: The Atlantic Monthly Press, 1988.
Cheryl Carpenter	*Kids, Drugs, and Crime.* Lexington, MA: Lexington Books, 1988.
Calvin Chatlos	*What You Should Know About the Cocaine Epidemic.* New York: Pedigree Books, 1987.
S.K. Chatterjee	*Drug Abuse and Drug-Related Crimes.* Norwell, MA: Kluwer Academic Publishing Group, 1989.
Paul Eddy, with Hugo Sabogal and Sara Walden	*The Cocaine Wars.* New York: W.W. Norton, 1988.
Patricia G. Erickson, Edward M. Adlaf, Glen F. Murray, and Reginald G. Smart	*The Steel Drug: Cocaine in Perspective.* Lexington, MA: Lexington Books, 1987.
Mathea Falco and Warren I. Cikins	*Toward a National Policy on Drug and AIDS Testing.* Washington, DC: The Brookings Institution, 1989.
Barry Glassner and Julia Loughlin	*Drugs in Adolescent Worlds.* London: Macmillan, 1987.
Guy Gugliotta and Jeff Leen	*Kings of Cocaine.* New York: Simon & Schuster, 1988.
Ronald Hamowy, ed.	*Dealing with Drugs: Consequences of Government Control.* Lexington, MA: Lexington Books, 1987.
Anne Swany Harrity and Ann Brey Christensen	*Kids, Drugs, and Alcohol.* Whitehall, VA: Betterway Publications, 1987.
Richard A. Hawley	*Drugs and Society: Responding to an Epidemic.* New York: Walker and Co., 1988.
Ray E. Herbert, ed.	*What Every Journalist Should Know About the Drug Abuse Crisis.* Washington, DC: Voice of America, 1988.
Abbie Hoffman	*Steal This Urine Test.* New York: Penguin Books, 1987.
James A. Inciardi	*The War on Drugs: Heroin, Cocaine, Crime, and Public Policy.* Palo Alto, CA: Mayfield Publishing Co., 1986.

Lloyd D. Johnston, Patrick M. O'Malley, and Jerald G. Bachman	*National Trends in Drug Use and Related Factors Among American High School Students and Young Adults, 1975-1986.* Washington, DC: U.S. Department of Health and Human Services, 1987.
Katherine Ketcham and Ginny Lyford Gustafson	*Living on the Edge: A Guide to Intervention for Families with Drug and Alcohol Problems.* New York: Bantam Books, 1989.
Mark A.R. Kleiman	*Marijuana: Costs of Abuse, Costs of Control.* Westport, CT: Greenwood Press, 1989.
Jonathan Kwitney	*The Crimes of Patriots.* New York: W.W. Norton, 1987.
Rensselaer W. Lee III	*The White Labyrinth: Cocaine and Political Power.* New Brunswick, NJ: Transaction Publishers, 1989.
Donald J. Mabry	*The Latin American Narcotics Trade and U.S. National Security.* Westport, CT: Greenwood Press, 1989.
Michele McCormick	*Designer Drug Abuse.* New York: Franklin Watts, 1989.
Scott B. Macdonald	*Dancing on a Volcano: The Latin American Drug Trade.* New York: Praeger Publishers, 1988.
Scott B. Macdonald	*Mountain High, White Avalanche: Cocaine and Power in the Andean States and Panama.* New York: Praeger Publishers, 1989.
Edmundo Morales	*Cocaine: White Gold Rush in Peru.* Tucson: University of Arizona Press, 1989.
David F. Musto	*The American Disease: Origins of Narcotic Control.* London: Oxford University Press, 1988.
Gabriel G. Nahas	*Cocaine: The Great White Plague.* Middlebury, VT: Paul S. Erickson, 1989.
Office for Substance Abuse Prevention	*Prevention Plus II: Tools for Creating and Sustaining Drug-Free Communities.* Rockville, MD: National Clearinghouse for Alcohol and Drug Information, 1989.
William Mack Perkins	*Raising Drug-Free Kids in a Drug-Filled World.* San Francisco: Harper & Row, 1987.
Peter Reuter, Gordon Crawford, and Jonathan Cave	*Sealing the Borders: The Effects of Increased Military Participation in Drug Interdiction.* Santa Monica, CA: The Rand Corporation, 1988.
Stephen E. Schlesinger and Lawrence K. Horberg	*Taking Charge: How Families Can Climb Out of the Chaos of Addiction.* New York: Simon & Schuster, 1988.
Robert Schwebel	*Saying No Is Not Enough.* New York: Newmarket Press, 1989.
Richard B. Seymour and David E. Smith	*Drugfree.* New York: Sarah Lazin Books, 1987.

Elaine Shannon	*Desperadoes: Latin Drug Lords, U.S. Lawmen, and the War America Can't Win.* New York: Viking Press, 1988.
Pamela J. Shoemaker, ed.	*Communicating Campaigns About Drugs.* Hillsdale, NJ: Lawrence Erlbaum Associates, 1989.
Arnold S. Trebach	*The Great Drug War.* New York: Macmillan, 1987.
United States General Accounting Office	*Drug Abuse Prevention.* Washington, DC: U.S. General Accounting Office, 1988.
William O. Walker	*Drug Control in the Americas.* Albuquerque: University of New Mexico Press, 1989.
Steven Wisotsky	*Beyond the War on Drugs.* Buffalo, NY: Prometheus Books, 1990.
Kay Wolff	*The Last Run.* New York: Viking Press, 1989.
Zig Ziglar	*Raising Positive Kids in a Negative World.* New York: Ballantine Books, 1989.

Index

255

259

260

Please remember that this is a library book,
and that it belongs only temporarily to each
person who uses it. Be considerate. Do
not write in this, or any, library book.